The

New Social Drug

CULTURAL, MEDICAL, AND LEGAL
PERSPECTIVES ON MARIJUANA

Edited by
DAVID E. SMITH, M.D.

PRENTICE-HALL, INC. A SPECTRUM BOOK *Englewood Cliffs, N. J.*

12/28/82

Copyright © 1970 by
PRENTICE-HALL, INC.
Englewood Cliffs, New Jersey

A SPECTRUM BOOK

Current Printing (last number):
10 9 8 7 6 5 4 3 2 1

C–13-615765-3
P–13-615757-2

Library of Congress Catalog Card Number: 77–104863

Printed in the United States of America

PRENTICE-HALL INTERNATIONAL, INC. (*London*)
PRENTICE-HALL OF AUSTRALIA, PTY. LTD. (*Sydney*)
PRENTICE-HALL OF CANADA, LTD. (*Toronto*)
PRENTICE-HALL OF INDIA PRIVATE LIMITED (*New Delhi*)
PRENTICE-HALL OF JAPAN, INC. (*Tokyo*)

Notes on the Editor and Contributors

DAVID E. SMITH, M.D., is Medical Director of the Haight-Ashbury Medical Clinic, Consultant on Drug Abuse at the San Francisco General Hospital, Assistant Clinical Professor of Toxicology at the San Francisco Medical Center of the University of California, and Lecturer in Criminology at the University of California, Berkeley. He also edits the *Journal of Psychedelic Drugs*.

JAMES T. CAREY, Ph.D., is Assistant Professor of Criminology at the University of California, Berkeley.

GILBERT GEIS, Ph.D., is Professor of Sociology at Long Beach State College.

ERICH GOODE, Ph.D., is Assistant Professor of Sociology at the State University of New York, Stoney Brook.

WILLIAM H. MCGLOTHLIN, Ph.D., is Research Psychologist at the University of California, Los Angeles.

CARTER MEHL, M.S., is Research Associate at the Haight-Ashbury Medical Clinic.

MARK MESSER, Ph.D., is Associate Professor of Sociology at the University of California, Santa Cruz.

FREDERICK H. MEYERS, M.D., is Professor of Pharmacology at the University of California Medical Center.

JUDITH M. NELSEN is a graduate student in the Department of Pharmacology at the Boston University School of Medicine.

J. FRED E. SHICK, M.D., is Resident in Psychiatry at the University of Chicago, and Research Associate at the Haight-Ashbury Medical Clinic.

ROGER C. SMITH, M.S., is Director of the Amphetamine Research Project at the University of California Medical Center.

MICHAEL A. TOWN, LL.M., is a member of the California Bar; A.B., Stanford University; J.D., University of California (Hastings College of the Law); LL.M., Yale Law School.

ANDREW T. WEIL, M.D. is a physician with the National Institute of Mental Health.

NORMAN E. ZINBERG, M.D., is a psychoanalyst, currently doing research in the Department of Psychiatry at the Tufts University School of Medicine.

Contents

Introduction

In 1919 America stood on the threshold of a new era—the national prohibition of alcohol. Led by the forceful Carry Nation and the evangelizing Billy Sunday, Americans had been indoctrinated to believe that if alcohol were banned, "men will walk upright, women will smile, and children will laugh. Hell will be forever rent." In response to such a vocal constituency, Congress, true to its penchant for legislating against the use of drugs, made the consumption of alcoholic beverages illegal. Unfortunately this simplistic approach brought exactly the opposite results. The "speakeasy" was created, as was a billion-dollar criminal syndicate. To counter this, the government had to expand its drug-policing forces, composed of incorruptible federal agents. A new language was created: "bone-dry," "white lightning," "hijacker," "flagger," "racketeer," and "scofflaw"; all these words owed their existence to prohibition. By 1928 an estimated twenty-five million dollars a day was being spent to quench America's thirst for alcohol. In 1933 prohibition was repealed, but during its existence of thirteen years, ten months and thirteen days an established criminal syndicate was born and still exists today, as well as a general disregard for drug laws by middle-class America. Alcohol was legalized not because we found out anything new or magical about the drug, but because prohibition produced a series of social changes that were intolerable.

Unfortunately, America does not learn its drug lessons well and in 1970 we are in the middle of another drug controversy that has many parallels to the alcohol situation. This controversy, of course, is national marijuana prohibition. In the late 1930s the Federal Narcotics Bureau spearheaded an all-out attack on marijuana. It claimed the drug led to insanity, crime, violence, and moral degeneration. This position was liberally supported by the alcohol lobby, primarily for *economic* reasons, since users of marijuana tend to reduce their alcohol consumption. As a result marijuana was mislabeled a narcotic and very strict legal penalties were imposed on those who used or sold the drug. When the La Guardia Report, published in 1944, disproved these allegations, the battle cry became "marijuana leads to heroin." This prohibition remained in force as government agencies effectively banned almost all marijuana research so that no new information could be developed to counter previous misconceptions.

In the last five years, however, resentment against the official practice of incarceration and "think stop" has manifested itself in increasing overt rebellion even by individuals with respected positions in our society. Health, Education and Welfare Undersecretary Roger O. Egeberg stated that penalties for marijuana possession are too strict and the drug should not be classified with "hard" substances such as heroin and LSD (Lysergic Acid Diethylamide). Dr. Stanley Yolles, Director of HEW's National Institute of Mental Health (NIMH), indicated that marijuana is the mildest of the hallucinogens and not a very dangerous drug. "Kids using the stuff" may have their sensitivity and emotional development impaired, but as far as dire catastrophe is concerned, it does not lead to addiction, it does not lead to a life of crime, and your first cigarette does not mean you are on the road to heroin.

The rebellion among the youth of our country, however, is much more direct; NIMH statistics indicate that between eight to twelve *million* Americans have had experience with marijuana; the major increase was among middle-class adolescents and young adults. All of these people, of course, are subject to felony convictions and incarceration of from two to ten years; the latter term has been actively supported by many conservatives in our society, including President Nixon, with his "omnibus bill" drug control legislation—although subsequently public pressure seems to have softened the administration's hard line position.

As pointed out by Erich Goode in "Marijuana and the Politics of Reality" [1] the polarization over the marijuana issue is at present primarily *political* rather than *scientific*. "Marijuana has become a symbol for a complex of positions, beliefs, and activities in which those who use the drug must also be politically radical, engage in loose sexual practices, and be unpatriotic." In other words, marijuana is a communist conspiracy; hence destructive legal penalties threatening the futures of millions of Americans are justified because they are participants in this conspiracy.

Without question, then, marijuana has served to reinforce our generation gap, for the cry among large segments of our population is "pot and peace. The hypocrisy that has gotten us involved in the war in Vietnam is the same that produced a situation in which our drug (marijuana) is illegal and your drug (alcohol) legal."

Representative Claude Pepper (Dem.-Fla.), as Chairman of the House Select Committee on Crime, has emphasized that "the marijuana controversy has become a political rather than a scientific debate in which many contend that government is attempting to legislate morality."

To make rational decisions, however, toward resolving the political

---

[1] See below, pp. 168–86.

conflict and eliminating marijuana prohibition, one must be informed of the latest information on this most complex social issue. This book analyzes the most important current issues to provide the reader with the necessary information to make an informed and rational response to questions about marijuana.

To begin such a discussion we must understand the nature of the drug we are talking about. Is it a narcotic, a hallucinogen, or a sedative? All of these classifications have been advanced and vigorously defended in modern times, and yet the drug marijuana (derived from the flowering tops of the female *Cannabis sativa* plant) has been associated with civilized man for more than 4,000 years; the first written account occurred in Chinese literature around 2700 B.C.

Part One of *The New Social Drug* deals with the issue of marijuana pharmacology and classification. Although at present no sound medical opinion would classify marijuana as a narcotic similar to the opiates, experts are divided as to its correct classification. Dr. William McGlothlin, among others, has described marijuana as a mild psychedelic and pointed out its close similarity to drugs such as LSD, with the primary difference being only in intensity of effect.[2] Dr. Frederick Meyers, however, feels that marijuana should be classified as a sedative-hypnotic-anesthetic and that its high dose perceptual effects are consistent with such anesthetics as laughing gas or nitrous oxide.[3] Dr. Leo Hollister feels that marijuana lies halfway between alcohol (a sedative-hypnotic) and LSD (a psychedelic), "combining the best of both worlds." [4] Goodman and Gilman, the prime pharmacological reference, hedges the issue by listing *Cannabis* in a "miscellaneous" drug classification.[5]

Certainly a great deal of the controversy in properly classifying marijuana arises from the difficulty in isolating and studying its active ingredients. Currently it is felt that tetrahydrocannabinal (THC) is the primary psychoactive agent in *Cannabis*. Isolation and synthesis of THC is a relatively recent phenomenon; it permits investigators to standardize dosage and administer THC under controlled circumstances to produce valuable information as to the pharmacological nature of marijuana.

THC has taken on greater social significance since large quantities

---

[2] See below, pp. 147–56.

[3] See below, pp. 35–39.

[4] L. E. Hollister; R. K. Richards; and H. K. Gillespie, "Comparison of Tetrahydrocannabinol and Synhexyl in Man," *Clinical Pharmacology and Therapeutics* 9 (1969): 783–91.

[5] Goodman and Gilman, *The Pharmacological Basis of Therapeutics* (New York: Macmillan, 1960): 170–75.

of various drugs labeled "THC" have been sold on the black market. Some newspapers have even described THC as "synthetic pot"; this has increased the extreme anxiety of parents and legislators alike. Although dozens of supposed THC samples have been analyzed, to date none has contained the chemical. Because of cost and difficulty in synthesis it is unlikely that THC will become a psychochemical of major social use. What we will see instead is black market advertising of drugs such as Benactazine ("Hog") and P.C.P. ("peace pill") sold as synthetic pot. At present the editor would agree with Dr. Meyers that marijuana should be considered primarily a sedative-hypnotic anesthetic, and that its desired effects (anxiety relief and euphoric intoxication) and adverse effects (nausea and high dose perceptual alteration) are closely related.

Part Two deals with marijuana abuse. Any acute or chronic drug response is dependent not only on the properties of the drug itself but also on the personality of the drug user and the social and cultural factors surrounding and influencing his drug use. Marijuana, like all drugs, has a certain abuse potential. Uncritical liberals, nevertheless, have stated publicly that marijuana as used in America is harmless in all cases. Inexperienced biased conservatives, on the other hand, have been quite vocal in proclaiming frequent acute psychotic episodes or "instant heroin addiction" as a consequence of smoking marijuana. Both positions are invalid.

San Francisco and the surrounding bay area has a very high incidence of occasional or regular marijuana use. This ranges from virtually 100 percent use in the Haight-Ashbury district of San Francisco to 30 percent use in many bay area high schools. As a result of this high density use, the editor, as consultant on drug abuse at the San Francisco General Hospital and as medical director of the Haight-Ashbury Medical Clinic, has had the opportunity to observe many nonabusing marijuana users and to treat in certain patients the problems resulting from acute and chronic marijuana toxicity. Case examples of acute and chronic toxicity will be presented in an attempt to define properly the abuse potential of marijuana; the examples will be followed by a detailed analysis of the use and abuse of marijuana in Haight-Ashbury. It is apparent from this work that a higher incidence of acute toxic reactions occurs with inexperienced users or individuals with rigid or disturbed personalities. It is also apparent that an individual who abuses one drug tends to abuse another (the multiple drug abuse theory), and that any association between marijuana and other drugs is due to the influence of personality and group factors. There is nothing in marijuana that leads one to heroin—current mythology to the contrary.

Part Three attempts to place use of the drug in proper perspective by discussing marijuana as a social issue. During the 1960's we have seen major segments of America's younger generation turn from enthusiasm for to alienated rejection of our country's dominant value system. This alienation has reached its peak in such areas as Haight-Ashbury, where thousands of young people have massed to form an environment based on the philosophy "drop out, turn on, tune in."

However, in analyzing the various youth protest movements— whether political activists and the Peace and Freedom Party, centered in Berkeley, or the Bohemians in Haight-Ashbury—one finds a number of common slogans: "end the war in Vietnam, eliminate racism, and legalize marijuana." A very definite drug culture involving young people in various states of rebellion has developed in the United States. One group of young marijuana smokers told me, "We smoke pot as a bond of trust in our battle against the establishment. *Oppression by the straights* solidifies our group."

This cultural conflict is going to intensify and very soon. Large numbers of American soldiers have been "turned on" to "grass" for the first time while in Vietnam. Reliable estimates have confirmed that more than half the U.S. soldiers in Vietnam have smoked marijuana; many antiwar protestors have stated that the only good result of this tragic war will be that a whole new segment of American society will henceforth prefer "grass" to alcohol. It is interesting that the politicians who are most vigorously supporting the war effort are also the most vocal in their attacks on marijuana and "its associated evils such as the hippies." It is ironic that the war of these politicians is serving as one of the major forces in strengthening marijuana's acceptance by American society.

In Part Three Dr. Gilbert Geis reviews the social and epidemiological aspects of marijuana use;[6] Dr. James Carey completes this part with a description of marijuana use among the new bohemians.[7]

Marijuana, then, has contributed to widening the generation gap in America. Alcohol is the social drug of this generation and pot is the social drug of the next generation. Many youthful protestors cannot vote. The youth say, "You start immoral wars and then draft us to fight your wars before we can even vote on the issue. You outlaw our drug, but keep your own personal vices, and all of it's part of the hypocrisy of the dominant culture . . . but all that's going to change!" It is apparent that drug laws will change, but in what direction is still not clear.

[6] See below, pp. 78–90.
[7] See below, pp. 91–104.

President Nixon's "omnibus bill" legislative attack on drug abuse lumped marijuana together with all other agents of abuse (including heroin and LSD) and called for increased possession penalties and reduction of illegal supply to push the price of the drug so high that students will not be able to afford it. He placed little emphasis on the education and treatment approach. Of even greater significance is the fact that the Nixon proposal could serve as a prelude to organized crime's assuming control of the marijuana market in a manner similar to the way it now controls the sale of heroin. A defense of this conservative and punitive approach to marijuana was well presented by Judge G. Joseph Tauro, chief justice of the Massachusetts Superior Court, who presided over the famous 1967 *Commonwealth vs. Leis* case (the most exhaustive court presentation on the validity of current marijuana legislation) in his presentation on "marijuana and relevant problems." [8]

Judge Tauro listed the following nine "areas of agreement," although he was vague about who agreed to these points:

There are certain important areas on which there is no substantial controversy among reputable and informed authorities.

First, marijuana is universally recognized as a mind-altering drug which in varying degrees and with unpredictable effect produces a state of intoxication sometimes referred to as "euphoric."

Second, in the United States marijuana is customarily used for the explicit purpose of inducing this state of intoxication.

Third, in varying degrees this state of intoxication can cause a lessening of psychomotor coordination and a distortion of the ability to perceive time, distance, and space. However, there is usually no interrelated diminution of muscular strength.

Fourth, the *habitual* use of marijuana is particularly prevalent among individuals with marginal personalities exhibiting feelings of inadequacy, anxiety, disaffiliation, alienation, and frustration or suffering from neuroses, psychoses, or other mental disorders. Such persons constitute a significant percent of our population, and it is precisely among this type of individual that marijuana may cause psychological dependence.

Fifth, marijuana may have a disinhibiting effect upon the user which tends to aggravate or exaggerate his pre-existing mental state or disposition. Thus its effects can vary with individuals and can vary during different occasions of use by the same individual.

[8] Judge G. Joseph Tauro, "Marijuana and Relevant Problems," remarks before the Commonwealth of Massachusetts Drug Dependency Conference, March 12, 1969.

Sixth, marijuana has no accepted medical use in modern medicine and serves no useful purpose in any other way.

Seventh, the use of marijuana is not part of the dogma of any recognized Western religion.

Eighth, marijuana has had a growing attraction for the young and the adolescent.

Last, but probably most significant, no one can guarantee with any degree of certainty that continued use of marijuana will not eventually cause permanent physical injury.

Tauro concluded that on the basis of these points marijuana "is a dangerous drug possessing a potential of harm both to the user and to society." He further indicated that because marijuana is harmful, the current system of punitive drug regulation is valid, and that anyone criticizing this system is both unscientific and irresponsible. He further concluded that "no foreign enemy poses a greater danger to our nation than a self-imposed danger of permitting drug use to become part of our culture, and no outside force would be more destructive."

The major errors in Judge Tauro's "areas of agreement" and conclusions reflect the confusion in the defense of current marijuana regulation. An excellent study by D. I. Manheimer, et al.[9] indicated that psychoactive drugs are already a major part of our culture and that millions of Americans regularly ingest a variety of stimulants, sedatives, and tranquilizers. In fact Americans are the greatest drug takers in the history of mankind and must look to doctors, drug advertising, and affluency to discover the real cause of their orientation to drug use. The desire to blame a foreign conspiracy is actually an attempt to shift the blame from the real culprit—ourselves.

The judge's nine points could also be applied in many cases to a widely accepted legal intoxicant, alcohol. Basically the question revolves around not whether we use drugs, but what drugs we do use. It is now impossible in an age of mass communications for a father to come home "roaring drunk" on Friday night and preach the dangers of marijuana on Saturday morning to his credulous son. All drugs have an abuse potential, and they should be regulated in proportion to it. Whether an individual uses a drug *destructively* depends more on his personality than on the agent itself. For example, individuals that have a history of alcohol abuse may, when they start using marijuana, decrease their alcohol consumption but then smoke marijuana to excess. Conversely, if we were to legalize marijuana, we would not in-

[9] D. I. Manheimer; G. D. Mellinger; and M. B. Malter, "The Use of Psychotherapeutic Drugs among Normal Adults," Family Research Center, Langley Porter Neuropsychiatric Unit, San Francisco Medical Center, 1969.

crease the *net* amount of drug abuse, but rather just produce a shift in the agent of abuse. Without question current marijuana legislation is designed to punish the users of one particular intoxicant and to imprison rather than rehabilitate the abusers of that agent; the latter position is particularly repugnant to a physician.

Many people advocate making regulations on the use of marijuana exactly like those regulating alcohol consumption. Certain influential groups—some motivated by profit, such as the liquor lobby, and others by power, such as the Federal Bureau of Narcotics—would fight such a proposal. Beyond these questionable considerations of profit and preservation of bureaucratic prerogatives, however, making marijuana laws like alcohol laws seems a dubious objective to the editor.

Alcohol abuse is the major drug problem in the United States; 80 percent of the adult population uses alcohol (alcohol is highly caloric and is used as a food substituent as well as an intoxicant) and one in twenty abuse it. In addition, alcohol is a factor in close to 50 percent of the nation's major auto accidents. How can we regulate marijuana so that the statutes are consistent with the abuse potential of the drug, so that the constitutional rights of the individual are not violated (as is the present case), yet not reproduce the errors made with current alcohol regulation? This is the concern of Part Four.

In Part Four, Roger C. Smith, criminologist, reviews the history of marijuana regulation in the United States.[10] Michael A. Town, a member of the California Bar, discusses privacy and the marijuana laws.[11] Dr. William McGlothlin proposes a rational view of marijuana regulation.[12] Dr. McGlothlin feels we must consider protection of the young, who are often too immature to properly handle psychoactive drugs, and the compulsive drug abuser, who seems unable to handle any drug no matter what his age. This must be done without compromising the rights of those who do not fall into either of these categories.

The book closes with Part Five, which discusses marijuana as a political issue, with articles by Dr. Mark Messer on the psychedelic revolution[13] and Dr. Erich Goode on marijuana and the politics of reality.[14] The articles defend the thesis that opposition to a rational approach to the marijuana question—an approach that includes such proposals, as the removal of *Cannabis* from the narcotic classification and the elimination of marijuana from the felony category (a provision that threatens the futures of millions of American youth)—is primarily political in nature. Unfortunately, it does not appear that this political

[10] See below, pp. 105–17.
[11] See below, pp. 118–46.
[12] See below, pp. 147–56.
[13] See below, pp. 157–67.
[14] See below, pp. 168–86.

irrationality will be modified in this generation; but if the editor may venture a prediction, when the old generation passes on, marijuana will be placed in proper perspective, for as Victor Hugo said, "Stronger than all the armies is an idea whose time has come."

Clinical and Psychological Effects of Marijuana in Man

Andrew T. Weil, M.D.

Norman E. Zinberg, M.D.

Judith M. Nelsen

In the spring of 1968 we conducted a series of pilot experiments on acute marijuana intoxication in human subjects. The study was not undertaken to prove or disprove popularly held convictions about marijuana as an intoxicant, to compare it with other drugs, or to introduce our own opinions. Our concern was simply to collect some long overdue pharmacological data. In this article we describe the primitive state of knowledge of the drug, the research problems encountered in designing a replicable study, and the results of our investigations.

Marijuana is a crude preparation of flowering tops, leaves, seeds, and stems of female plants of Indian hemp *Cannabis sativa* L.; it is usually smoked. The intoxicating constituents of hemp are found in the sticky resin exuded by the tops of the plants, particularly the females. Male plants produce some resin but are grown mainly for hemp fiber, not for marijuana. The resin itself, when prepared for smoking or eating, is known as "hashish." Various *Cannabis* preparations are used as intoxicants throughout the world; their potency varies directly with the amount of resin present (1). Samples of American marijuana differ greatly in pharmacological activity, depending on their composition (tops contain most resin; stems, seeds, and lower leaves least) and on the conditions under which the plants were

"*Clinical and Psychological Effects of Marijuana in Man*" was published in Science 162 (December 13, 1968): 1234–42. Copyright © 1968 by the American Association for the Advancement of Science. Reprinted by permission of the publisher and Andrew T. Weil, M.D.

The work was conducted in the Behavioral Pharmacology Laboratory of the Boston University School of Medicine, sponsored and supported by its division of psychiatry, and at the Boston University Medical Center, Boston, Massachusetts.

grown. In addition, different varieties of *Cannabis* probably produce resins with different proportions of constituents (2). Botanists feel that only one species of hemp exists, but work on the phytochemistry of the varieties of this species is incomplete (3). Chronic users claim that samples of marijuana differ in quality of effects as well as in potency; that some types cause a preponderance of physical symptoms, and that other types tend to cause greater distortions of perception or of thought.

Pharmacological studies of *Cannabis* indicate that the tetrahydrocannabinol fraction of the resin is the active portion. In 1965, Mechoulam and Gaoni (4) reported the first total synthesis of $(-)$-Δ^1-*trans*-tetrahydrocannabinol (THC), which they called "the psychotomimetically active constituent of hashish (marijuana)." Synthetic THC is now available for research in very limited supply.

In the United States, the use of *Cannabis* extracts as therapeutics goes back to the 19th century, but it was not until the 1920's that use of marijuana as an intoxicant by migrant Mexican laborers, urban Negroes, and certain Bohemian groups caused public concern (3). Despite increasingly severe legal penalties imposed during the 1930's, use of marijuana continued in these relatively small populations without great public uproar or apparent changes in numbers or types of users until the last few years. The fact that almost none of the studies devoted to the physiological and psychological effects of *Cannabis* in man was based on controlled laboratory experimentation escaped general notice. But with the explosion of use in the 1960's, at first on college campuses followed by a spread downward to secondary schools and upward to a portion of the established middle class, controversy over the dangers of marijuana generated a desire for more objective information about the drug.

Of the three known studies on human subjects performed by Americans, the first (see 5) was done in the Canal Zone with 34 soldiers; the consequences reported were hunger and hyperphagia [excessive eating], loss of inhibitions, increased pulse rate with unchanged blood pressure, a tendency to sleep, and unchanged performance of psychological and neurological tests. Doses and type of marijuana were not specified.

The second study, known as the 1944 La Guardia Report (6), noted that 72 prisoners, 48 of whom were previous *Cannabis* users, showed minimum physiological responses, but suffered impaired intellectual functioning and decreased body steadiness, especially well demonstrated by nonusers after high doses. Basic personality structures remained unchanged as subjects reported feelings of relaxation, disinhibition, and self-confidence. In that study, the drug was administered orally as an extract. No controls were described, and doses and quality of marijuana were unspecified.

Williams *et al.* in 1946 (*7*) studied a small number of prisoners who were chronic users; they were chiefly interested in effects of long-term smoking on psychological functioning. They found an initial exhilaration and euphoria which gave way after a few days of smoking to indifference and lassitude that somewhat impaired performance requiring concentration and manual dexterity. Again, no controls were provided.

Predictably, these studies, each deficient in design for obtaining reliable physiological and psychological data, contributed no dramatic or conclusive results. The 1967 President's Commission on Law Enforcement and the Administration of Justice described the present state of knowledge by concluding (*3*): ". . . no careful and detailed analysis of the American experience [with marijuana] seems to have been attempted. Basic research has been almost nonexistent. . . ." Since then, no other studies with marijuana itself have been reported, but in 1967 Isbell (*8*) administered synthetic THC to chronic users. At doses of 120 μg/kg [micrograms per kilogram] orally or 50 μg/kg by smoking, subjects reported this drug to be similar to marijuana. At higher doses (300 to 400 μg/kg orally or 200 to 250 μg/kg by smoking), psychotomimetic effects occurred in most subjects. This synthetic has not yet been compared with marijuana in nonusers or given to any subjects along with marijuana in double-blind fashion.

Investigations outside the United States have been scientifically deficient, and for the most part have been limted to anecdotal and sociological approaches (*9–12*). So far as we know, our study is the first attempt to investigate marijuana in a formal double-blind experiment with the appropriate controls. It is also the first attempt to collect basic clinical and psychological information on the drug by observing its effects on marijuana-naive human subjects in a neutral laboratory setting.

Research Problems

That valid basic research on marijuana is almost nonexistent is not entirely accounted for by legislation which restricts even legitimate laboratory investigations or by public reaction sometimes verging on hysteria. A number of obstacles are intrinsic to the study of this drug. We now present a detailed description of our specific experimental approach, but must comment separately on six general problems confronting the investigator who contemplates marijuana research.

1. Concerning the route of administration, many pharmacologists dismiss the possibility of giving marijuana by smoking because, they say, the dose cannot be standardized (*13*). We consider it not only possible but important to administer the drug to humans by smoking rather than by the oral route for the following reasons. (i) Smoking is the way nearly all Americans use marijuana. (ii) It is possible to have subjects smoke marijuana cigarettes in such a way that drug dosage is reasonably uniform for all subjects. (iii) Standardization of dose is not assured by giving the drug orally because little is known about gastrointestinal absorption of the highly water-insoluble cannabinols in man. (iv) There is considerable indirect evidence from users that the quality of the intoxication is different when marijuana or preparations of it are ingested rather than smoked. In particular, ingestion seems to cause more powerful effects, more "LSD-like" effects, longer-lasting effects, and more hangovers (*12, 14*). Further, marijuana smokers are accustomed to a very rapid onset of action due to efficient absorption through the lungs, whereas the latency for onset of effects may be 45 or 60 minutes after ingestion. (v) There is reported evidence from experiments with rats and mice that the pharmacological activities of natural hashish (not subjected to combustion) and hashish sublimate (the combustion products) are different (*14*).

2. Until quite recently, it was extremely difficult to estimate the relative potencies of different samples of marijuana by the techniques of analytical chemistry. For this study, we were able to have the marijuana samples assayed spectrophotometrically (*15*) for THC content. However, since THC has not been established as the sole determinant of marijuana's activity, we still feel it is important to have chronic users sample and rate marijuana used in research. Therefore, we assayed our material by this method as well.

3. One of the major deficiencies in previous studies has been the absence of negative control or placebo treatments, which we consider essential to the design of this kind of investigation. Because marijuana smoke has a distinctive odor and taste, it is difficult to find an effective placebo for use with chronic users. The problem is much less difficult with nonusers. Our solution to this dilemma was the use of portions of male hemp stalks (*16*), devoid of THC, in the placebo cigarettes.

4. In view of the primitive state of knowledge about marijuana, it is difficult to predict which psychological tests will be sensitive to the effects of the drug. The tests we chose were selected because, in addition to being likely to demonstrate effects, they have been used to evaluate many other psychoactive drugs. Of the various physiological parameters available, we chose to measure (i) heart rate, because

previous studies have consistently reported increases in heart rate after administration of marijuana (for example, 5); (ii) respiratory rate, because it is an easily measured vital sign, and depression has been reported (11, 17); (iii) pupil size, because folklore on effects of marijuana consistently includes reports of pupillary dilatation, although objective experimental evidence of an effect of the drug on pupils has not been sought; (iv) conjunctival appearance, because both marijuana smokers and eaters are said to develop red eyes (11); and (v) blood sugar, because hypoglycemia [lowered blood sugar] has been invoked as a cause of the hunger and hyperphagia commonly reported by marijuana users, but animal and human evidence of this effect is contradictory (6, 10, 11). [The La Guardia Report, quoted by Jaffee in Goodman and Gilman (18), described hyperglycemia as an effect of acute intoxication.] We did not measure blood pressure because previous studies have failed to demonstrate any consistent effect on blood pressure in man, and we were unwilling to subject our volunteers to a nonessential annoyance.

5. It is necessary to control set and setting. "Set" refers to the subject's psychological expectations of what a drug will do to him in relation to his general personality structure. The total environment in which the drug is taken is the setting. All indications are that the form of marijuana intoxication is particularly dependent on the interaction of drug, set, and setting. Because of recent increases in the extent of use and in attention given this use by the mass media, it is difficult to find subjects with a neutral set toward marijuana. Our method of selecting subjects (described below), at the least, enabled us to identify the subjects' attitudes. Unfortunately, too many researchers have succumbed to the temptation to have subjects take drugs in "psychedelic" environments or have influenced the response to the drug by asking questions that disturb the setting. Even a question as simple as, "How do you feel?" contains an element of suggestion that alters the drug-set-setting interaction. We took great pains to keep our laboratory setting neutral by strict adherence to an experimental timetable and to a prearranged set of conventions governing interactions between subjects and experimenters.

6. Medical, social, ethical, and legal concerns about the welfare of subjects are a major problem in a project of this kind. Is it ethical to introduce people to marijuana? When can subjects safely be sent home from the laboratory? What kind of follow-up care, if any, should be given? These are only a few specific questions with which the investigator must wrestle. Examples of some of the precautions we took are as follows. (i) All subjects were volunteers. All were given psychiatric screening interviews and were clearly informed that they might be asked to smoke marijuana. All nonusers tested were persons

who had reported that they had been planning to try marijuana. (ii) All subjects were driven home by an experimenter; they agreed not to engage in unusual activity or operate machinery until the next morning and to report any unusual, delayed effects. (iii) All subjects agreed to report for follow-up interviews 6 months after the experiment. Among other things, the check at 6 months should answer the question whether participation in the experiment encouraged further drug use. (iv) All subjects were protected from possible legal repercussions of their participation in these experiments by specific agreements with the Federal Bureau of Narcotics, the Office of the Attorney General of Massachusetts, and the Massachusetts Bureau of Drug Abuses and Drug Control (*19*).

Subjects

The central group of subjects consisted of nine healthy male volunteers, 21 to 26 years of age, all of whom smoked tobacco cigarettes regularly but had never tried marijuana previously. Eight chronic users of marijuana also participated, both to "assay" the quality of marijuana received from the Federal Bureau of Narcotics and to enable the experimenters to standardize the protocol, using subjects familiar with their responses to the drug. The age range for users was also 21 to 26 years. They all smoked marijuana regularly, most of them every day or every other day.

The nine "naive" subjects were selected after a careful screening process. An initial pool of prospective subjects was obtained by placing advertisements in the student newspapers of a number of universities in the Boston area. These advertisements sought "male volunteers, at least 21 years old, for psychological experiments." After nonsmokers were eliminated from this pool, the remaining volunteers were interviewed individually by a psychiatrist who determined their histories of use of alcohol and other intoxicants as well as their general personality types. In addition to serving as a potential screening technique to eliminate volunteers with evidence of psychosis, or of serious mental or personality disorder, these interviews served as the basis for the psychiatrist's prediction of the type of response an individual subject might have after smoking marijuana. (It should be noted that no marijuana-naive volunteer had to be disqualified on psychiatric grounds.) Only after a prospective subject passed the interview was he informed that the "psychological experiment" for which he had volunteered was a marijuana study. If he consented to participate, he was asked to sign a release, informing him that he would be "expected to smoke cigarettes containing marijuana or an inert substance."

He was also required to agree to a number of conditions, among them that he would "during the course of the experiment take no psychoactive drugs, including alcohol, other than those drugs administered in the course of the experiment." It proved extremely difficult to find marijuana-naive persons in the student population of Boston, and nearly two months of interviewing were required to obtain nine men. All those interviewed who had already tried marijuana volunteered this information quite freely and were delighted to discuss their use of drugs with the psychiatrist. Nearly all persons encountered who had not tried marijuana admitted this somewhat apologetically. Several said they had been meaning to try the drug but had not got around to it. A few said they had no access to it. Only one person cited the current laws as his reason for not having experimented with marijuana. It seemed clear in the interviews that many of these persons were actually afraid of how they might react to marijuana; they therefore welcomed a chance to smoke it under medical supervision. Only one person (an Indian exchange student) who passed the screening interview refused to participate after learning the nature of the experiment.

The eight heavy users of marijuana were obtained with much less difficulty. They were interviewed in the same manner as the other subjects and were instructed not to smoke any marijuana on the day of their appointment in the laboratory.

Subjects were questioned during screening interviews and at the conclusion of the experiments to determine their knowledge of marijuana effects. None of the nine naive subjects had ever watched anyone smoke marijuana or observed anyone high on marijuana. Most of them knew of the effects of the drug only through reports in the popular press. Two subjects had friends who used marijuana frequently; one of these (No. 4) announced his intention to "prove" in the experiments that marijuana really did not do anything; the other (No. 3) was extremely eager to get high because "everyone I know is always talking about it very positively."

Setting

Greatest effort was made to create a neutral setting. That is, subjects were made comfortable and secure in a pleasant suite of laboratories and offices, but the experimental staff carefully avoided encouraging any person to have an enjoyable experience. Subjects were never asked how they felt, and no subject was permitted to discuss the experiment with the staff until he had completed all four sessions. Verbal interactions between staff and subjects were minimal and formal. At the end of each session, subjects were asked to complete a brief form asking whether they thought they had smoked marijuana that night; if so, whether a high dose or a low dose; and how confident they were of their answers. The experimenters completed similar forms on each subject.

Marijuana

Marijuana used in these experiments was of Mexican origin, supplied by the Federal Bureau of Narcotics (20). It consisted of finely chopped leaves of *Cannabis*, largely free of seeds and stems. An initial batch, which was judged to be of low potency by the experimenters on the basis of the doses needed to produce symptoms of intoxication in the chronic users, was subsequently found to contain only 0.3 percent of THC by weight. A second batch, assayed at 0.9 percent THC, was rated by the chronic users to be "good, average" marijuana, neither exceptionally strong nor exceptionally weak compared to their usual supplies. Users consistently reported symptoms of intoxication after smoking about 0.5 gram of the material with a variation of only a few puffs from subject to subject. This second batch of marijuana was used in the experiments described below; the low dose was 0.5 gram, and the high dose was 2.0 grams.

All marijuana was administered in the form of cigarettes of standard size made with a hand-operated rolling machine. In any given experimental session, each person was required to smoke two cigarettes in succession (Table 1).

TABLE 1. Composition of the Dose*

Dose	Marijuana in Each Cigarette (g)	Total Dose Marijuana [Two Cigarettes] (g)	Approximate Dose THC
Placebo	—	—	—
Low	0.25	0.5	4.5 mg
High	1.0	2.0	18 mg

* The placebo cigarette consisted of placebo material, tobacco filler, and mint leaves for masking flavor. The low dose was made up of marijuana, tobacco filler, and mint leaves. The high dose consisted of marijuana and mint leaves.

Placebo material consisted of the chopped outer covering of mature stalks of male hemp plants; it contained no THC. All cigarettes had a tiny plug of tobacco at one end and a plug of paper at the other end so that the contents were not visible. The length to which each cigarette was to be smoked was indicated by an ink line. Marijuana and placebos were administered to the naive subjects in double-blind fashion. Scented aerosols were sprayed in the laboratory before smoking, to mask the odor of marijuana. The protocol during an experimental session was as follows. The sessions began at approximately 5:30 p.m.

Time	Procedure
0:00	Physiological measurements; blood sample drawn
0:05	Psychological test battery No. 1 (base line)
0:35	Verbal sample No. 1
0:40	Cigarette smoking
1:00	Rest period
1:15	Physiological measurements; blood sample drawn
1:20	Psychological test battery No. 2
1:50	Verbal sample No. 2
1:55	Rest period (supper)
2:30	Physiological measurements
2:35	Psychological test battery No. 3
3:05	End of testing

Experimental Sessions

Chronic users were tested only on high doses' of marijuana with no practice sessions. Each naive subject was required to come to four sessions, spaced about a week apart. The first was always a practice session, in which the subject learned the proper smoking technique and during which he became thoroughly acquainted with the tests and the protocol. In the practice session, each subject completed the entire protocol, smoking two hand-rolled tobacco cigarettes. He was instructed to take a long puff, to inhale deeply, and to maintain inspiration for 20 seconds, as timed by an experimenter with a stopwatch. Subjects were allowed 8 to 12 minutes to smoke each of the two cigarettes. One purpose of this practice smoking was to identify and eliminate individuals who were not tolerant to high doses of nicotine, thus reducing the effect of nicotine on the variables measured during subsequent drug sessions (21). A surprising number (five) of volunteers who had described themselves in screening interviews as heavy cigarette smokers, "inhaling" up to two packs of cigarettes a day, developed acute nicotine reactions when they smoked two tobacco cigarettes by the required method. Occurrence of such a reaction disqualified a subject from participation in the experiments.

In subsequent sessions, when cigarettes contained either drug or placebo, all smoking was similarly supervised by an experimenter with a stopwatch. Subjects were not permitted to smoke tobacco cigarettes while the experiment was in progress. They were assigned to one of the three treatment groups listed in Table 2.

TABLE 2. Order of Treatment

Group	Drug Session		
	1	2	3
I	High	Placebo	Low
II	Low	High	Placebo
III	Placebo	Low	High

Physiological and Psychological Measures

The physiological parameters measured were heart rate, respiratory rate, pupil size, blood glucose level, and conjunctival vascular state. Pupil size was measured with a millimeter rule under constant illumination with eyes focused on an object at constant distance. Conjunctival appearance was rated by an experienced experimenter for dilation of blood vessels on a 0 to 4 scale with ratings of 3 and 4 indicating "significant" vasodilatation. Blood samples were collected for immediate determinations of serum glucose and for the serum to be frozen and stored for possible future biochemical studies. Subjects were asked not to eat and not to imbibe a beverage containing sugar or caffeine during the 4 hours preceding a session. They were given supper after the second blood sample was drawn.

The psychological test battery consisted of (i) the Continuous Performance Test (CPT)—5 minutes; (ii) the Digit Symbol Substitution Test (DSST)—90 seconds; (iii), CPT with strobe light distraction—5 minutes; (iv) self-rating bipolar mood scale—3 minutes; and (v) pursuit rotor—10 minutes.

The Continuous Performance Test was designed to measure a subject's capacity for sustained attention (22). The subject was placed in a darkened room and directed to watch a small screen upon which six letters of the alphabet were flashed rapidly and in random order. The subject was instructed to press a button whenever a specified critical letter appeared. The number of letters presented, correct responses, and errors of commission and omission were counted over the 5-minute period. The test was also done with a strobe light flickering at 50 cycles per second. Normal subjects make no or nearly no errors on this test either with or without strobe distraction; but sleep deprivation, organic brain disease, and certain drugs like chlorpromazine adversely affect performance. Presence or absence of previous exposure to the task has no effect on performance.

The Digit Symbol Substitution Test is a simple test of cognitive function (see Fig. 1). A subject's score was the number of correct answers

FIGURE 1. Digit Symbol Substitution Test*

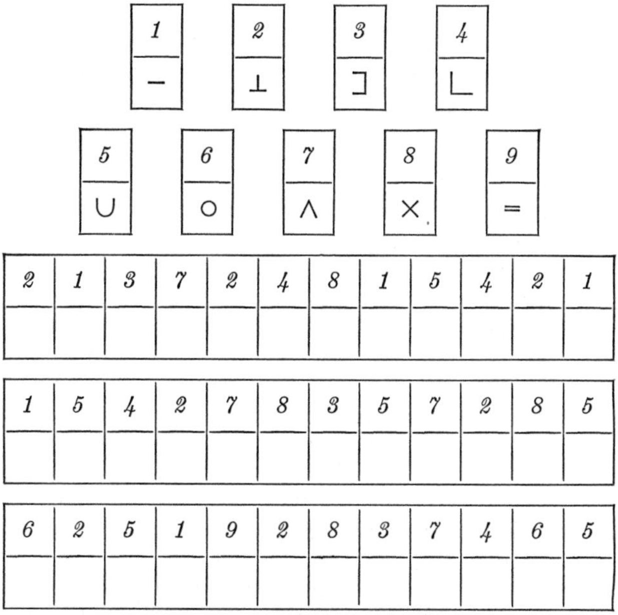

* This is a sample of the test used in these studies. On a signal from the examiner the subject was required to fill as many of the empty spaces as possible with the appropriate symbols. The code was always available to the subject during the 90-second administration of the test. [This figure appeared originally in *Psychopharmacologia* 5, 164 (1964).]

in a 90-second period. As in the case of the CPT, practice should have little or no effect on performance.

The self-rating bipolar mood scale used in these experiments was one developed by Smith and Beecher (23) to evaluate subjective effects of morphine. By allowing subjects to rate themselves within a given category of moods, on an arbitrary scale from +3 to −3, it minimizes suggestion and is thus more neutral than the checklists often employed in drug testing.

The pursuit rotor measures muscular coordination and attention. The subject's task was to keep a stylus in contact with a small spot on a moving turntable. In these experiments, subjects were given ten 30-second trials in each battery. The score for each trial was total time in contact with the spot. There is a marked practice effect on this test, but naive subjects were brought to high levels of performance during their practice session, so that the changes due to practice were reduced during the actual drug sessions. In addition, since there was a different order of treatments for each of the three groups of naive subjects, any session-to-session practice effects were minimized in the statistical analysis of the pooled data.

At the end of the psychological test battery, a verbal sample was collected from each subject. The subject was left alone in a room with a tape recorder and instructions to describe "an interesting or dramatic experience" in his life until he was stopped. After exactly 5 minutes he was interrupted and asked how long he had been in the recording room. In this way, an estimate of the subject's ability to judge time was also obtained.

Results

1. *Safety of marijuana in human volunteers.* In view of the apprehension expressed by many persons over the safety of administering marijuana to research subjects, we wish to emphasize that no adverse marijuana reactions occurred in any of our subjects. In fact, the five acute nicotine reactions mentioned earlier were far more spectacular than any effects produced by marijuana.

In these experiments, observable effects of marijuana were maximum at 15 minutes after smoking. They were diminished between 30 minutes and 1 hour, and they were largely dissipated 3 hours after the end of smoking. No delayed or persistent effects beyond 3 hours were observed or reported.

2. *Intoxicating properties of marijuana in a neutral setting.* With the high dose of marijuana (2.0 grams), all chronic users became "high" (24) by their own accounts and in the judgment of experimenters who had observed many persons under the influence of marijuana. The effect was consistent even though prior to the session some of these

subjects expressed anxiety about smoking marijuana and submitting to tests in a laboratory.

On the other hand, only one of the nine naive subjects (No. 3) had a definite "marijuana reaction" on the same high dose. He became markedly euphoric and laughed continuously during his first battery of tests after taking the drug. Interestingly, he was the one subject who had expressed his desire to get high.

3. *Comparison of naive and chronic user subjects.* Throughout the experiments it was apparent that the two groups of subjects reacted differently to identical doses of marijuana. We must caution, however, that our study was designed to allow rigorous statistical analysis of data from the naive group—it was not designed to permit formal comparison between chronic users and naive subjects. The conditions of the experiment were not the same for both groups: the chronic users were tested with the drug on their first visit to the laboratory with no practice and were informed that they were to receive high doses of marijuana. Therefore, differences between the chronic and naive groups reported below—although statistically valid—must be regarded as trends to be confirmed or rejected by additional experiments.

4. *Recognition of marijuana versus placebo.* All nine naive subjects reported that they had not been able to identify the taste or smell of marijuana in the experimental cigarettes. A few subjects remarked that they noticed differences in the taste of the three sets of cigarettes but could not interpret the differences. Most subjects found the pure marijuana cigarettes (high dose) more mild than the low dose or placebo cigarettes, both of which contained tobacco.

The subjects' guesses of the contents of cigarettes for their three sessions are presented in Table 3. It is noteworthy that one of the

TABLE 3. Subject's Appraisal of the Dose

Actual Dose	Guessed Dose			Fraction Correct
	Placebo	Low	High	
Placebo	8	1		8/9
Low	3	6		6/9
High	2	6	1	1/9

two subjects who called the high dose a placebo was the subject (No. 4) who had told us he wanted to prove that marijuana really did nothing. There were three outstanding findings: (i) most subjects receiv-

ing marijuana in either high or low dose recognized that they were
getting a drug; (ii) most subjects receiving placebos recognized that
they were receiving placebos; (iii) most subjects called their high dose
a low dose, but none called his low dose a high dose, emphasizing the
unimpressiveness of their subjective reactions.

5. *Effect of marijuana on heart rate.* The mean changes in heart
rate from base-line rates before smoking the drug to rates at 15 and
90 minutes after smoking marijuana and placebo (Table 4) were

TABLE 4. Change in Heart Rate (Beat/Minute)
After Smoking the Best Material*

Subject	15 Minutes			90 Minutes		
	Placebo	Low	High	Placebo	Low	High
Naive subjects						
1	+16	+20	+16	+20	− 6	− 4
2	+12	+24	+12	− 6	+ 4	− 8
3	+ 8	+ 8	+26	− 4	+ 4	+ 8
4	+20	+ 8			+20	− 4
5	+ 8	+ 4	− 8		+22	− 8
6	+10	+20	+28	−20	− 4	− 4
7	+ 4	+28	+24	+12	+ 8	+18
8	− 8	+20	+24	− 3	+ 8	−24
9		+20	+24	+ 8	+12	
Mean	+7.8	+16.9	+16.2	+0.8	+7.6	−2.9
S.E.	2.8	2.7	4.2	3.8	3.2	3.8
Chronic subjects						
10		+32			+ 4	
11		+36			+36	
12		+20			+12	
13		+ 8			+ 4	
14		+32			+12	
15		+54			+22	
16		+24				
17		+60				
Mean		+33.2			+15.0	
S.E.		6.0			5.0	

* Results are recorded as a change from the base line 15 minutes and 90 minutes
after the smoking session.

tested for significance at the .05 level by an analysis of variance;
Tukey's method was applied for all possible comparisons (Table 5).

TABLE 5. Significance of Differences (at the .05 level)
in Heart Rate*

Comparison	15 Minutes	90 Minutes
Low dose versus placebo	Significant	Significant
High dose versus placebo	Significant	Not significant
Low dose versus high dose	Not significant	Significant
Chronic users versus high dose	Significant	Significant

* Results of Tukey's test for all possible comparisons.

In the naive subjects, marijuana in low dose or high dose was followed by increased heart rate 15 minutes after smoking, but the effect was not demonstrated to be dose-dependent. The high dose caused a statistically greater increase in the heart rates of chronic users than in those of the naive subjects 15 minutes after smoking.

Two of the chronic users had unusually low resting pulse rates (56 and 42), but deletion of these two subjects (No. 11 and No. 15) still gave a significant difference in mean pulse rise of chronic users compared to naives. Because the conditions of the sessions and experimental design were not identical for the two groups, we prefer to report this difference as a trend that must be confirmed by further studies.

6. *Effect of marijuana on respiratory rate.* In the naive group, there was no change in respiratory rate before and after smoking marijuana. Chronic users showed a small but statistically significant increase in respiratory rate after smoking, but we do not regard the change as clinically significant.

7. *Effect of marijuana on pupil size.* There was no change in pupil size before and after smoking marijuana in either group.

8. *Effect of marijuana on conjunctival appearance.* Significant reddening of conjunctivae due to dilatation of blood vessels occurred in one of nine subjects receiving placebo, three of nine receiving the low dose of marijuana, and eight of nine receiving the high dose. It occurred in all eight of the chronic users receiving the high dose and was rated as more prominent in them. The effect was more pronounced 15 minutes after the smoking period than 90 minutes after it.

9. *Effect of marijuana on blood sugar.* There was no significant change in blood sugar levels after smoking marijuana in either group.

10. *Effect of marijuana on the Continuous Performance Test.* Performance on the CPT and on the CPT with strobe distraction was unaffected by marijuana for both groups of subjects.

11. *Effect of marijuana on the Digit Symbol Substitution Test.* The

significance of the differences in mean changes of scores at the .05 level was determined by an analysis of variance by means of Tukey's method for all possible comparisons. Results of these tests are summarized in Tables 6 and 7.

TABLE 6. Significance of Differences (at the .05 level)
for the Digit Symbol Substitution Test*

Comparison	15 Minutes	90 Minutes
Low dose versus placebo	Significant	Significant
High dose versus placebo	Significant	Significant
Low dose versus high dose	Significant	Not significant
Chronic users versus high dose	Significant	Significant

* Results of Tukey's test for all possible comparisons.

The results indicate that: (i) Decrements in performance of naive subjects following low and high doses of marijuana were significant at 15 and 90 minutes after smoking. (ii) The decrement following marijuana was greater after high dose than after low dose at 15 minutes after taking the drug, giving preliminary evidence of a dose-response relationship. (iii) Chronic users started with good base-line performance and improved slightly on the DSST after smoking 2.0 grams of marijuana, whereas performance of the naive subjects was grossly impaired. Experience with the DSST suggests that absence of impairment in chronic users cannot be accounted for solely by a practice effect. Still, because of the different procedures employed, we prefer to report this difference as a trend.

12. *Effect of marijuana on pursuit rotor performance.* This result is presented in Table 8. Again applying Tukey's method in an analysis of variance, we tested differences in mean changes in scores (Table 9). Decrements in performance of naive subjects after both low and high doses of marijuana were significant at 15 and 90 minutes. This effect on performance followed a dose-response relation on testing batteries conducted at both 15 minutes and 90 minutes after the drug was smoked.

All chronic users started from good baselines and improved on the pursuit rotor after smoking marijuana. These data are not presented, however, because it is probable that the improvement was largely a practice effect.

13. *Effect of marijuana on time estimation.* Before smoking, all nine naive subjects estimated the 5-minute verbal sample to be 5 ± 2

TABLE 7. Digit Symbol Substitution Test*

Subject	15 Minutes			90 Minutes		
	Placebo	Low	High	Placebo	Low	High
			Naive subjects			
1	− 3		+ 5	− 7	+ 4	+ 8
2	+10	− 8	−17	− 1	−15	− 5
3	− 3	+ 6	− 7	−10	+ 2	− 1
4	+ 3	− 4	− 3		− 7	
5	+ 4	+ 1	− 7	+ 6		− 8
6	− 3	− 1	− 9	+ 3	− 5	−12
7	+ 2	− 4	− 6	+ 3	− 5	− 4
8	− 1	+ 3	+ 1	+ 4	+ 4	− 3
9	− 1	− 4	− 3	+ 6	− 1	−10
Mean	+0.9	−1.2	−5.1	+0.4	−2.6	−3.9
S.E.	1.4	1.4	2.1	1.9	2.0	2.0
			Chronic users			
10			− 4			−16
11			+ 1			+ 6
12			+11			+18
13			+ 3			+ 4
14			− 2			− 3
15			− 6			+ 8
16			− 4			
17			+ 3			
Mean			+0.25			+2.8
S.E.			1.9			4.7

* Change in scores from base line (number correct) 15 and 90 minutes after the smoking session.

minutes. After placebo, no subject changed his guess. After the low dose, three subjects raised their estimates to 10 ± 2 minutes, and after the high dose, four raised their estimates.

14. *Subjective effects of marijuana.* When questioned at the end of their participation in the experiment, persons who had never taken marijuana previously reported minimum subjective effects after smoking the drug, or, more precisely, few effects like those commonly reported by chronic users. Non-users reported little euphoria, no distortion of visual or auditory perception, and no confusion. However, several subjects mentioned that "things seemed to take longer." Below are examples of comments by naive subjects after high doses.

TABLE 8. Pursuit Rotor (Naive Subjects)*

Sub-ject	15 Minutes			90 Minutes		
	Placebo	Low	High	Placebo	Low	High
1	+1.20	−1.04	−4.01	+1.87	−1.54	−6.54
2	+0.89	−1.43	−0.12	+0.52	+0.44	−0.68
3	+0.50	−0.60	−6.56	+0.84	−0.96	−4.34
4	+0.18	−0.11	+0.11	+0.06	+1.95	−1.37
5	+3.20	+0.39	+0.13	+2.64	+3.33	+0.34
6	+3.45	−0.32	−3.46	+2.93	+0.22	−2.26
7	+0.81	+0.48	−0.79	+0.63	+0.16	−0.52
8	+1.75	−0.39	−0.92	+2.13	+0.40	+1.02
9	+3.90	−1.94	−2.60	+3.11	−0.97	−3.09
Mean	+1.8	−0.6	−2.0	+1.6	+0.3	−1.9
S.E.	0.5	0.3	0.8	0.4	0.5	0.8

* Changes in scores (averages of sten trials) from base line (seconds).

Subject 1: "It was stronger than the previous time (low dose) but I really didn't think it could be marijuana. Things seemed to go slower."

Subject 2: "I think I realize why they took our watches. There was a sense of the past disappearing as happens when you're driving too long without sleeping. With a start you wake up to realize you were asleep for an instant; you discover yourself driving along the road. It was the same tonight with eating a sandwich. I'd look down to discover I'd just swallowed a bite but I hadn't noticed it at the time."

Subject 6: "I felt a combination of being almost drunk and tired, with occasional fits of silliness—not my normal reaction to smoking tobacco."

Subject 8: "I felt faint briefly, but the dizziness went away, and I

TABLE 9. Significance of Differences (at the .05 level)
for the Pursuit Rotor*

Comparison	15 Minutes	90 Minutes
Low dose versus placebo	Significant	Significant
High dose versus placebo	Significant	Significant
Low dose versus high dose	Significant	Significant

* Results of Tukey's test for all possible comparisons, 15 and 90 minutes after the smoking session.

felt normal or slightly tired. I can't believe I had a high dose of marijuana."

Subject 9: "Time seemed very drawn out. I would keep forgetting what I was doing, especially on the continuous performance test, but somehow every time an 'X' (the critical letter) came up, I found myself pushing the button."

After smoking their high dose, chronic users were asked to rate themselves on a scale of 1 to 10, 10 representing "the highest you've ever been." All subjects placed themselves between 7 and 10, most at 8 or 9. Many of these subjects expressed anxiety at the start of their first battery of tests after smoking the drug when they were feeling very high. Then they expressed surprise during and after the tests when they judged (correctly) that their performance was as good as or better than it had been before taking the drug.

15. The effect of marijuana on the self-rating mood scale, the effect of marijuana on a 5-minute verbal sample, and the correlation of personality type with subjective effects of marijuana will be reported separately.

Discussion

Several results from this study raise important questions about the action of marijuana and suggest directions for future research. Our finding that subjects who were naive to marijuana did not become subjectively "high" after a high dose of marijuana in a neutral setting is interesting when contrasted with the response of regular users who consistently reported and exhibited highs. It agrees with the reports of chronic users that many, if not most, people do not become high on their first exposure to marijuana even if they smoke it correctly. This puzzling phenomenon can be discussed from either a physiological or psychosocial point of view. Neither interpretation is entirely satisfactory. The physiological hypothesis suggests that getting high on marijuana occurs only after some sort of pharmacological sensitization takes place. The psychosocial interpretation is that repeated exposure to marijuana reduces psychological inhibition, as part of, or as the result of a learning process.

Indirect evidence makes the psychological hypothesis attractive. Anxiety about drug use in this country is sufficiently great to make worthy of careful consideration the possibility of an unconscious psychological inhibition or block on the part of naive drug takers. The subjective responses of our subjects indicate that they had imagined a marijuana effect to be much more profoundly disorganizing than what they experienced. For example, subject No. 4, who started with a bias against the possibility of becoming high on marijuana, was able to control subjectively the effect of the drug and report that he had received a placebo when he had actually gotten a high dose. As anxiety about the drug is lessened with experience, the block may decrease, and the subject may permit himself to notice the drug's effects.

It is well known that marijuana users, in introducing friends to the drug, do actually "teach" them to notice subtle effects of the drug on consciousness (25). The apparently enormous influence of set and setting on the form of the marijuana response is consistent with this hypothesis, as is the testimony of users that, as use becomes more frequent, the amount of drug required to produce intoxication decreases—a unique example of "reverse tolerance." (Regular use of many intoxicants is accompanied by the need for increasing doses to achieve the same effects.)

On the other hand, the suggestion arising from this study that users and nonusers react differently to the drug, not only subjectively but also physiologically, increases the plausibility of the pharmacological-sensitization hypothesis. Of course, reverse tolerance could equally well be a manifestation of this sensitization.

It would be useful to confirm the suggested differences between users and nonusers and then to test in a systematic manner the hypothetical explanations of the phenomenon. One possible approach would be to continue to administer high doses of marijuana to the naive subjects according to the protocol described. If subjects begin reporting high responses to the drug only after several exposures, in the absence of psychedelic settings, suggestions, or manipulations of mood, then the likelihood that marijuana induces a true physiological sensitization or that experience reduces psychological inhibitions, permitting real drug effects to appear, would be increased. If subjects fail to become high, we could conclude that learning to respond to marijuana requires some sort of teaching or suggestion.

An investigation of the literature of countries where anxieties over drug use are less prominent would be useful. If this difference between responses of users and nonusers is a uniquely American phenomenon, a psychological explanation would be indicated, although it would not account for greater effects with smaller doses after the initial, anxiety-reducing stage.

One impetus for reporting the finding of differences between chronic and naive subjects on some of the tests, despite the fact that the experimental designs were not the same, is that this finding agrees with the statements of many users. They say that the effects of marijuana are easily suppressed—much more so than those of alcohol. Our observation, that the chronic users after smoking marijuana performed on some tests as well as or better than they did before taking the drug, reinforced the argument advanced by chronic users that maintaining effective levels of performance for many tasks—driving, for example (26)—is much easier under the influence of marijuana than under that of other psychoactive drugs. Certainly the surprise that the chronic users expressed when they found they were performing more effectively on the CPT, DSST, and pursuit rotor tests than they thought they would is remarkable. It is quite the opposite of the false sense of improvement subjects have under some psychoactive drugs that actually impair performance.

What might be the basis of this suppressibility? Possibly, the actions of marijuana are confined to higher cortical functions without any general stimulatory or depressive effect on lower brain centers. The relative absence of neurological—as opposed to psychiatric—symptoms in marijuana intoxication suggests this possibility (7).

Our failure to detect any changes in blood sugar levels of subjects after they had smoked marijuana forces us to look elsewhere for an explanation of the hunger and hyperphagia commonly reported by users. A first step would be careful interviewing of users to determine whether they really become hungry after smoking marijuana or whether they simply find eating more pleasurable. Possibly, the basis of this effect is also central rather than due to some periphral physiological change.

Lack of any change in pupil size of subjects after they had smoked marijuana is an enlightening finding especially because so many users and law enforcement agents firmly believe that marijuana dilates pupils. (Since users generally observe each other in dim surroundings, it is not surprising that they see large pupils.) This negative finding emphasizes the need for data from carefully controlled investigations rather than from casual observation or anecdotal reports in the evaluation of marijuana. It also agrees with the findings of others that synthetic THC does not alter pupil size (8, 27).

Finally, we would like to comment on the fact that marijuana appears to be a relatively mild intoxicant in our studies. If these results seem to differ from those of earlier experiments, it must be remembered that other experimenters have given marijuana orally, have given doses much higher than those commonly smoked by users, have administered potent synthetics, and have not strictly controlled the laboratory setting. As noted in our introduction, more powerful effects are often reported by users who ingest preparations of marijuana. This may mean that some active constituents which enter the body when the drug is ingested are destroyed by combustion, a sug-

gestion that must be investigated in man. Another priority consideration is the extent to which synthetic THC reproduces marijuana
intoxication—a problem that must be resolved before marijuana research proceeds with THC instead of the natural resin of the whole
plant.

The set, both of subjects and experimenters, and the setting must be
recognized as critical variables in studies of marijuana. Drug, set, and
setting interact to shape the form of a marijuana reaction. The researcher who sets out with prior conviction that hemp is psychotomimetic or a "mild hallucinogen" is likely to confirm his conviction
experimentally (*10*), but he would probably confirm the opposite
hypothesis if his bias were in the opposite direction. Precautions to
insure neutrality of set and setting, including use of a double-blind
procedure as an absolute minimum, are vitally important if the object
of investigation is to measure real marijuana-induced responses.

Conclusions

1. It is feasible and safe to study the effects of marijuana on human
   volunteers who smoke it in a laboratory.
2. In a neutral setting persons who are naive to marijuana do not have
   strong subjective experiences after smoking low or high doses of the
   drug, and the effects they do report are not the same as those described
   by regular users of marijuana who take the drug in the same neutral
   setting.
3. Marijuana-naive persons do demonstrate impaired performance on
   simple intellectual and psychomotor tests after smoking marijuana; the
   impairment is dose-related in some cases.
4. Regular users of marijuana do get high after smoking marijuana in a
   neutral setting but do not show the same degree of impairment of
   performance on the tests as do naive subjects. In some cases, their performance even appears to improve slightly after smoking marijuana.
5. Marijuana increases heart rate moderately.
6. No change in respiratory rate follows administration of marijuana by
   inhalation.
7. No change in pupil size occurs in short term exposure to marijuana.
8. Marijuana administration causes dilatation of conjunctival blood vessels.
9. Marijuana treatment produces no change in blood sugar levels.
10. In a neutral setting the physiological and psychological effects of a
    single inhaled dose of marijuana appear to reach maximum intensity
    within one-half hour of inhalation, to be diminished after 1 hour, and
    to be completely dissipated by 3 hours.

References

1. R. J. Bouquet, *Bull. Narcotics*, 2, 14 (1950).
2. F. Korte and H. Sieper, in *Hashish: Its Chemistry and Pharmacology*, G. E. W. Wolstenholme and J. Knight, Eds. (Little, Brown, Boston, 1965), pp. 15–30.
3. Task Force on Narcotics and Drug Abuse, the President's Commission on Law Enforcement and the Administration of Justice, *Task Force Report: Narcotics and Drug Abuse* (1967), p. 14.
4. R. Mechoulam, and Y. Gaoni, *J. Amer. Chem. Soc.* 67, 3273 (1965).
5. J. F. Siler, W. L. Sheep, L. B. Bates, G. F. Clark, G. W. Cook, W. A. Smith, *Mil. Surg.* (November 1933), pp. 269–280.
6. Mayor's Committee on Marijuana, *The Marijuana Problem in the City of New York*, 1944.
7. E. G. Williams, C. K. Himmelsbach, A. Winkler, D. C. Ruble, B. J. Lloyd, *Public Health Rep.* 61, 1059 (1946).
8. H. Isbell, *Psychopharmacologia* 11, 184 (1967).
9. I. C. Chopra and R. N. Chopra, *Bull. Narcotics* 9, 4 (1957).
10. F. Ames, *J. Ment. Sci.* 104, 972 (1958).
11. C. J. Miras, in *Hashish: Its Chemistry and Pharmacology*, G. E. W. Wolstenholme and J. Knight, Eds. (Little, Brown, Boston, 1965), pp. 37–47.
12. J. M. Watt, in *Hashish: Its Chemistry and Pharmacology*, G. E. W. Wolstenholme and J. Knight, Eds. (Little, Brown, Boston, 1965), pp. 54–66.
13. AMA Council on Mental Health *J. Amer. Med. Ass.* 204, 1181 (1968).
14. G. Joachimoglu, in *Hashish: Its Chemistry and Pharmacology*, G. E. W. Wolstenholme and J. Knight, Eds. (Little, Brown, Boston, 1965), pp. 2–10.
15. We thank M. Lerner and A. Bober of the U.S. Customs Laboratory, Baltimore, for performing this assay.
16. We thank R. H. Pace and E. H. Hall of the Peter J. Schweitzer Division of the Kimberly-Clark Corp. for supplying placebo material.
17. S. Garattini, in *Hashish: Its Chemistry and Pharmacology*, G. E. W. Wolstenholme and J. Knight, Eds. (Little, Brown, Boston, 1965), pp. 70–78.
18. J. H. Jaffee, in *The Pharmacological Basis of Therapeutics*, L. S. Goodman and A. Gilman, Eds. (Macmillan, New York, ed. 3, 1965), pp. 299–301.
19. We thank E. L. Richardson, Attorney General of the Commonwealth of Massachusetts, for permitting these experiments to proceed and N. L. Chayet for legal assistance. We do not consider it appropriate to de-

scribe here the opposition we encountered from governmental agents and agencies and from university bureaucracies.

20. We thank D. Miller and M. Seifer of the Federal Bureau of Narcotics (now part of the Bureau of Narcotics and Dangerous Drugs, under the Department of Justice) for help in obtaining marijuana for this research.

21. The doses of tobacco in placebo and lowdose cigarettes were too small to cause physiological changes in subjects who qualified in the practice session.

22. K. E. ROSVOLD, A. F. MIRSKY, I. SARASON, E. D. BRANSOME, L. H. BECK, J. Consult. Psychol. 20, 343 (1956); A. F. Mirsky and P. V. Cardon, Electroencephalogr. Clin. Neurophysiol. 14, 1 (1962); C. Kornetsky and G. Bain, Psychopharmacologia 3, 277 (1965).

23. G. M. SMITH and H. K. BEECHER, J. Pharmacol. 126, 50 (1959).

24. We will attempt to define the complex nature of a marijuana high in a subsequent paper discussing the speech samples and interviews.

25. H. S. BECKER, Outsiders: Studies in the Sociology of Deviance (Macmillan, New York, 1963), chap. 3.

26. Although the motor skills measured by the pursuit rotor are represented in driving ability, they are only components of that ability. The influence of marijuana on driving skill remains an open question of high medico-legal priority.

27. L. E. HOLLISTER, R. K. RICHARDS, H. K. GILLESPIE, in preparation.

28. Sponsored and supported by Boston University's division of psychiatry, in part through PHS grants MH12568, MH06795–06, MH7753–06, and MH33319, and the Boston University Medical Center. The authors thank Dr. P. H. Knapp and Dr. C. Kornetsky of the Boston University School of Medicine, Department of Psychiatry and Pharmacology, for consistent support and excellent advice, and J. Finkelstein of 650 Madison Avenue, New York City, for his support at a crucial time.

Pharmacologic Effects of Marijuana

Frederick H. Meyers, M.D.

There is an unnecessary aura of uncertainty and confusion in the discussions of the pharmacology of marijuana and its various preparations and constituents. Part of the uncertainty is generated by those who believe that marijuana is a frighteningly dangerous drug in no way comparable to any accepted social drug, and, at the other extreme, by those individuals of increasing number who claim it is a purely beneficent drug in no way comparable to any acceptable social drug. Additional reluctance to summarize the pharmacology of marijuana stems from the assumption that research on its pharmacology is scant, dated, and of poor quality. Certainly much research remains to be done. However, the inability to present a consistent formulation of the pharmacology of marijuana may be due not so much to lack of data as to the failure to apply some unifying concept to the fragmentary information available.

Most drugs can be put into classes or categories. When this is done information derived from the previous study of other drugs in a particular class can be used to predict the effects of the drug under scrutiny. The period of study is shortened and an organizing concept is provided. For example, the study of the latest barbiturate to be synthesized is simplified by the exhaustive studies on the prototypes of its class of drugs.

There is a class of drugs made up of the sedative-hypnotics (alcohol, barbiturates) and the general anesthetics (ether, halothane and other "Freons" including those in hair spray, nitrous oxide, phencyclidine or PCP, the solvents in glue). If the effects of large doses of a sedative—like a dose of barbiturate taken with suicidal intent or an anesthetic dose of Pentothal—are examined, it is apparent that all of the drugs listed have qualitatively similar effects differing mostly in their physical state. Gases and volatile liquids are selected for use as general anesthetics because their transfer across the alveoli of the lungs allows for rapid onset of action, minute-to-minute control of dosage, and rapid recovery. The sedatives are given to achieve a longer

"Pharmacologic Effects of Marijuana" was published in the Journal of Psychedelic Drugs 2, no. 1 (Fall 1968): 31–36. Copyright © 1968 by David E. Smith, M.D. Reprinted with minor changes by permission of the publisher and the author.

Completion of this report was supported by a United States Public Health Service research grant (MH–15436) from the National Institute of Mental Health.

less intense effect and, if solids such as barbiturates are selected, they are more easily dispensed.

Having defined one drug class, the sedative-hypnotics, let us examine the following hypothesis: marijuana has all of the properties of a sedative-hypnotic. It seems distinctive from this class mostly because our experience is limited to its use by smoking, which provides for a rapidly appearing effect but also for a rapid decay of the effect as the absorbed drug is redistributed in the body. With the oral use of hashish or synthetic *Cannabis* equivalents, the apparent distinctiveness from alcohol or barbiturates disappears.

To establish that the hypothesis mentioned above is correct almost beyond question, this paper will list the properties of a sedative-hypnotic (Table 1) and then discuss the observations establishing that the constituents of *Cannabis* have the same actions.

TABLE 1. Actions That Characterize Sedative-Hypnotics and General Anesthetics (7)

Mechanism of Action:

Ascending Reticular Activating System Specifically Depressed

Descriptive:

A. Effect of Graded Doses (Stages of Anesthesia):
 1. Sedation and relief of anxiety
 2. Disinhibition or excitement
 3. Anesthesia
 4. Respiratory and vasomotor (medullary) depression

B. With Chronic Administration:
 1. Anticonvulsant
 2. Spinal cord depression (voluntary muscle relaxation)
 3. Physical dependence (withdrawal state)
 4. Liability for abuse
 5. Therapeutic effect: relief of anxiety, induction of sleep

Throughout the discussion the following cautions should be remembered.

1. Effects are described that aid in the classification of the drug. It does not follow that these effects appear regularly in the ordinary use of marijuana in our culture, where the usual pattern is smoking rather than ingestion and where comparatively weak "grass" is the mode.
2. The assumption is made that hashish, grass, THC, and synhexyl exert qualitatively similar effects. (Synhexyl, or pyrahexyl, differs from the

THC, assumed to be the most important active component, by one CH_2 group. It has been available in adequate amounts and has been studied far more thoroughly than other natural or synthetic THC's. Studies in humans establish the similarities of effects.) (4)

Effects of Graded Doses

If marijuana is a sedative-hypnotic, the administration of progressively larger doses should lead to a sequence of changes comparable to the stages of general anesthesia. It can be shown in animals that large doses do produce anesthesia and that after huge doses the animal does die from respiratory depression.

The interpretation of the effects of smaller doses, however, appears controversial to some observers because the "high" is assumed to be a manifestation of stimulation by the drug.

To understand the effect of smaller doses of marijuana, one must differentiate between manifest behavior, i.e., excitement or depression, and the underlying pharmacologic effect of stimulation or depression. Marijuana, like alcohol, is a depressant in its effects on the nervous system; the "high" is a result of depression of the higher centers and consequent release of lower centers from chronic inhibitory influences. Increasing the dosage, whether of marijuana, alcohol, or ether, leads to pure depression as the excitement stage is passed. There is other laboratory evidence for the depressant effect of the tetrahydrocannabinols, for example, the ability to prolong the sleep induced by other sedatives.

As marijuana is used in this country, the period of disinhibition or drunkenness is quite brief. Psychomotor ability and probably judgment are impaired during this period. The disinhibition also causes euphoria and relief of anxiety; it also explains the social use and possible misuse of all of the drugs of this class.

An additional area of confusion or controversy is introduced when marijuana is characterized as a "mild hallucinogen." The effect in question is better described as a dreamy state with an increased tendency to fantasize and to accept suggestion. Such a dreamy, hypnogogic state can be induced with almost any one of the sedatives or anesthetics under favorable conditions. The use of nitrous oxide to produce such a state was described by Humphry Davy almost as soon as he isolated the gas. The Pentothal interview and the recent use of PCP (Sernylan®) are additional examples, and a transient "hallucinatory" state has also been described during the therapeutic use of chlordiazepoxide (Librium). (9)

Effects of Continuous Use

1. *Physical dependence and withdrawal.* Physical dependence as a factor maintaining drug misuse has undoubtedly been greatly over-emphasized. Alcohol, for example, undoubtedly provides the number 1 drug problem in our culture, but only rarely causes delirium tremens. Nevertheless, if a drug is to be classified as a sedative-hypnotic, it must be demonstrated that the abrupt discontinuance of large doses results in a state of hyperexcitability.

Clinical observations of hashish smokers suggest that withdrawal symptoms are unusual or mild. Experimentally, i.e., for purposes of classification, a withdrawal state can be shown. For example, subjects were given large doses of pyrahexyl orally for 26 to 31 days. On the third day following discontinuation of the drug most patients were restless and slept poorly. One subject experienced agitation progressing to disorientation and the symptoms were abolished within four to five hours by the administration of pyrahexyl. Another passed through a hypomanic state on the fourth day. Under the same experimental conditions subjects were allowed free access to marijuana cigarettes for 39 days. The average patient smoked 17 cigarettes per day but no withdrawal sate was demonstrated. (10)

2. *Liability for misuse.* The question of whether the use of marijuana as a social drug can, like the use of alcohol as a social drug, sometimes lead to the development of a compulsive pattern of use is, of course, an emotionally loaded question. Certainly the hazards of smoking the weak marijuana preparations available in this country are minimal. If one looks outside of our culture to the Muslim world, it appears that a compulsive pattern of use with results comparable to those of chronic alcoholism is indeed possible.

3. *Other effects.* There are other pharmacologic actions of *Cannabis* preparations that are useful in classifying the drug but that are of interest primarily to the laboratory investigator. For example, the tetrahydrocannabinols are anticonvulsant and depress polysynaptic transmission within the spinal cord.

None of the preparations of *Cannabis* has therapeutic applications, and none of the questions associated with its use as a social drug would be altered if it did. The use of synhexyl as an antidepressant is, however, often mentioned. Review of the paper by Stockings (8) usually cited in this regard will establish that he actually used the drug for the relief of anxiety. He clearly characterizes his ambulant patients as neurotic and describes the development after the administration of synhexyl of mild intoxication, euphoria, and dreamy apathy.

MECHANISM OF ACTION

The ability of a sedative or anesthetic to cause loss of consciousness is due to the sensitivity of the reticular activating system to their depressant effects. When electrodes are implanted into the reticular formation and several functionally related areas in the brain, the effect of synhexyl cannot be distinguished from that of Pentothal. (3)

Conclusion

Thus the effects of marijuana, both operationally and in its mechanism of action, correspond exactly to those of other sedatives and anesthetics, especially alcohol. The apparent distinctiveness of marijuana is due mostly to the use of a route of administration that permits the rapid development of an effect and to properties of the active components that lead to rapid decrease in the effects. One is driven to the conclusion that the differences between the dominant attitudes and consequent laws toward marijuana and alcohol are unrelated to the pharmacologic effects of the drugs but are due to a conflict between the mores of the dominant and one or more of the subcultures in this country.

References

1. Bose, B. C.; Saifi, A. Q.; and Bhagwat, A. W. 1963. Effect of Cannabis indica on hexobarbital sleeping time and tissue respiration of rat brain. *Arch. int. Pharmacodyn* 141: 520–24.

2. Bose, B. C. et al. 1963. Chemical and pharmacological investigations of Cannabis indica. Part I. *Arch. int. Pharmacodyn* 146: 99–105.

3. Boyd, E. S., and Meritt, D. A. 1966. Effects of barbiturates and tetrahydrocannabinol derivative on recovery cycles of medial lemniscus, thalamus and reticular formation in the cat. *J. Pharmacol. Exper. Therap.* 151: 376–84.

4. Hollister, L. E.; Richards, R. K.; and Gillespie, H. K. 1968. Comparison of tetrahydro cannabinol and synhexyl in man. *Clin. Pharmacol. Therap.* 9: 783–91.

5. Loewe, S. 1946. Studies on the pharmacology and acute toxicity of compounds with marijuana activity. *J. Pharmacol. Exper. Therap.* 88: 154–61.

6. Dagirmanjian, R., and Boyd, E. S. 1962. Some pharmacological effects of two tetrahydrocannabinols. *J. Pharmacol. Exper. Therap.* 135: 25–33.

7. MEYERS, F. H., JAWETZ, E., and GOLDFIEN, A. 1968. *Review of Medical Pharmacology*. Los Altos: Lange Publications.
8. STOCKINGS, G. T. 1947. A new euphoriant for depressive mental states. *Brit. Med. J.* 1: 918–22.
9. VISCOTT, D. S. 1968. Chlordiazepoxide and hallucinations. *Arch. Gen. Psychiat.* 19: 370–76.
10. WILLIAM, E. G. et al. 1946. Studies on marijuana and pyrahexyl compound. *Public Health Reports* 61: 1059–83.

Use of Marijuana

in the

Haight-Ashbury Subculture

J. Fred E. Shick, M.D.

David E. Smith, M.D.

Frederick H. Meyers, M.D.

Marijuana has been adopted by a significant portion of the youthful subculture as a social drug. Despite marijuana's central importance in helping us understand current patterns of drug use, only limited information on it is available, especially concerning its relation to the use of other drugs. The present study was feasible because the Haight-Ashbury Medical Clinic provided access to people who widely used marijuana and other drugs.

The Haight-Ashbury Clinic was established in San Francisco in anticipation of the influx of persons into that neighborhood during the summer of 1967; beginning on June 6, 1967, it started to provide free care for acute medical problems as well as for problems related to drug use. By the time this study was made the clinic and its volunteer staff had gained acceptance by the community and was providing care for as many as 200 persons per day.

By September 1967, when our survey was conducted, the well-publicized hippie group had been diluted by a large number of transient youths who were exploring, rather than being committed to,

"Use of Marijuana in the Haight-Ashbury Subculture" was published in the Journal of Psychedelic Drugs 2, no. 1 (Fall 1968): 49–66. Copyright © 1968 by David E. Smith, M.D. Reprinted with minor changes by permission of the publisher and J. Fred E. Shick, M.D.

The authors are grateful to the Indiana University Medical School Research Computation Center for providing computer time under a Public Health Service grant (FR–00162). Completion of this article was supported by a Public Health Service research grant (MH–15436) from the National Institute of Mental Health.

the hip philosophy. To describe the people of the neighborhood at that time as being hippies is to deny the diversity of those who had come to the Haight with differing backgrounds, motivations, expectations, as well as degree of drug experience. Furthermore, the community subsequently changed to include a substantial proportion of compulsive methamphetamine ("speed") users, and the presence of that group was evident at the time of our survey.

The availability of a favorable population and the high regard in which the Haight-Ashbury Clinic was held by that population encouraged us to believe that accurate data could be collected to test our subjective impressions.

Methods

Members of the clinic staff, themselves Haight-Ashbury residents and members of the community, were trained to administer a questionnaire designed to present limited, simple, and self-explanatory choices. The survey included multiple choice questions providing demographic and personal data, present employment, past incidence of psychiatric counseling and hospitalization, drug preferences, and questions detailing the respondents' own use of marijuana, hard liquor, beer and wine, other sedative-hypnotic drugs, oral and intravenous amphetamines, the psychedelic drugs, heroin, cocaine, and opium.

A total of 413 usable questionnaires were completed during the month of September 1967, which sampled both from those who came to the clinic and from other congregation areas (e.g., Golden Gate Park), and community agencies (e.g., Huckleberries for Runaways) within the Haight-Ashbury neighborhood of 20 square blocks. The sample, admittedly a sample of opportunity, is as representative as possible of the Haight-Ashbury's hippie population present at the time. The demographic data agrees well with the findings of other investigators. (1)

Among the community there was a well-known mistrust of the straight society and a history of a lack of cooperation with other investigators who had attempted even less comprehensive surveys. We therefore decided that in addition to protecting the anonymity of the respondent, it would be necessary to have members of the "New Community," as clinic personnel, administer the drug survey in order to obtain adequate and truthful answers concerning drug use. The reputation of the clinic minimized any suspicion that the information collected would be used against the community or any individual. Community leaders were assured that the data would be published only after a reasonable interval. The survey was well received by the community and the refusal rate was less than one percent.

Data from the surveys were transferred onto IBM cards; then several computer programs were written to select and tabulate the information on selected groups from the sample. The statistics are for the most part expressed in percentage form, and an analysis of variance is applied to obtain the standard error and confidence interval for the statistic obtained. Where the percentage statistic of two samples is to be compared and the equality of population means tested, a two-tailed student's T test is applied to the hypothesis of the equality of the means or percentages. In this study the confidence interval expressed is 95 percent or p = .05. Likewise for a difference to be labeled as "significant," a two-tailed test with a p = .05 or less is required unless otherwise stated.[1]

The characteristics of the population living in the Haight-Ashbury neighborhood have not been constant over any but very brief periods. As the drug-centered community evolved, the relative proportion of individuals who prefer one or another drug or pattern of drug use has changed. At the time of this survey the hippie influence was still influential but waning, and the use of high dose intravenous methamphetamine (speed) was growing. In order to follow changes in the neighborhood and to test several hypotheses related to sociological aspects of drug use, extensive surveys were carried out at two subsequent times based on random sampling techniques.

The present paper focuses on the patterns of marijuana use and its relationship to the abuse of other drugs. We have briefly characterized the total sample of respondents regardless of their pattern of marijuana use and then discussed areas of difference among various patterns of use.

The Community as Revealed by the Sample

The types of people that this community comprises vary in proportion from one time to another. During the summer and fall of 1967, the time interval that the present study represents, Haight-Ashbury could be described as composed primarily of sons and daughters of the white middle class, who often had some college education and who frequently experimented with various drugs.

Our sample consisted of 413 respondents: 222 males and 191 females. Our analysis substantiates that the population was drawn

[1] See Jerome C. R. Li, *Statistical Inference* (Ann Arbor, Mich.: Edwards Brothers, Inc., 1966).

largely from families of the middle class. The occupation of the head of the household served as an index of socioeconomic class; 51.6 percent of our respondents' fathers had occupations in the professional, managerial, or sales categories, and 44.3 percent of the fathers had some college education. Of the entire sample of 413 respondents, 79.9 percent identified themselves as single and 10.7 percent as married. With regard to race, 86.2 percent of the sample identified themselves as Caucasian; less than 1 percent of the sample was Negro. The sample included 16 American Indians (3.9 percent). The mean age of the respondents was 20.5 ± 1.5 years; 51.8 percent had at least some college education. Some 43 percent of the respondents had not lived with their parents for three years or more.

It is remarkable that about half of the respondents were from states other than California. Only 16.2 percent had been raised in the Bay Area of San Francisco; 34.1 percent had been raised in another large metropolitan area such as New York City, Los Angeles, or Chicago; and 41.4 percent had spent most of their lives in cities of less than 200,000 or in rural areas. One hundred eighty-one (44 percent) were living outside of California before they began to participate in the Haight-Ashbury scene, whereas only 128 (31 percent) were living in the Bay Area.

The use of marijuana was practically universal in this population. It was generally used as a social drug, much as the parents of the respondents use alcohol. In answer to the question, "Have you ever used marijuana?" 94.6 percent of the males and 98.4 percent of the females responded affirmatively; 90.8 percent (375) of the total sample had used the drug in Haight-Ashbury, though not necessarily exclusively there, as we shall discuss later. Three hundred eighty-one, or 92.4 percent, had used marijuana within a month prior to the time of the survey, and 87 percent of the total had used LSD or a similar hallucinogenic drug at least once.

It is important to emphasize that this population had a particularly high level of familiarity with various drugs. Some 87 percent had consumed hard liquor, 55 percent had used other drugs of the sedative-hypnotic type, not to mention the 96 percent who had tried marijuana. One fourth of the total sample had tried heroin, though not necessarily intravenously, although only 8 persons were presently abusing that narcotic. About 58 percent had tried smoking opium, or what was thought to be opium, which is an important distinction when discussing "street drugs." Some 87 percent had tried one of the various psychedelics, most frequently LSD. About 35 percent had tried intravenous amphetamine; 75 percent had tried the oral amphetamines; and 36 percent admitted to some personal experience with cocaine. Thus our population differed from other drug using populations in several aspects, and the results of our study should not necessarily be construed as applying to other drug using subcultures.

Levels of Marijuana Use by the Respondents

FREQUENCY OF USE AND PRESENT AGE

It is difficult to speak of the abuse of marijuana in the United States because of the low concentration of active ingredients in the "grass" arriving or grown in the United States at the time of our study and because of its inherent low potential for abuse. Drug abuse may be defined as the use of a drug to the extent that it interferes with one's health, economic, or social functioning. Certainly our questions were not sensitive enough to identify the rare person whose functioning was hindered by his use of marijuana. For the purpose of this analysis we differentiated three groups of marijuana users, namely the occasional user, the regular user, and the habitual user. Our sample consisted of 51 occasional users, 161 regular users, and 177 habitual users of the drug. The occasional user was defined as the individual choosing an answer on the questionnaire indicating use of up to four times in the month preceding the time of the questionnaire. A regular user indicated use of four to thirty times, and a habitual user more than 30 times during the previous month.

Questions regarding the amount of drug used on each occasion were, unfortunately, often regarded as ambiguous by respondents and were not used to determine the level of marijuana use. The loss of data was not great since the variable potency of the product and

TABLE 1. Ages of Marijuana Users*

	Occasional Users	Regular Users	Habitual Users	Total
Males (222):				
Number	26	75	104	222
Age Range	16–26	15–30	15–34	15–34
Mean Age	21.4 ± .6	20.8 ± .3	20.99 ± .3	21.0 ± .2
Females (191):				
Number	25	86	73	191
Age Range	15–34	9–37	13–29	9–37
Mean Age	21.7 ± .8	20.4 ± .3	19.4 ± .3	20.2 ± .2

* 95 percent confidence limits are given.

varying techniques of smoking could not have been evaluated in any case. The use of certain drugs was found to differ in some respects between the sexes, and we believe that their motivations to drug use often were dissimilar. So for the most part the analysis was made of males and females as separate groups and the statistics were then compared. Our sample had a mean age of 20.65 ± .15 years and a range of 9 to 37 years. The ages of the various groups of marijuana users is detailed in Table 1. The mean age of all males was 21.04 ± .2 (range 15 to 34 years), which is significantly older than all females (20.2 ± .23 [range 9–37 years]), as illustrated in Table 1. The mean age of the female habitual user of marijuana was significantly younger than either that of her male counterpart (20.99 ± .3) or the females as a whole (20.2 ± .2). This same finding was reflected in the significantly increased number of female habitual users in the 16- to 20-year-old age bracket (Table 2).

TABLE 2. Male and Female Users by Age Groups*

| | Age Range: | | | |
	16–20 Years	21–25 Years	26–30 Years	Total Sample
(1) Number	112	86	16	413
(2) Mean Age†	18.8	22.6	27.4	20.7
(3) Age† First Tried MJ	15.8 ± .2	18.2 ± .4	20.4 ± .1	17.1 ± .2
(4) Difference Between 2 & 3	3.0	4.4	7.0	3.6
(5) Percent Habitual MJ Users	49.6 ± 6.5%	33.3 ± 7.8%	35.7 ± 17.7%	42.9 ± 4.8%

* 95 percent confidence limits are given.
† In years.

AGE AT INTRODUCTION TO USE

The entire sample had first tried marijuana at a mean age of 17.07 ± .2 years of age (range 5 to 35 years). The age for first trying the drug tended to vary with the level of marijuana use. That is, the occasional user had first tried marijuana at a mean age of 18.6 ± .7; the regular user at the age of 17.4 ± .3; and the habitual user at the age of 16.2 ± .3. The difference between the age of first trying marijuana and the present age indicated a trend within the groups of male users that is not present among the females. The male occasional user had first tried marijuana on an average of 2.9 years ago, the male regular user 3.4 years ago, and the male habitual user 4.6 years ago. These findings are summarized in Table 3.

The older age group (25 to 30 years), average age of 27.4 years, had the greatest percentage of occasional users, in contrast to the

TABLE 3. Age for First Trying Marijuana*

	Occasional User	Regular User	Habitual User	Total
Males (222):				
(1) Present Mean Age	21.4 ± .8	20.8 ± .3	20.99 ± .3	21.0 ± .2
(2) Mean Age For First Trying MJ	18.7 ± .7	17.4 ± .4	16.4 ± .3	17.1 ± .2
(3) Difference Between Row 1 & 2	2.9	3.4	4.6	3.9
Females (191):				
(1) Present Mean Age	21.7 ± .8	20.4 ± .3	19.4 ± .3	20.2 ± .2
(2) Mean Age For First Trying MJ	18.7 ± .7	17.4 ± .3	16.0 ± .3	17.1 ± .2
(3) Difference Between Row 1 & 2	3.0	3.0	3.4	3.1

* 95 percent confidence limits are given.

17 year olds (ages 16 to 20), who had the least number of occasional users. Furthermore, the percentage of habitual users in the 25- to 30-year-old age bracket tended to be lower than in the younger age groups (Table 2).

The data in Table 3, analyzed without considering other pertinent data, could lead to the conclusion that the longer one uses marijuana, the greater his use of the drug becomes. But this conclusion is *not* supported by the data in Table 2, for the older age group had one of the smallest percentages of habitual users, although they had been using the drug for the greatest length of time. In fact, the greatest percent of habitual users and least percentage of occasional users were found among the 16- to 20-year-olds in both the male and female samples.

Our study supports the impression that in the past few years marijuana has been used by increasingly younger persons. In the 25- to 30-year age bracket (mean age 27.4 years) the age of first trying marijuana was about 21, while in the 16- to 20-year-old bracket (mean age 18.8 years) the age was significantly younger, about 16 years. And most of the 10- to 15-year-olds in our sample had tried marijuana within the year, while the 25- to 30-year-olds had tried it on an average of 7 years ago (Table 2). Some 90 to 95 percent of all groups of users agreed they would continue to use the drug, and among the older groups the agreement was unanimous.

CHARACTERISTICS OF THE THREE GROUPS

The habitual user, besides having used marijuana more frequently than the other users, also used greater amounts of the drug more frequently, as one might expect. There was a detectable difference between the amount used each time by the females and the males. There was a tendency (significant at the 90 percent level of confidence) for the females to use less of the drug than the males each time they used it, irrespective of their frequency of use.

Almost 55 percent of the respondents had at one time used or were using marijuana habitually, but it is interesting how often the habitual level of use could be replaced by only occasional use. This was reflected in the eight occasional users (15.7 percent), who had at one time had a peak habitual use of marijuana and the one quarter (23.6 percent) of the regular users, who at one time had used the drug habitually. It is rare to find such decreases in level of use among the users of drugs with more abuse potential, e.g., intravenous methamphetamine; such findings certainly reflect the low abuse potential for the marijuana found circulating in the United States.

The occasional user differed from the regular and habitual user in several important attitudes about his continued use of marijuana. Only three quarters of the occasional users admitted that they still used the drug. Furthermore, significantly fewer of the occasional users (77.1 percent) admitted that they planned to continue using the drug, compared with the regular or habitual users, who were almost unanimous (95–99 percent) about their intention to continue. Finally, only 13.3 percent of the females and 20.1 percent of the males of the total sample admitted that they had ever worried about their use of marijuana. Only 11 percent of the sample had ever refrained from using any drug because of the dangerous drug or narcotic drug laws.

An analysis of the relationship of the demographic data to the level of marijuana use was remarkable in that no trends were apparent. For instance, there was no correlation between the population of the area in which the user was raised and his level of use. With socio-economic level, the occupation of the head of the household serving as the index, there was no detectable relationship to the level of marijuana use, although the sample from the working classes was small. Fifty percent of the sample had an educational background of at least some college education. A detailed analysis of the level of schooling achieved and the present level of marijuana use gave no hint of a relationship. It was apparent, however, that there was a particularly large number of people with some graduate education who were also occasional users of marijuana. Otherwise marijuana use appeared to be unrelated to the educational level achieved by members of our population.

THE POSSIBLE HAZARD OF RESIDENCE
IN AN ENVIRONMENT OF HIGH USE

We looked particularly at the respondent's time in Haight-Ashbury and his present level of marijuana use. Do those who stay longer have higher levels of use because of increased availability, associations made in the area, and the like? Conclusive evidence is difficult to gain from our questionnaire, since so few had arrived before 1967 (only 70 respondents, or 17 percent, had come to Haight before 1967). We are awaiting more data from the surveys conducted in 1968 to deal conclusively with this question. At this time it can be said, however, that there was no statistically significant difference in the frequency of marijuana use between those who arrived in the summer of 1967 and those who had arrived earlier in that year.

The individual's experience with marijuana was by no means entirely in Haight-Ashbury; his first introduction to the drug was usually outside the community. This is evidenced by a difference of at least two years between the age of his first trying marijuana and the age when he arrived in Haight (Table 3). Many users (73.6 percent) had come to Haight-Ashbury during the first nine months of 1967. In addition, 17.7 percent of the occasional users and 3.1 percent of the regular users had never used marijuana in Haight, and more than half were Haight-Ashbury residents at the time of the study. A significantly lower percentage of the 25- to 30-year-olds had used marijuana in Haight-Ashbury, which perhaps reflects a greater mobility and diversity of experience and acquaintances.

The Use of Marijuana and the Abuse of Other Drugs

ALCOHOL–MARIJUANA CORRELATES.[2]

The use of the legal ethyl alcohol-containing drugs by this population was particularly interesting, especially when comparing and contrasting the use of marijuana to the use of alcohol. Evidence has been presented that marijuana may be similar in its pharmacologic action to alcohol—that it is a member of the sedative-hypnotic class of drugs. (2) It was our impression that within this community marijuana was being used as an alcohol substitute. Fifty-two of the total sample (12.8 percent) had never tried hard liquor, yet only about 2 percent (eight) had never tried marijuana. Only 65.6 percent of the entire group of respondents had used any form of ethanol in Haight-Ashbury, although 90.8 percent had used marijuana there. The average age of the sample was 20.7 years, and almost half were of the legal age to use and purchase alcoholic beverages.

The abuse of hard liquor in this sample was quite small when compared to the abuse of other drugs, notably the psychedelics and

[2] In this paper the terms alcohol, ethyl alcohol, and ethanol are used interchangeably.

intravenous amphetamines. Only about 3 percent of the sample were dependent drinkers of hard liquor and only about one half of them were assuredly abusing the drug in terms of the amount they consumed on each occasion. It is striking that among a population with a very high level of marijuana use and much experience with psychedelic drugs (where 50 percent habitually used marijuana and 15 percent abused the psychedelic drugs), less than 3 percent abused the ethyl alcohol-containing drugs, hard liquor, beer and wine, in terms of frequency and amount consumed on each occasion.

The males in the survey had first tried hard liquor at about the same age of 13 years, irrespective of their present age, yet there was a difference among the females. The younger females, 16 to 20 years of age, had first tried hard liquor at a significantly earlier age than their 25- to 30-year-old counterparts. The younger females had begun at age 12 to 13, about the same age as all age groups of the males. Perhaps this reflects a change in social attitude toward the use of liquor by females in our society.

But we were concerned with a relationship between the use of marijuana and the use of alcohol and so examined in detail the peak and present levels of the use of both drugs. Our questionnaire distinguished between two types of ethanol use. There were questions concerning the respondents' consumption of hard liquor and their pattern of consumption of beer and wine. Again we determined who in each group was abusing the drug by applying our previously stated definition for abuse. First the respondents' use of hard liquor was compared to their use of marijuana.

Because there was a small sample of hard liquor abusers (number sampled = 12), it was difficult to show any statistical trend about the abusers' use of marijuana. A few isolated trends stood out, however, which began to confirm our impression that in this population a high level of marijuana use was associated with a low level of hard liquor consumption. For instance, among the female occasional users of marijuana, a significantly higher percentage (20 percent) used hard liquor in an abusive pattern than did the regular or habitual users of marijuana. And among the female habitual users of marijuana, their use of hard liquor was quite low. The lowest percentage of hard liquor abuse was among the habitual users of marijuana, although because of the small sample this was not a statistically significant difference.

There was much suggestion in the data that people who had abused hard liquor previously were now at a low level of liquor use but at the same time sustained a high level of marijuana use. Here is a specific example of a sample of males who had abused liquor previously. Of these 26 males, 20 had only minimally consumed hard liquor during the month that this survey was conducted, although their use of marijuana in the same period was almost completely in the regular or habitual use level. All of the 20 had used psychedelic drugs. These 20 who were now at a low level of hard liquor consumption did use the drug in excessive quantities on the rare occasions when they consumed hard liquor; that is, two thirds used it to get drunk, sick, or pass out on these occasions. Three quarters of these former abusers of hard liquor stated that they did not plan to continue drinking hard liquor, all planned to continue using marijuana, and practically all attributed the change in their hard liquor consumption to having taken marijuana and/or LSD.

Of the total sample, 309 had decreased or stopped their consumption of hard liquor, 79 percent attributed this change to their having taken marijuana and/or LSD. Again, 90 percent were regular or habitual users of marijuana, among a community that condones marijuana use much as the middle class condones the consumption of alcohol. Certainly it is dangerous to suggest a cause and effect relationship between taking marijuana and decreasing alcohol consumption; to underscore this point we would add that when asked about their preferred drug or drug of choice, so to speak, 61.8 percent of these persons preferred the psychedelics and not marijuana as first choice; marijuana as a second choice drug, however, was quite commonly preferred (56.6 percent).

MARIJUANA–LSD CORRELATES

There was a high degree of association in our sample between the use of psychedelics and the use of marijuana. And it is our impression, supported by statistics from this survey and in agreement with the impressions of others, that in this community in the summer and fall of 1967 the use of LSD and the use of marijuana were practically inseparable. One must remember that in the summer of 1967 this community consisted of people who used primarily the psychedelics and marijuana. In fact the "hippie ethic" and the "New Community" had part of its basis in the use of the psychedelics, and only secondarily used marijuana.

Unwilling to accept established conceptions about drugs, this population has experimented a great deal with a variety of drugs. And as we began to examine the abusers of each drug included in our survey, it became clear that the abuse of one drug was often associated with the abuse of another drug, often within the same time period. We were able to distinguish an abuser group—a group of persons who only experimented with various drugs—as well as a group who used drugs regularly but infrequently abused them. This latter group of users used primarily the psychedelics and marijuana.

There were the experimenters, only 27.4 percent of the total sample, who have made no significant use of any of the illegal drugs but only 14.5 percent of the sample who *never* have had more than an occasional use of any illegal drug except marijuana. Then there were the persons who regularly used marijuana and one or another of the psychedelics but had no abusive pattern of use of any drug (amphetamines, heroin, liquor, psychedelics); these persons made up one third of the community. Finally, there were the drug abusers (19.4 percent of the sample), most commonly of the psychedelics, whose use of other drugs was usually on the abusive level. This we call the abuser group. Among the regular marijuana–LSD users only 9 percent had abused another drug during the same period, while among the abuser group almost 32 percent had abused another drug.

The drug most commonly used in Haight-Ashbury, aside from the almost universal use of marijuana, was the class of psychedelics. And these were the drugs most commonly abused. The next most commonly abused drugs were the intravenous amphetamines, commonly methamphetamine. Of the total sample, 84 percent had tried one of the psychedelics at least once (usually LSD) and two thirds had used the psychedelic drugs at least once during the month of September 1967. LSD was the drug most commonly abused. Of those who had abused any illegal drug except marijuana (the abuser group) 74 percent had abused LSD or another of the psychedelics. By contrast only 9.9 percent of this group abused heroin. A significant 44.4 percent of the sample of abusers abused *only* the psychedelics; these persons had an associated habitual use (86 percent) of marijuana. Of the persons who used only the psychedelics but did not abuse them, 75 percent abused no other drug, although marijuana was used by one half habitually.

The habitual use of marijuana was significantly more frequently associated with the abuse of the psychedelics than with the abuse of any other drug (Table 4); 85 percent of the psychedelic abusers also used marijuana habitually, and this is significantly higher ($p < .05$) ["<" means "less than"] than the frequency of habitual marijuana use in any other abuser group. By contrast, among the regular users of the psychedelics (i.e., those who used the psychedelics and marijuana almost exclusively) only 52 percent used marijuana habitually. The abuse of the intravenous amphetamines was negligible in this group of regular LSD users; only 11 of 175 had abused the intravenous amphetamines. But among abusers of the psychedelics, 23.3

TABLE 4. Male and Female Abuser Groups
and Marijuana Use*

	Psyche-delics	Intravenous Amphet-amines	Abusers of: Oral Amphet-amines	Heroin	Total Sample
Number of Abusers	60	30	9	8	413
Percent Habitual MJ Users	85.0 ± 11.9%	63.3 ± 17.2%	55.6 ± 32.6%	50.0 ± 34.6%	42.9 ± 4.2%

* 95 percent confidence limits are given.

percent also abused amphetamine intravenously in the same period as their abuse of LSD.

It is interesting to compare the age of the abusers and regular users of the psychedelics when first trying marijuana and hard liquor. The mean age of the psychedelic abuser (19.8 ± 0.4 years) was significantly younger than the regular LSD–marijuana user. Likewise, among psychedelic abusers the mean age of first trying marijuana was younger (15.2 ± 0.4 years) than among the LSD-marijuana (regular LSD users) user group (16.8 ± 0.2 years). But the difference between the mean ages of first trying marijuana and the present ages of the respondents differed by only one year. The mean age for first trying hard liquor was significantly younger among the abuser group than among the regular LSD–marijuana user group. We do not believe that the age for first trying marijuana and the level of use of drugs is causally related, but the significantly younger age for trying hard liquor and marijuana among abusers may reflect early conditions that predispose one to abuse drugs. Certainly the high level of abuse of one drug associated with the abuse of other drugs supports the multiple drug abuse theory, explained in the discussion.

MARIJUANA-AMPHETAMINE CORRELATES

Of the total sample of 413 respondents, 34.1 percent had tried using amphetamines by intravenous administration at least once. Of these 21.3 percent (7.3 percent of the total sample) were abusing the drug at the time of our study. The intravenous amphetamines were the second most commonly abused drug within our sample. Among the various levels of marijuana use (occasional, regular, habitual) there were no significant differences between the percentages of intravenous amphetamine abusers in each group: a range of from five percent of the occasional users to 11 percent of the habitual marijuana users. Among the habitual users of marijuana, however, there was a significantly greater frequency ($p < .10$) of experimental and periodic use of intravenous amphetamine than in the occasional or regular marijuana use categories. This simply reflected a greater frequency of drug use among those who had extensive acquaintance with drugs and who frequently experimented with various drugs and means of administration.

Apparently the level of intravenous amphetamine use had no relationship to the level of marijuana use, for the perecentage distribution of the various levels of marijuana use was statistically the same whether among experimental users, periodic users, or abusers of the intravenous amphetamines (Table 5). From 8 to 13 percent were oc-

TABLE 5. Marijuana Use Among Male and Female
Intravenous (I.V.) Amphetamine Users and Abusers*

	I.V. Amphetamine Pattern of Use:		
	Experi-mental	Periodic	Abuser	Total Sample
Number in Group	74	37	30	413
Marijuana Use Pattern (percent)				
Occasional	$8.2 \pm 6.3\%$	$5.4 \pm 6.1\%$	$13.3 \pm 12.2\%$	$12.4 \pm 3.2\%$
Regular	$34.3 \pm 10.9\%$	$21.6 \pm 13.3\%$	$23.3 \pm 15.1\%$	$39.0 \pm 4.7\%$
Habitual	$56.2 \pm 11.4\%$	$59.5 \pm 15.8\%$	$63.3 \pm 17.2\%$	$42.9 \pm 4.8\%$
No Response	1.3%	13.5%	0.1%	5.7%

* 95 percent confidence limits are given.

casional users of marijuana; 22 to 34 percent were regular users of marijuana; and 56 to 63 percent were habitual users of marijuana. The habitual level of marijuana use was the most frequent within the various levels of intravenous amphetamine use and abuse, as it was among the total sample of 413. It is true that habitual marijuana use was significantly more frequent among respondents who were using any intravenous amphetamines at all than among the total sample of 413. But other levels of marijuana use, namely occasional and regular use, were no more frequent among users or abusers of intravenous amphetamines than among the sample as a whole.

If we consider only the abusers of the various drugs we find that the frequency of habitual marijuana use was significantly greater ($p < .05$) among the abusers of the psychedelics than among any other abuser group. Although the frequency of habitual marijuana use was significantly greater among the abusers of the intravenous amphetamines than among the general population of Haight, it cannot be considered significantly greater than the other abuser groups, namely oral amphetamines or heroin, because of the small sample from these groups.

Originally it was our impression that the frequency of marijuana use among abusers of the intravenous amphetamines would be quite high because of observations that marijuana was being used to aid the person who was "coming down" from intravenous amphetamine intoxication, much as a sedative would be used. This practice may account for the significantly greater frequency of habitual marijuana use among the intravenous amphetamine abusers than among the sample as a whole.

It is, however, difficult to account for the high association between habitual marijuana use and abuse of the psychedelics, except to explain that these were the most "socially acceptable" drugs within this subculture; their association may simply reflect the social preference. It may also be true that marijuana was used to modulate the psychedelic experience either as a "downer" (a sedative) or in an attempt to heighten the experience.

Summary of Drug Preference

Certain questions in the survey concerned a respondent's drug preferences. His drug of choice was that drug that he considered best to fulfill the goals that he associated with taking drugs. A unique feature of our respondents in this population was their preference for psychedelics; 46.8 percent of the respondents listed LSD as their first choice, and 25.5 percent listed marijuana first. Although 8 percent of the sample were abusing intravenous amphetamines, only 3 percent listed that drug as first choice. The preference for LSD existed among practically all groups of users and abusers within this community. Marijuana was listed by 53.9 percent of the respondents as second choice, and LSD was listed second by 19.4 percent.

Discussion

A few concepts and definitions must be reviewed before discussing the problems of multiple drug use and the inverse or direct relation between the use of one drug and another. Why, for example, was the inverse relationship between hard liquor consumption and marijuana use just described in this population not repeated when the consumption of beer and wine by the marijuana users was considered?

CLASSIFICATION OF DRUGS SUBJECT TO MISUSE

Psychoactive drugs may be classified in several groups according to their mode of action. We have discussed hard liquor, which is a sedative-hypnotic. Other members of this general classification include the other ethanol-containing drugs (in our survey beer and wine), the barbiturates, and drugs formerly termed "minor tranquilizers" but now known to be sedatives, such as meprobamate (Miltown), chlordiazepoxide (Librium), and diazepam (Valium). Furthermore, there is evidence to support the classification of marijuana as a sedative drug. (2) A second group of drugs is the opiate derivatives: heroin, morphine, crude opium, and narcotic synthetics. It is generally agreed that marijuana is *not* a member of this class of drugs. A third group of drugs are selective central nervous system stimulants, conveniently termed the psychedelic or hallucinogenic drugs, such as LSD-25, STP (DOM), MDA, mescaline, and psylocybin. Marijuana is said by some to be a "mild hallucinogen" and was compared in some studies to peyote or mescaline in its effects (3), which implies its inclusion in this class of drugs. It must be remembered that the occurrence of hallucinations, or what has been termed pseudo-hallucinations (4) with a particular drug, does not automatically place it in the class of psychedelic drugs. Nitrous oxide, ethanol, and amphetamine may produce hallucinations at certain stages of intoxication or withdrawal. The authors of this article prefer its classification as a sedative and have assembled evidence in support of this hypothesis. (2) A fourth group of drugs are the general stimulants of the central nervous system— drugs of the amphetamine type, including oral and intravenous amphetamine ("speed") and nicotine and caffeine. In passing we should note how similar are the psychedelic drugs and the amphetamines in pharmacologic action and chemical structure (Figure 1).

PATTERNS OF DRUG USE

It is of central importance to distinguish between the use and the abuse of a particular drug, whether one talks about alcohol, marijuana, or the amphetamines. Any drug may be used or it may be abused. For example, many people drink alcohol but do not become alcoholics. How then do we define abuse? Abuse may be defined as the use of a drug to the point where it seriously interferes with the user's health, social or economic functioning, but what factors are operating in relation to the person who is using or abusing drugs? Both the best and

Figure 1. CHEMICAL STRUCTURES

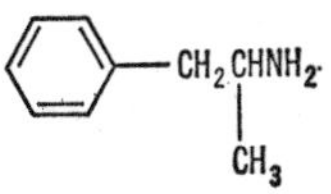

Amphetamine

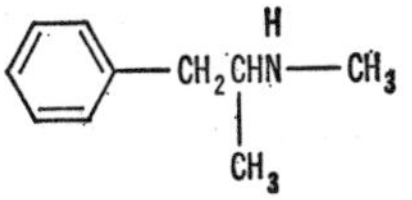

Methamphetamine

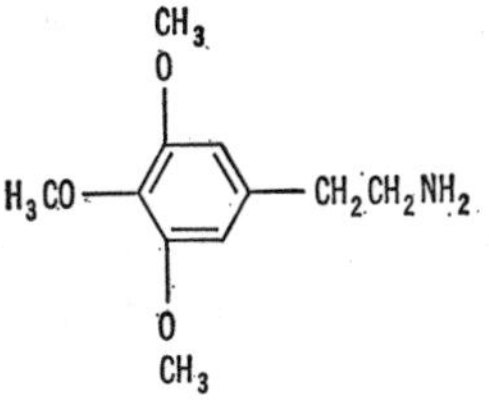

Mescaline

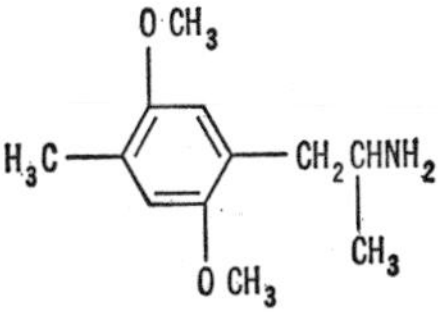

DOM (STP)
2, 5-dimethoxy-4-methyl-
amphetamine

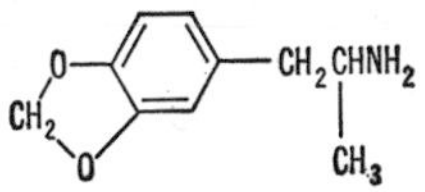

MDA
2, 3-Methylenedioxy-
amphetamine

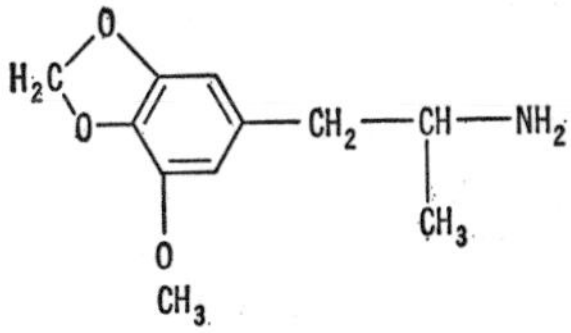

MMDA
3-methoxy-4, 5-methylene-
dioxyamphetamine

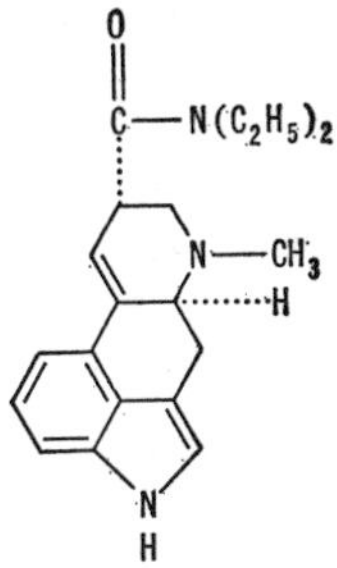

LSD-25
Lysergic acid
diethylamide

the worst consequences of drug use tend to be attributed to the drug itself. It is important to realize, however, that there are other factors operating besides the obvious pharmacologic effects. There are three groups of factors that influence drug use: the drug factors (i.e., pharmacologic tolerance, physical dependence, abstinence syndrome, behavioral toxicity, and metabolism), the individual factors, and the group factors. These have been discussed elsewhere by one of the authors. (7) These factors interrelate to determine the individual's particular pattern of drug use. The various ways in which persons use drugs may be most easily considered by discussing four patterns of drug use: the experimental use, the social use, the ritual use, and the compulsive use. The elective *experimental* or episodic use of drugs implies primarily the use of drugs infrequently, though the person may perhaps use an astounding variety of drugs experimentally. The *social* pattern of use is the occasional or periodic use of drugs in a social setting, where attaining a state of intoxication is of secondary importance to the facilitation of social interaction and the alleviation of the social anxiety by the drug. The paradigm here may be the use of alcohol by the middle class as a social drug. The *ritual* pattern of use, somewhat less familiar but quite important when considering drug-using subcultures, is the use of a drug as a part (sacrament, perhaps) of a ritual, or more generally drug use to achieve previously defined goals, often of a philosophic or psychotherapeutic type, which may or may not be realistic. The use of peyote by the Native American Church is an example of this pattern of use. The *compulsive* pattern includes the need to continue the use of the drug even in the face of deterioration of the user's functioning, as well as the tendency not to return to lower levels of use or to lower doses but usually to increase the dose, regardless of pharmacologic tolerance. The drug abuser (whether the alcoholic, the heroin abuser, the oral sedative abuser, or the like) represents this compulsive pattern of drug use.

MULTIPLE DRUG ABUSE

There are several theories about drug abuse and the drug abuser, but a particularly useful one, and one that is supported by our data from this drug-centered community, is the multiple drug abuse theory. The person who has an abusive pattern of use of one drug is more likely to abuse another drug, either concomitantly or when the first drug becomes less available. This theory implies that there are people who are prone to abuse (or compulsively use) any drug, although they may prefer one drug to another for its effect or lack of side effects. It is not meant to imply that all abusers exhibit a particular personality or type of psychopathology. Furthermore, such a theory should not be applied to the social or ritual use of drugs, e.g., marijuana by the youthful subculture or LSD by an indoctrinated hippie, nor should its emphasis on individual susceptibility obscure pertinent group factors.

The multiple drug abuse theory assumes that abuse of drugs by an individual may extend beyond a single class of drugs, for instance the amphetamines, into another group with different properties such as alcohol, a sedative drug. This type of abuse—abuse of drugs in differing classes—is known as *horizontal* abuse. An example would be the amphetamine abuser who also abuses the psychedelic drugs or the narcotics, such as heroin. A different pattern of abuse may be called *vertical* abuse—the abuse of different drugs within the same drug classification. An example of this form of abuse is the alcoholic who also abuses another sedative, for instance chlordiazepoxide (Librium). The use of drugs within the same class may lead to an additive effect of the two drugs being used together in the same time period; that is, the effect of one drug adds its effect to the effect of the other drug. This result is twice that of other drugs used alone in the same dosage.

INTERCHANGEABLE USE OF MARIJUANA AND ALCOHOL

Now these concepts may be applied to our study, in particular to the use of beer, wine, and marijuana by the population that we studied. We noted that our data tended to support our impression that marijuana was being used as an alcohol substitute within this subculture, and that the consumption of alcohol had declined for many of the respondents, although their use of marijuana was quite high. To suggest any cause for such a change or the exact nature of that cause would be highly speculative, but we should mention that 80 to 90 percent of a given sample attributed their decrease in alcohol consumption to their having taken marijuana and/or LSD, and agreed that their use of marijuana and LSD came before the decline in their use of alcohol. The role LSD has played in such a change is difficult to evaluate, but certainly a greater percentage prefer LSD to marijuana.

Nevertheless, if we look at the group whose consumption of hard liquor had decreased or stopped, we find that although their use of beer and wine had also decreased for the most part, significantly fewer of these persons had discontinued their consumption of beer and wine and more planned to continue their consumption of these beverages in the future. Only 23 percent of this sample of persons whose consumption of hard liquor has decreased or stopped planned to continue drinking hard liquor; but 58 percent planned to continue drinking beer and wine. Objective evidence, however, indicates that their consumption of hard liquor was usually at a lower level of use.

There were 31 persons who had abused ethanol in some form (hard liquor or beer and wine) but who were presently consuming minimal amounts of alcohol; 9 of them had stopped drinking hard liquor altogether. All were habitual users of marijuana and all had continued drinking beer and wine but in nonabusive amounts.

Why do not attitudes and practices toward beer and wine follow the decreased consumption of hard liquor among the marijuana users in this population? There are many possible explanations and probably not any single explanation will suffice. But we have on several occasions talked to members of this community who spoke of their concurrent use of marijuana and wine. A group would smoke several "joints" of marijuana and then consume a bottle of wine. They insisted that this practice led to becoming much more "stoned"; the experience of marijuana and wine together was said to be better than the use of either drug alone. The occurrence of such a practice would explain the statistics; moreover, it would be an example of the additive effect of two drugs being used together. It is known that alcoholics will try to get sedative drugs to decrease their consumption of alcohol; this is certainly the practice in the medical treatment of withdrawal from alcohol to substitute one safer, longer acting sedative drug for ethanol, a shorter acting sedative with a low degree of safety. If one considers marijuana a sedative drug like ethanol or the barbiturates, then this is an example of vertical abuse. Heroin abusers at times will abuse a barbiturate in order to decrease their dependence on heroin—an example of horizontal abuse; the reported contamination of LSD with methamphetamine to increase the subjective effects aims at a similar result.[3]

MARIJUANA USE AND THE SEQUENTIAL THEORY OF DRUG ABUSE

The habitual use of marijuana is often associated with the abuse of other drugs not in the same pharmacologic class. The habitual use of marijuana is frequently associated with the use of the psychedelic drugs, for example, which is a case of vertical abuse if marijuana is considered to be a psychedelic or horizontal abuse if it is considered a sedative. In any event there were many examples of high levels of marijuana use associated with high levels of use or abuse of other drugs within this community. Marijuana is involved in both horizontal and vertical use within this community as a social drug, a spree drug, and a depressant to antagonize stimulant drugs.

The sequential theory of drug abuse, that the use of marijuana will lead to the abuse of heroin in particular, has been the subject of much debate. Most authorities now agree that there is little basis in fact for such a statement. (3) Our data strongly supports its refutation.

Only 8 of the total sample of 413 respondents were heroin abusers. The percentage of heroin abusers presently using marijuana habitually was significantly lower than the high percentage of habitual marijuana

---

[3] Illegal LSD is sometimes mixed with methamphetamine to decrease the amount of LSD needed to produce an effect.

use among the abusers of the psychedelics, and tended to be lower than the frequency of habitual marijuana use among any other abuser group. Only half the heroin abusers habitually used marijuana, yet 85 percent of the abusers of the psychedelics habitually used it. The levels of marijuana use among the abusers of the various drugs are shown in Table 4.

This survey suggests a surprisingly high incidence of experience with opium among the respondents. For reasons mentioned below, we believe that our questions did not provide a valid measure of the amount of opium actually used. Of our total sample, 58.3 percent admitted to having tried opium at some time, and 36.3 percent stated that they had used opium while in the Haight-Ashbury neighborhood. However, more detailed interviews with residents and dealers suggest that many of their answers were based on the very dubious assumption that they had used "opium-cured grass" at one time or another. The small amount of opium brought into the community in the past was used in small amounts and in a group setting very much as marijuana was used.

As alluded to above and as explained in other papers (6) the selling of drugs on the street in this community involves what might be termed a "Madison Avenue approach." Drugs are being sold under constantly changing guises, fantastic claims are made about each drug, and the user has a preconception about the expected effect of a particular drug sold to him, even before he has experienced it. Many drugs are billed as containing one ingredient when in fact they contain something else.

There have been actual attempts at "curing" marijuana in solutions of such drugs as DMT or cocaine, but such curings are hardly frequent enough to account for the often-heard patter of the seller about "opium, DMT, or cocaine-cured grass." The different effects one may experience with marijuana purchased in Haight is more rationally explained by attributing them to the amount of active ingredient, rather than attributing them to a contaminant in the marijuana, as the community often does. It is known that attempts at curing marijuana in sugar have been successful; hence stories of DMT or opium curing should not be dismissed as mere fiction.

References

1. DAVIS, F., and MUNOZ, L. 1968. Heads and freaks: patterns and meanings of drug use among hippies. *Journal of Health and Social Behavior* 9: 156–64.

2. MEYERS, F. H. 1968. Pharmacologic effects of marijuana. *Journal of Psychedelic Drugs* 2, no. 2: 30–36. See above pp. 35–39.

3. McGLOTHLIN, W. H. 1964. *Hallucinogenic drugs: a perspective with special reference to peyote and cannabis.* Santa Monica, Calif.: The RAND Corporation.

4. SMITH, D. E. 1967. LSD: An Historical Perspective. *Journal of Psychedelic Drugs* 1, no. 1: 1–7.

5. SMITH, D. E., and ROSE, A. J. 1967. "LSD": Its use, abuse, and suggested treatment. *Journal of Psychedelic Drugs* 1: 117–23.

6. MEYERS, F. H.; ROSE, A. J.; and SMITH, D. E. 1968. Incidents involving the Haight-Ashbury population and some uncommonly used drugs. *Journal of Psychedelic Drugs* 1, no. 2: 136–46.

7. MEYERS, F. H.; JAWETZ, E.; and GOLDFIEN, A. 1968. *Review of Medical Pharmacology.* Los Altos, Calif.: Lange Medical Publications.

An Analysis of Marijuana Toxicity

David E. Smith, M.D.

Carter Mehl, M.S.

Marijuana use in the United States, once restricted primarily to the urban poor and the rural southwest, is rapidly becoming a middle-class phenomenon. Its use by college and high school students has increased tremendously in the 1960s, and in the last few years it has spread downward to junior high and elementary school children, as well as upward to young professionals and businessmen. Concurrent with the increase in the number of marijuana users has been an increasing desire for information about the consequences of smoking marijuana. Unfortunately, much of what passes for information is really misinformation distorted by the biases of the source. Thus on the one hand we have many law enforcement officers, judges, teachers, and physicians claiming that marijuana is addictive and that its use leads to moral degradation, psychological instability, and antisocial behavior. On the other hand, we have increasing numbers of young "pot" smokers claiming that marijuana is completely harmless. It seems reasonable to say that this divergence of opinion is largely due to different value systems and life styles of these various groups. Marijuana has served to widen the generation gap; Goode, in his excellent article "Marijuana and the Politics of Reality" [see below, pp. 168–86], indicated that this difference might never be resolved because of the vast differences that exist in the perception of reality between the two generations. (1)

Despite the confused legal and social situation in the last few years the tight controls on marijuana research have begun to loosen, and a body of factual information is emerging that will perhaps shed some light on this controversy. With increasingly widespread use of marijuana, an accurate evaluation of the possible dangers of such use takes on increased social significance. This paper reports the preliminary results of a toxicological analysis of a large group of marijuana users.

Several studies on marijuana use in other countries—notably India —have indicated addiction, physical degradation, and psychiatric disorders as consequences of long term marijuana use. These studies,

This study was supported by California State Grant MR/Pharmacology: Marijuana Research 2-444943-20540.

however, were of users of hashish (the gummy resin from the leaves of the female *Cannabis sativa* plant) which is more potent than the marijuana preparations commonly used in the United States. Furthermore, social and cultural factors are important determinants in the effects of marijuana use; hence cross cultural comparisons are risky. For example, in India heavy hashish smoking is primarily a lower caste phenomenon, as are disease and malnutrition. It is impossible to tell whether the same degree of organic deterioration would result even if no drugs were used. The best studies in this country indicate that marijuana as commonly used in the United States is *not addictive* and does not of itself cause criminal behavior, moral deterioration, or psychological instability. It can, however, produce toxic reactions, both acute and chronic. A description of the nature of these reactions and an examination of their causes are the specific concerns of this article.

Methods

In studying marijuana toxicity we made a survey of a population using marijuana with clinical methods and participant observation. The survey and most of the clinical case studies came from contacts made through the Haight-Ashbury Medical Clinic, through interviews held in the bay area suburbs and through lectures on drug abuse across the country. This clinic has a two-year history of sympathetic treatment of young people with medical and psychiatric problems, often related to drug use. During this period approximately 40,000 patients (2) were treated, 95 percent of whom had experience with marijuana. (3) The clinic has gained the trust and acceptance of drug users in the bay area; and includes as patients college students, professionals, and working-class people, as well as residents of the Haight-Ashbury district.

Opportunity for a good deal of naturalistic observation also came through clinic contacts. The clinic provides ready access to a large marijuana-using population since about 90 percent of the thousands of patients seen each year use marijuana. Furthermore, the senior author has had both clinical and social contact with marijuana users during his professional travels to many parts of the country, and the junior author has immersed himself in several pot-using subcultures in the bay area, which has allowed him access to information not ordinarily available to a clinician.

It is worth mentioning here what appears to us to be difficulties with statistical and clinical reports in this area. Ungerleider *et al.* (4)

reported the results of a statistical survey of 2,700 professionals (psychiatrists, psychiatric residents, general practitioners, internists, and psychologists) in Los Angeles County. The survey was primarily concerned with adverse reactions to LSD, but it included a reporting of 1,887 adverse marijuana reactions. Unfortunately no definition of "adverse reaction" was offered, and in view of the statement of one respondent (he considered all LSD reactions adverse), we wonder what sorts of marijuana reactions were reported as adverse. A good deal of the marijuana use observed by professionals consists of youths who experimented with marijuana who were then brought in for treatment by anxious parents. Neither marijuana smoking as a form of rebellion, nor parental anxiety should be considered adverse marijuana reactions. On the other hand, mild overdose reactions are unlikely to be observed by professionals because they are normally treated by the user's friends or by the marijuana user himself. Therefore, it seems that a survey of professionals is not an effective way of estimating the incidence of adverse reactions in a drug-using population. Statistical study of adverse marijuana reactions requires direct access to a marijuana using population and at least a general definition of what constitutes an adverse reaction.

Toxic Reactions to Marijuana

Toxic reactions to marijuana may be considered as any effects that result in physical or psychological damage, that are subjectively experienced as unpleasant by the user, or that produce significant interference with adequate social functioning. We specifically exclude the relaxed euphoric feelings the user describes as being "high" or "stoned."

Actual physical damage resulting from marijuana use is as yet unproved. Claims of brain damage from chronic use in India are not well supported as nutritional deficiency as a possible cause was not analyzed or controlled experimentally. Since marijuana in the United States is ordinarily smoked we can suspect as a chronic effect increased susceptibility to respiratory disease, as with tobacco smoking, though this effect has not yet been documented with marijuana. If an individual smokes 10 or more tobacco cigarets for 15 or more years, his chances of getting lung cancer are 20 times higher than those of the non-smoker. Such levels would be impossible for the marijuana smoker to achieve without continuous yearly intoxication to the point of virtual anesthesia, and therefore it is highly unlikely that a link between marijuana smoking and lung cancer will be established. Death in human beings from marijuana overdose is almost impossible although death by coma can be produced in animals by deliberate massive overdose.

Unpleasant experiences induced by marijuana and its effects which hinder social functioning are best discussed in terms of acute and chronic toxicity. Acute toxic reactions are those unpleasant effects, usually of rapid onset, resulting from a single marijuana experience. Typical examples are nausea, anxiety, paranoia, and disorientation. Chronic toxic reactions are those undesirable effects that result only from prolonged marijuana use. Inasmuch as chronic physical damage from marijuana has not yet been satisfactorily demonstrated, the main chronic toxic reaction seems to be an impairment of social functioning in the form of an amotivational syndrome or generalized loss of desire to work or face challenges.

Acute Toxic Reactions

Many marijuana users report a variety of minor symptoms which should not be considered adverse reactions. They include such things as reddening and burning of the eyes, dryness of the mouth, excessive hunger, and lethargy. These are so minor as not to merit further discussion, and are best thought of as minor side effects.

Somewhat more serious effects that may occur with marijuana intoxication are paranoia, disorientation, confusional states, short-term memory loss, and a variety of perceptual alterations. Whenever these effects are desired by the marijuana user (as the last three often are), they cannot be considered toxic reactions. When, however, they are considered unpleasant by the user, and particularly whenever they produce concern or fear, they constitute acute toxic reactions. Anxiety reactions, psychotic breaks, and overdose reactions are the major acute toxic reactions. These may be so serious as to lead the user to seek professional help. We will discuss these major reactions in the context of their primary causative factors.

Toxic reactions to any psychoactive drug depend on the nature and strength of the drug used, the personality and mood of the user, and the social context in which the drug is used. Any instance of marijuana toxicity will involve all three factors; proper analysis requires evaluation of all three variables.

DRUG FACTORS

In examining toxic marijuana reactions there is a tendency to overemphasize the role of the drug. When we first began seeing acute toxic reactions in experienced marijuana users, we (and many of the users) suspected that there were adulterants in the marijuana. Now, however, we minimize this possibility for three reasons.

1. In the few cases where we have been able to chemically analyze the drug producing the acute toxic reaction, it has invariably been demonstrated to be unadulterated marijuana.
2. In most cases careful questioning revealed that either the user had smoked from the same batch previously without ill effects or other people shared his "grass" with no unusual effect, which indicates that an adulterant is not a factor.
3. Street talk of marijuana cured with opium, cocaine, DMT [Dimethyl tryptamine], or some other psychoactive substance far exceeds the amount of marijuana actually so treated.

Random analysis of the more potent marijuana circulating in Haight-Ashbury (given such names as "super grass") indicated that it was unadulterated, although it did contain a high concentration of THC (the active ingredient in marijuana). Hence, the "effects one may experience with marijuana purchased in the Haight is more rationally explained in terms of the amount of active ingredient, rather than attributing it to a contaminant in the marijuana as the community often does." (3)

The amount of the active ingredient and the quantity smoked, together with the tolerance of the user, interact to determine the degree of intoxication. This is important in that acute adverse reactions are more likely when one is highly intoxicated than when only mildly "stoned." The greater the amount of active ingredient, the more intoxicated the marijuana user feels. This response, however, is modified by the user's tolerance level. Interestingly enough a form of reverse tolerance with marijuana has been reported by Weil. (5) Novices generally require more marijuana than experienced users to feel "high." Recent work by Jones et al. (6) has indicated that this represents the psychosocial effect of learning how to get "high"; Jones found a greatly increased incidence of placebo reactions with the experienced marijuana user than with the novice. Our clinical research, however, indicates that tolerance to marijuana is even more complicated than this, for we found several regular heavy users who could smoke ten or more "joints" per day and yet be only mildly "high," which indicates an increased tolerance with very heavy use. Furthermore, several experienced users have indicated to us that they get high more easily after a period of nonuse than during periods of regular daily use. This suggests that the degree of marijuana tolerance is best described as a J–shaped function: that is, the novice has a moderate degree of tolerance; with increasing exposure to marijuana tolerance appears to drop so that the occasional user has a low degree of tolerance; and with increasingly heavier use tolerance rises again so that a very heavy user has a high degree of tolerance. We indicate a J–shaped function because a very heavy user can undoubtedly tolerate more marijuana than a novice without ill effects. This J–shaped function may be a partial explanation of why heavy users rarely suffer acute toxic reactions. It appears that the initial negative tolerance is a learned phenomenon as suggested by Becker (14), but that the later increased tolerance may be pharmacologic in origin.

This lack of experience with marijuana by the novice user may also explain the "first time" cannabis induced toxic psychosis reported by investigators such as Talbott et al. (16) who cited 12 acute toxic psychosis in Viet Nam soldiers after their first exposure to marijuana. However, Talbott also emphasized the importance of environment on the drug reaction, questioning whether there are factors in Viet Nam, not present in the United States, that predispose to psychosis. He also supported our finding that most adverse marijuana reactions do not come to the attention of medical facilities.

The most common acute toxic reaction with marijuana is nausea, dizziness and a very heavy, "drugged" feeling where every motion seems an extreme effort. The following case is an example.

Case 1: A 23-year-old white female secretary, an experienced marijuana user, shared several "joints" with a few friends in a quiet setting. She got very high, and about an hour after smoking she felt that she was nauseated and had diarrhea. With effort she stood up and walked to the bathroom, but neither vomited nor had a bowel movement. When she left the bathroom she felt dizzy and looked very pale. After sitting down again and eating something she felt better, but she remained weak and slightly nauseated until she fell asleep later that night. There was no hangover or residual symptoms the next day.

This is analogous to an alcohol overdose—getting too drunk. In fact, regular marijuana users often describe these symptoms as "getting too stoned." The main difference is that generally there is no hangover with marijuana.

We are aware of this type of reaction through our rather direct contact with a marijuana-using population and find it not at all rare. The average physician, psychiatrist, or psychologist, however, would likely be unaware of this condition, since it, like drunkenness, is generally treated at home without professional help.

The route of administration of the drug can also be an important factor. Smoking allows self-titration so that the user can stop with the first signs of a toxic reaction. Taking the drug orally is more likely to lead to a toxic reaction because overdosage cannot be so easily prevented. Six subjects in the La Guardia report (7) suffered brief psychotic episodes, all after the drug was ingested rather than smoked. Furthermore, the study reported in general a greater incidence of unpleasant symptoms with eating than with smoking the drug.

PSYCHOLOGICAL FACTORS

The effect marijuana has on an individual depends to a large extent on his personality structure, his expectations and attitude toward marijuana, and his mood at the time of use. The great variability of these factors makes the effects of marijuana rather unpredictable; hence in this country it is generally considered unsuitable as a medicinal agent. These same psychological factors—personality, mood and setting—are largely responsible for the most serious acute toxic reactions.

Marijuana can precipitate an acute psychotic reaction in a marginally adjusted or poorly organized personality. The following is an example.

Case 2: A 21-year-old white unemployed male experienced an acute psychosis after smoking marijuana with three other people in Golden Gate Park. When he came to the Haight-Ashbury Medical Clinic—about one hour after smoking marijuana—he was talking in such a fashion that he would increase his speed until he simply babbled. He would then return to a fairly rational state only to begin babbling again. Flight of ideas, depersonalization, and transformation of personality were evident. One hundred milligrams of Thorazine given over a two-hour period returned him to a reasonably normal state. During the next four days he "tripped out" several times, though he used no drugs during this period. It was difficult to determine whether these were true "drug flashbacks" or recurrent psychotic episodes (8).

Further questioning indicated that he had recurrent feelings of depersonalization and hallucinations during these four days. He was on welfare, had recently been arrested, had a history of epilepsy, had a brief psychotic break at age 12, and gave the impression of a marginally adjusted borderline psychotic. Two weeks after his initial adverse reaction he reported that he felt fine, and no further follow-up could be obtained. In cases such as this the psychosis is characteristic of the personality structure of the user, not of the drug. The drug intoxication merely triggers the psychosis, as happens with a variety of other drugs, including alcohol, amphetamine, and LSD.

Even with better organized personalities marijuana can precipitate severe, though less profoundly disorganizing, psychological changes, particularly in the presence of excessive stress. The intoxicated state may produce a keener awareness of existing stresses and may hinder the ability to maintain structural defenses. The following case illustrates this reaction.

Case 3: A 27-year-old white female student complained of a depressive reaction to marijuana on three separate occasions. She has been a casual user for five years. The adverse reaction on these three occasions was characterized by a feeling of isolation and detachment from people, lack of energy, and excessive sleeping over the period of a week to ten days following marijuana use. In each case she was in a socially awkward or frightening situation while under the influence of the drug. Furthermore, the first two instances occurred in the context of a more general social stress: she was in a foreign country traveling with friends for whom she felt an excessive amount of responsibility. In the third instance she still felt "stoned" upon awakening the day after marijuana use and began to fear that she was schizophrenic or going crazy. Approximately one month later she came to the clinic.

Further questioning revealed that her mother was excessively dependent; consequently the patient assumed the primary responsibility for the care of her younger siblings. As a result she had a great deal of trouble breaking away from home and making a life of her own. She had a tendency to adopt an undue amount of responsibility for others' problems. She was usually slightly manic: always very much on the go and involved in more things than she could generally handle comfortably. It appears that the patient was a manic-depressive personality, and that in stressful situations laced with excessive responsibility marijuana triggered the depression. After gaining some insight into her problems, the patient has set some limits for herself and seemed to be gaining firmer control over her life.

Again, the prolonged reaction is a result of personality problems which the drug merely serves to unmask. A long term psychotic state induced by marijuana (as opposed to a brief psychotic reaction lasting a few hours) in a well-integrated stable personality, if it occurs at all, is exceedingly rare in this country. Some studies in other countries indicate that *Cannabis* is an important cause of psychosis, but most American authors disagree that the drug is causative in these cases.

In both cases two and three patients had been occasional users of marijuana for several years. Both were quite familiar with the drug. It was the confluence of various psychosocial stresses quite distinct from marijuana use that helped precipitate the toxic reactions described above. In many cases, however, it is the marijuana use itself that creates the stressful situation. Since marijuana use in the United States is illegal and most of us have been exposed to strong warnings about its dangers, the novice experimenting with marijuana often finds himself in an emotionally charged situation. He may fear discovery and arrest with consequent loss of respect, loss of job, straining of family relations, and possible incarceration. He may harbor secret fears that marijuana intoxication will produce physical damage, will make him lose control and do things he does not want to do, or will drive him insane. Such a strong negative attitude toward marijuana can, of itself, produce sufficient stress to create a state of panic when the influence of the drug is felt. The altered mental state produced by the drug seems only to confirm the fears, and a full-blown anxiety reaction develops. The following case illustrates this point.

Case 4: A 34-year-old single, hard working, white male business executive, in his capacity as president of a small and rapidly growing company, had a good deal of responsibility. He was well dressed, drove quality cars, had his own airplane, and fit the role of the dashing urban bachelor. He was a regular user of alcohol, attended many cocktail parties, and was a heavy smoker of cigarettes—approximately two packs per day. At the suggestion of various friends and out of curiosity he decided to smoke marijuana. He shared one marijuana cigarette with two other individuals; then they all went to dinner. During the course of his conversaiton he noted that he would forget what he had just said; as a result he became very disturbed. His anxiety increased because he felt he was losing control of himself; he said later it was like what he thought would happen if one lost his mind. The other two individuals who had smoked approximately the same dosage were having a very good time and showed no adverse effects. This individual, however, became quite panic stricken and was taken home and given a sedative. After a good night's sleep there were no residual effects, but the individual described his marijuana experience as being most unpleasant, and said he greatly preferred alcohol. Subsequent interviews indicated that the threat of being arrested while under the influence of marijuana was also one of his major concerns.

Even if a negative mood or set is not present, the unexpected nature of marijuana and the fear of altered reality may prove disastrous to the user. Anxiety may also result from a misunderstanding of the physical symptoms of marijuana intoxication. We have seen cases where the mild increase in heart rate that occurs with the early stages of marijuana intoxication was interpreted under increased sensory awareness as resembling the onset of a heart attack with a subsequent anxiety state. More commonly, though, the altered state of consciousness adds to the picture. The altered time sense may give a feeling of disorientation, and an increased sensory awareness may make breathing or talking seem to require a great deal of effort. All this may produce a sense of loss of control over one's body or mind, which creates great anxiety, as in the following case.

Case 5: A 26-year-old professional man experienced an anxiety reaction the second time he smoked marijuana. His first experience with the drug was in combination with alcohol and he had no distinct experience of being high on marijuana. His second experience was with friends who were experienced users. After becoming quite high, he noticed altered time perception and found that his words came slowly and with great difficulty when he tried to speak. This loss of control proved very frightening; he even feared he might be going insane. When the group moved to a different environment he developed a full-blown anxiety reaction with some paranoid ideation. He was given Thorazine at the Haight-Ashbury Medical Clinic. About four hours later, after returning to his friend's house, he fell asleep. The next day he was lethargic, uncoordinated, and unable to work properly.

He reported that at the time of this experience he was under a good deal of psychological stress and was seeing a psychotherapist. He recalled that at the time he feared for his professional career if he were to be caught with marijuana, but that the primary fear was loss of control and fear of going insane. Since then he has smoked marijuana several times with only pleasant results.

These last two cases are examples of novice anxiety reactions— anxiety reactions of an inexperienced user that resulted from unfamiliarity with and (often repressed) fear of marijuana. As in the last case, this kind of reaction does not necessarily occur the first time marijuana is smoked; if it is going to occur at all, it generally occurs at the first instance of strong intoxication. In view of the generally high tolerance of the novice, this may well be the fourth or fifth intoxication.

Recently fully half of the acute toxic reactions we have seen at the Haight-Ashbury Medical Clinic have been novice anxiety reactions, and a majority of them have involved "straight" people over 25 years of age. We can expect such anxiety reactions whenever people with rigid personality structures committed to the current dominant value system experiment with illegal psychoactive drugs. As more young professionals, businessmen, and middle-class parents (at the urging of their children) experiment with marijuana, we can expect an increase in these acute toxic reactions.

SOCIAL FACTORS

The effects one experiences with marijuana intoxication are greatly influenced by the setting—the immediate environment in which the drug is used. Young couples smoking "grass" together are likely to experience increased erotic feelings, whereas a student listening to classical music under the influence of "grass" will likely describe his experience as aesthetic. In many circles marijuana is used at parties as a social lubricant to relax inhibitions, reduce tension, and promote a feeling of social warmth—much as alcohol is used at cocktail parties.

A marijuana user is particularly susceptible to the influence of the people around him while he is intoxicated. If companions are disliked or seen as threatening, a toxic reaction may result, as in the following case.

Case 6: An 18-year-old white female at a midwestern college was having numerous experiences with marijuana and with sexual exploration, both of which were foreign to her previous way of life; she felt liberated and part of the "new morality." One evening, however, she had one marijuana cigarette with friends and a boy whom she had only recently met. When he made rather vigorous sexual advances, she became quite frightened and cried hysterically. She cried for about four hours until reassurance by friends gradually brought this under control. Following this acute panic reaction she became quite depressed. Her father had to withdraw her from school and she sought psychiatric help. After about six months she was able to resolve the various conflicts that were plaguing her and returned to school.

The girl's unresolved sexual conflicts were a root cause in this reaction, but it took the threatening environment to precipitate the anxiety reaction.

The larger social context of marijuana use is also important. As mentioned previously, a member of the dominant culture committed to middle-class values is fairly likely to be fearful when experimenting with marijuana. On the other hand, a member of the Haight-Ashbury community, where marijuana is the drug of choice, is extremely unlikely to be paranoid about its use.

Most acute toxic marijuana reactions seen at the Haight-Ashbury Medical Clinic involve students and relatively "straight" young adults from surrounding areas; it is exceedingly rare for a "hip" resident of Haight to present himself with an acute marijuana reaction, because even if he overdoses himself he does not seek medical attention but merely "sleeps it off." There are probably several factors involved here, such as the fact that most Haight residents are experienced users who have learned to "handle their grass," but an important factor is undoubtedly the social acceptance of marijuana use. Group reassurance as to the harmlessness of marijuana is undoubtedly therapeutic in preventing anxiety reactions.

Spontaneous Recurrences

The spontaneous recurrence, in a drug-free state, of the intoxicating effects of a psychoactive drug is commonly called a flashback. LSD flashbacks have been widely reported in the literature (9, 10, and 11), and we have seen many cases at the Haight-Ashbury Medical Clinic. Keeler et al. have reported four cases of marijuana flashbacks (12).

A flashback in and of itself does not constitute a toxic reaction. For example, two of the cases reported by Keeler (12) found these recurrent states not at all unpleasant. If, however, the spontaneous recurrence produces anxiety or impairs physiological or social functions, then it constitutes a toxic reaction.

In discussions of the spontaneous recurrence of a drug effect, it is important to make clear what should *not* be considered a flashback. Users of marijuana sometimes report that when they are with a group of friends, all of whom have smoked marijuana and are feeling quite high, they themselves feel high, though they have not smoked the drug. The phenomenon is referred to as a "contact high." This is the result of social suggestion—not a flashback—and is related to the great susceptibility of the marijuana user to environmental influences as described by Jones (6).

Keeler (12) points out that recurrence of psychopathology that was present during the drug intoxication does not constitute a flashback. However, it is often difficult to make this distinction, as in the following case.

Case 7: A 24-year-old white male laborer came to the Haight-Ashbury Medical Clinic and complained of a marijuana flashback. He has been a casual user of marijuana—and only marijuana—for about four years. About a month and a half previously he and his wife had shared two joints and got very high. Both experienced perceptual distortions, paranoia, and fear. On the day he came to the clinic while at work, the patient started feeling high. He experienced paranoia and a sense of loss of control; he felt like his "mind was closing." When he came to the clinic he still felt high and was somewhat agitated. He was given reassurance and a phenothiazine tranquilizer. He had no recurrence of this during a one-month follow-up.

This is probably best considered a recurrent anxiety state rather than a true marijuana flashback, but the decision is difficult because the patient was not very articulate. It is interesting, nonetheless, that most flashbacks occur after an adverse drug reaction or "bad trip." In addition, Shick et al. (16) suggested a much higher incidence with amphetamine-LSD combinations.

Keeler (12) reports still another effect that should not be considered a flashback. Several people experienced increased perceptual awareness under the influence of marijuana and some degree of this enhancement remained with them.

It is hoped that these negative examples will help clarify the concept of a marijuana flashback; a precise, straightforward definition is difficult to give. Keeler (12) suggests that "spontaneous recurrence of drug effect may be relatively common," but we have yet to see a case we would definitely describe as a flashback. We are inclined to the view that flashback effects, though real, are quite rare.

Chronic Marijuana Toxicity

Toxic reactions from the cumulative effects of chronic marijuana use are poorly defined. The brain damage resulting from chronic alcoholism, for example, is a secondary effect of associated malnutrition; such effects do not result from chronic marijuana use in this country, since marijuana acts as an appetite stimulant, and the chronic user continues to eat well.

Reports from India (13) indicate that chronic heavy use of *charas* (a potent *Cannabis* preparation equivalent to hashish) may produce increased susceptibility to respiratory and digestive ailments and a kind of social indifference, but that regular use of *bhang* (a mild preparation comparable to the marijuana used in the United States) poses no social problem.

Chronic heavy marijuana use in the United States is often associated with social maladjustment. It is difficult to know whether the long term use of marijuana leads to changed social values and behavior, or whether changing social values lead to chronic marijuana use. Perhaps more likely the values and behavior interact to produce concomitant change, the marijuana use helping to alter values that in turn reinforce the drug use.

Whatever the causal relations are, it is true that a chronic heavy marijuana user can develop an *amotivational syndrome* (8). He loses his desire to work, to compete, and to face any challenges. His interests and major concerns may center around marijuana to the point that his drug use becomes compulsive. He may drop out of school or leave work, ignore personal hygiene, experience a loss of sex drive, and avoid most social interaction. The picture in terms of social consequences is then similar to that of a chronic alcoholic, but *without* the physical deterioration.

It is important to realize, however, that such effects depend on the personality and social environment of the user and are not inevitable results of chronic marijuana use. Marijuana use may in fact have a beneficial effect on certain adolescents facing identity problems, as the following case demonstrates.

> *Case 8:* A 15-year-old white male in a wealthy bay area suburb improved his performance in school after he began smoking marijuana. Prior to this time he suffered from free floating adolescent anxiety about "who he was" and "where he was going." There was very little family communication, although his parents continually advised him about his future objectives. The boy stated he was not needed economically or any other way in the family or the community. When he started smoking pot, however, he became a "head" (psychedelic drug user) and entered into the "head subculture" whereby he established a new identity for himself. Temporary resolution of this adolescent identity crisis resolved his anxiety and he was able to perform much better in school.

In summary, marijuana toxicity cannot be understood if one focuses only on the drug itself. One individual with a particular personality structure and set in a particular environment may react one way to marijuana, whereas another individual with different personality and environmental circumstances may react in an opposite way to the same drug dosage. Analysis of marijuana toxicity, then, requires a thorough understanding of the personality and social variables in addition to the individual drug factors.

References

1. GOODE, E. 1969. Marijuana and the politics of reality. *Journal of Health and Social Behavior* 10, no. 2: 83–94 [see below, pp. 168–86].

2. SMITH, D. E. April 1969. Health problems in a "hippie" subculture: Observations by the Haight-Ashbury Medical Clinic. *Clinical Pediatrics* 8, no. 4: 313–16.

3. SHICK, J. F. E.; SMITH, D. E.; and MEYERS, F. H. 1968. Use of marijuana in the Haight-Ashbury subculture. *Journal of Psychedelic Drugs* 2, no. 1: 49–66 [see below, pp. 41–62].

4. UNGERLEIDER, T. J.; FISCHER, D. D.; GOLDSMITH, S. R.; FULLER M.; and FORGY, E. September 1968. A statistical survey of adverse reactions to LSD in Los Angeles County. *American Journal of Psychiatry* 125: 3.

5. WEIL, A. T.; ZINBERG, N. E.; and NELSON, J. M. 1968. Clinical and Psychological effects of marijuana in man. *Science* 162: 1234–42 [See above, pp. 11–34].

6. JONES, R. T.; and STONE, G. C. May 1969. Psychological studies of marijuana and alcohol in man. Presented at the 125th Annual Meeting of the American Psychiatric Association.

7. *Mayor's Committee on Marijuana*, New York City. 1944. Lancaster, Pa.: Catrell Press.

8. SMITH, D. E. 1968. The acute and chronic toxicity of marijuana. *Journal of Psychedelic Drugs* 2, no. 1: 37–47.

9. FROSCH, W.; ROBBINS, E.; and STERN, M. 1965. Untoward reactions to LSD requiring hospitalization. *New England Journal of Medicine* 273: 1235–39.

10. ROSENTHAL, S. 1964. Persistent hallucinosis following repeated administration of hallucinogenic drugs. *American Journal of Psychiatry* 121: 238–44.

11. SMART, R. G.; and BATEMAN, K. 1967. Unfavorable reactions to LSD. *Journal of Canadian Med. Association* 97: 1214–21.

12. KEELER, M. D.; REIFLER, C. B.; and LIPZIN, M. D. September 1968. Spontaneous recurrence of the marijuana effect. *American Journal of Psychiatry* 125:3.

13. CHOPRA, I. C.; and CHOPRA, R. N. 1957. The Use of Cannabis Drugs in India. *Bulletin on Narcotics* 9, no. 1: 4–29.

14. BECKER, H. S. 1963. Becoming a marijuana smoker. In *The Outsiders,* pp. 41–85. New York: The Macmillan Company.

15. SHICK, J. F. E.; SMITH, D. E., and MEYERS, F. H. 1969. Use of Amphetamine in the Haight-Ashbury subculture. *Journal of Psychedelic Drugs* 2, no. 2.

16. TALBOTT, J. A.; and TEAGUE, J. W. 1969. Marijuana Psychosis. *Journal of the American Medical Association* 210, no. 2: 299–302.

Social and Epidemiological Aspects of Marijuana Use

Gilbert Geis, Ph.D.

To a sociologist, the marijuana picture today borders on the sur-realistic. Much discussion concerns the pharmacological properties of marijuana and the consequences—short- and long-term—of its use. Additional debate centers about the adequacy and/or fairness of legal sanctions and judicial dispositions for marijuana offences. Both of these items, however, beg the central issue regarding marijuana use today, an issue that is fundamentally social and epidemiological: it is the fact that respected and respectable people are themselves smoking marijuana or are facing the fact that their children do so or are likely to do so.

It matters not much, I think, whether marijuana will prove to be somewhat more or somewhat less harmful than we now believe it to be. There are things much more dangerous than marijuana that remain well beyond the reach of the criminal law. It may be noted, for instance, that overindulgence in food presents considerably more serious problems for the well-being of our society than use of marijuana. Overweight people kill themselves prematurely, make poor soldiers, and waste valuable commodities. Yet nobody seriously proposes the creation of new crimes, labeled first- and second-degree obesity, or the establishment of an S.S. corps (for Supermarket Surveillance), or restrictions on the import of Israeli halvah, Swiss chocolate, or Italian spaghetti—commodities that poison the bloodstream and make us vulnerable targets for a foreign takeover.

What does matter, excruciatingly so, is that marijuana is becoming

"Social and Epidemiological Aspects of Marijuana Use" was presented at the National Symposium on Psychedelic Drugs and Marijuana, under the auspices of the Illinois State Medical Society, on April 11, 1968, and was published in the Journal of Psychedelic Drugs 2, no. 1 (Fall 1968): 67–77. Copyright © 1968 by David E. Smith, M.D. Reprinted with minor changes by permission of the publisher and the author.

embedded as part of the way of life of obviously responsible, obviously otherwise conforming persons. The implications of the epidemiological situation pose problems regarding tactical withdrawal from an entrenched moral position. Our problem with marijuana is not unlike the long-standing problem of our official position in Vietnam (if a political aside may be permitted). It is not by chance alone, in this respect, that congressional attention has to be drawn in recent months to the supposedly high rate of marijuana use among American troops in Vietnam. Like sex indulged in under the banner of tomorrow-we-die-on-the-battlefield, marijuana use by combat troops raises delicate questions of a "moral armistice" in the manner that terminal cancer patients are permitted to have as much morphine or LSD as is necessary for their comfort. Presumably, as graduate students are drafted in large numbers into the armed forces, the marijuana problem will become aggravated; perhaps films such as "The Menace of Marijuana" will replace those on venereal disease as leading candidates for military cinema oscars.

How Things Went to Pot

It hardly needs saying that the precise parameters of marijuana usage are very difficult to locate. The well-publicized episode of a 58-year-old elementary school principal in a northern California town, who recently told a legislative committee that it had been her habit for the past 18 years to come home from the classroom to a puff of pot, illustrates what is undoubtedly a widespread phenomenon of regular and undetected marijuana usage. In the same vein is the story of a California law school dean who suggested that the statutes against marijuana would undoubtedly be repealed within the next ten years. It was his understanding that a large number of his students were currently using marijuana, and his presumption that many of these persons would be elected to the state legislature in coming years.

Anecdotal material does not, however, provide adequate fare for an epidemiological inventory regarding marijuana. Such an inventory might begin by noting that Chinese and Indian sources have reported on the presence of marijuana as far back as the 1300s. The drug was adopted in literary, intellectual, and artistic circles in Europe about 1800. It then made its way to Latin America and Mexico, but was virtually unknown in the United States until the 1920s.

Enactment of the Marijuana Tax Act in 1937 clearly set the ground rules for official handling of the drug. In 1930, when the Federal Bureau of Narcotics was established, only 16 states had outlawed marijuana, and theirs were relatively mild proscriptions, rarely enforced.[1] In 1933 the ill-fated Volstead Act and prohibition were abandoned, though by 1937 virtually all states had declared marijuana illegal. The congressional hearings in that year on the Marijuana Tax Act represent illustrations of the federal legislative process at its poorest; with single-minded dedication committee members moved from an untenable set of original postulates to a fallacious set of preordained conclusions, making certain to push aside any refractory material along the way.[2]

Fundamental to passage of the Marijuana Tax Act and to state laws was an unstated linkage between marijuana and the behavior and reputation of groups then using the drug in the United States. As we shall see, acts viewed as unattractive, family behavior patterns viewed as unappetizing, and similar conditions believed to be unesthetic, items that were indigenous to Negro and Spanish-speaking groups, were implicitly related to the presence of marijuana. It was the same process by which the idiosyncracies of the aberrant in other times and other places have been tied to such things as their style of dress, their heresies, and their ceremonies. Today, in similar manner, campaigns against crime in the streets often represent camouflaged methods for retaliatory tactics against minority group members, who most often commit such crimes, but against whom frontal assaults are no longer fashionable.

The Little Flower and Pot

Mayor Fiorello LaGuardia of New York City, while serving in the House of Representatives, had been impressed by testimony that use of marijuana among U.S. troops in Panama posed no serious problem either to mental health or discipline. Given this background, LaGuardia tended to doubt the horror stories regarding marijuana; he therefore arranged for a medically-supervised investigation of the drug. The subsequent report of the work of the mayor's committee, begun in 1939 and published in 1944, provides by far the best epidemiological material we have on marijuana for the 1930–40 period.

---

[1] David Solomon, "Marihuana Myths," in Solomon, ed., *The Marihuana Papers* (Indianapolis: Bobbs-Merrill, 1966), p. xv.

[2] U.S. House of Representatives, Committee on Ways and Means, Hearings on the Taxation of Marihuana, 75th Cong., 1st Sess., 1937. See also Joseph S. Oteri and Harvey A. Silverglate, "In the Marketplace of Free Ideas: A Look at the Passage of the Marihuana Tax Act," in J. L. Simmons, *Marihuana: Myths and Realities* (North Hollywood, Calif.: Brandon House, 1967), pp. 136–162; and Howard S. Becker, "The Marihuana Tax Act," in *The Outsiders: Studies in the Sociology of Deviance* (New York: Free Press, 1963), pp. 595–846.

Field work for the sociological segment of the mayor's committee report was undertaken, oddly enough, by six officers from the narcotic squad of the police department. Their investigation was directed toward answering six questions. The first two concerned the extent of marijuana use in New York and the method by which marijuana was distributed. They found that use of the drug was heaviest in Harlem and secondarily in one section of midtown Manhattan, although marijuana was used to some extent in other areas of the city as well. Most of the users were either Negro or Latin American, in their twenties, and unemployed. There were an estimated 500 peddlers in Harlem, and about 500 "tea-pads" where marijuana was consumed on the premises.

The third question dealt with how users viewed marijuana. The smokers felt that it made them feel better and that it was not harmful in any way. Persons would voluntarily cease using marijuana for long periods without signs of discomfort. Finally, it did not appear that marijuana served as a stepping stone to heroin or other addictive drugs.

Because of claims that marijuana use was responsible for sexual degeneracy and sex crimes, the field workers looked for possible relationships between marijuana and eroticism. They found none. The evidence also failed to substantiate the existence of a causal relationship between marijuana use and crime. In cases where an individual both smoked marijuana and engaged in crime, it appeared that the criminal activity came first. Finally, the study looked into the relationship between marijuana use and juveniles. It found very little marijuana use in the New York City high schools or junior high schools, and no tendency for juvenile delinquency to develop out of the little use there was. The report on the sociological part of the study concluded that "the publicity concerning the catastrophic effects of marijuana smoking in New York City is unfounded." [3]

Issued almost midway through the second world war, the sound and sophisticated material in the mayor's committee report has never received the careful attention it merits, though its conclusions regarding the nonaddictive qualities of marijuana are widely known.

Both support for and perversion of the approach of the mayor's committee is, however, nicely illustrated by a number of wartime studies of marijuana use by military personnel. All the studies, for instance, note a disproportionate number of Negroes among marijuana

[3] See Dudley D. Shoenfeld, "The Sociological Study," in *Mayor's Committee on Marihuana, New York City* (Lancaster, Pa.: Cattell Press, 1944), pp. 1–25. The summary of the report has been taken in large measure from the excellent presentation by David O. Arnold, "The Meaning of the LaGuardia Report: The Effects of Marihuana," in Simmons, *op. cit.*, pp. 111–35.

users referred to neuropsychiatric services. In a study of patients at
Fort McClellan, Alabama, 55 were Negroes, one white;[4] all but one
of the 35 marijuana cases at March Air Field Base in California were
Negroes,[5] and 95 percent of the marijuana cases among servicemen
in India were also Negroes.[6]

The Fort McClellan study illustrates as well as anything might the
often feudal and futile process of generalizing from a sample whose
characteristics are not measured by adequate sampling or control
techniques. Thus the Fort McClellan researchers concluded that "the
preponderance of Negroes is due, we believe, to the peculiar need
marijuana serves for them." Marijuana, they felt, "enables the Negro
addict to feel a sense of mastery denied him by his color," [7] a conclusion made somewhat less than prescient by the spread of use today to persons who possess an obvious sense of mastery of both themselves and the world about them.[8] In addition, the Fort McClellan
study went on to detail a past history of personal horrors among the
users that, three decades later, sounds like nothing more than a description of life and its consequences for a large part of the population
of the Negro ghetto.

The LaGuardia report and the clinical material from the military
doctors have been further supplemented by studies of marijuana use
among jazz musicians, members of an occupational group that perhaps more than any other has traditionally been associated with a
pattern of heavy recourse to drugs.

A study by Charles Winick indicates that jazz musicians were
heavy users of alcohol in the early years of this century, but moved
toward marijuana during the 1930s. Following the second world war,
however, heroin began to gain popularity. From interviews conducted
during 1954 and 1955 with 357 jazz musicians, whose average age was
33, regarding the drug use habits of their colleagues, Winick estimated that 82 percent had used marijuana at least once, 54 percent
were occasional users, and 23 percent were regular users. More than
half had tried heroin, 24 percent used it occasionally, and 16 percent
regularly. Though a majority of the musicians tended to believe that

    [4] Sol Charen, and Luis Perelman, "Personality Studies of Marihuana Addicts,"
American Journal of Psychiatry 102 (March 1946): 674–82.
    [5] Eli Marcovitz, and Henry J. Myers, "The Marihuana Addict in the Army,"
War Medicine 6 (December 1944): 382–91.
    [6] Herbert S. Gaskill, "Marihuana, An Intoxicant," *American Journal of Psychia-
try* 102 (September 1945): 202–94.
    [7] Charen and Perelman, "Personality Studies," p. 674.
    [8] "Fifteen percent of the students at Princeton admit smoking pot—two-thirds
of them in the upper academic 20 percent, a third of them members of varsity
athletic teams." Antoni Gollan, "The Great Marihuana Problem," *National Review*
20, 4 (January 30, 1968): 78.

marijuana hindered rather than improved performing ability, a number pointed out that use of the drug seemed necessary for them to face the demands of their job; that without it they would be unable to perform at all. The study also indicated that marijuana may aid in buttressing occupational solidarity and insularity. If true, the story often told to Winick that a jazz band had performed such marijuana-euphemistic numbers as "Tea for Two" and "Tumbling Tumbleweed" at a police benefit dance must have been a source for great ingroup merriment.[9]

By using a similar group of subjects interspersed with marijuana users other than musicians, Howard Becker has contributed the view that continued recourse to marijuana depends upon a series of events, beginning with learning to smoke the drug in a manner that will produce real effects, then learning to enjoy the perceived sensations. "In short," Becker suggests "the marijuana user learns to answer 'Yes' to the question: 'Is it fun?'" The further direction that his drug experience will take then comes to depend upon intervening factors, including such things as moral judgments, availability of the drug, fear of arrest, and social reactions.[10]

Out of the Frying Pot

Since 1968 we have acquired adequate longitudinal information with which to examine the continuing careers of persons in the lower socioeconomic class, who have been the principal marijuana users until very recent times. This information comes from a St. Louis study by Lee Robins and George Murphy, which indicated more widespread use of marijuana than many persons had suspected, as well as a striking diminution of marijuana use with advancing age.

Study subjects were young Negro men who had been born in St. Louis between 1930 and 1934, had attended local elementary schools, and were residing in St. Louis in 1966. Of the 221 persons interviewed in the study, 109 had tried at least one of four drugs; 103 had used marijuana, 28 had used heroin, 37 had used amphetamines, and 32 had used barbiturates. It is noteworthy that all the heroin addicts, as distinguished from heroin experimenters, had arrest records, and that all addicts admitted their heroin use to study interviewers, who them-

[9] Charles Winick, "The Use of Drugs by Jazz Musicians," *Social Problems,* Vol. 3 (winter 1959–1960), pp. 240–253; Winick, "Marihuana Use by Young People," in Ernest Harms, ed., *Drug Addiction in Youth* (New York: Pergamon Press, 1965), pp. 19–35.

[10] Howard S. Becker, "Becoming a Marihuana User," *American Journal of Sociology* 59 (November 1953): 235–42.

selves were previously unaware of it. In regard to marijuana, only a very small percentage of either occasional or regular users had ever come to the attention of the police. It is notable that half of the marijuana users had never taken any other drug, that three out of four of the heroin users began with marijuana, and that one out of four of the marijuana users began using the drug before his sixteenth birthday. Sixty-nine percent had begun using marijuana by the time they were 20 years old, and only nine percent from age 24 and afterwards.[11]

During the year preceding that in which they were interviewed, 22 of the men (about ten percent) reported that they had used drugs. Three had used heroin, and a fourth, then imprisoned, had been using heroin prior to his arrest.[12]

The drug-use rate uncovered by the St. Louis investigation may be slightly inflated by omission of rural and small town migrants, but it indicates nonetheless a quite pervasive pattern of marijuana use among a minority group in a midwestern city where drugs are not considered as notable a problem as they are in seaports and Mexican border cities.

Weed-Filled Recreation Sites

Marijuana use today has obviously moved from the lower socio-economic segments of our population into our demographic mainstream. The spread of marijuana to the middle and upper strata of the society is, however, a quite recent phenomenon, one that makes the most penetrating numeration outdated in short order. As a recent magazine recently put the matter: "Statistics on the problem are nonexistent, and its extent is tough to gauge. School officials normally ignore it or hush it up; students with first-hand knowledge are prone to boastful exaggeration; arrests are relatively rare." [13] Despite this situation, however, we do have some information regarding current marijuana use that provides a basis for observations about the direction in which such use is likely to proceed.

It is necessary, first, to continue to examine the lower socioeconomic groups, partly because they use the drug more than other groups, and partly because they provide the liaison to marijuana use in other segments of the society.

[11] Lee Robins, and George E. Murphy, "Drug Use in a Normal Population of Young Negro Men," *American Journal of Public Health* 57 (September 1967): 158–59.

[12] Ibid., p. 158.

[13] "The Pot Problem," *Time Magazine*, March 12, 1965, p. 49.

The clearest insight into present drug customs in deprived areas must certainly be that reported by Herbert Blumer and his colleagues in 1967. Blumer's work had been designed to induce youthful drug users to abstain from further usage, a mission in which it totally failed. "The real reason for the lack of success," project workers noted, "was the strong collective belief held by the youths that their use of drugs was not harmful and their ability to put up effective arguments, based usually on personal experience and observation, against claims of such harm." [14]

Frustrated as reformers, the project team decided to become researchers. As such, by their rather immodest appraisal, they were preeminently successful. "We believe," they write, "that we have penetrated more deeply and fully into an analysis of the world of youthful drug users than is true of any published accounts."

Two major types of drug users were identified among youths in the Oakland flatlands, an area populated primarily by lower-class Negroes and Mexican-Americans, where the project was run. These youths were labeled either as *rowdy* or as *cool*. Rowdies, a small minority, were aggressive and used any and all drugs but preferred alcohol. Cool youths fell into three types: pot heads (or weed heads), mellow dudes, and players. Mellow dudes, by far the most prevalent group, would "try anything once" but did not seek out drugs. Their orientation was hedonistic, their pleasures primarily sexual. They used pills and crystals (methamphetamine hydrochloride or methedrine) as well as marijuana.

The pot head, member of a sizeable group, is exclusively a user of marijuana. He has been described in the following terms:

He uses no drugs other than marijuana and may even prefer soda pop to drinking alcohol. He is respected by other adolescents, presenting an image of a calm, sensible, solitary figure, soft-spoken, personable, and thoroughly knowledgeable about what is "happening" in the adolescent world. He takes pride in his appearance, always wearing sharp slacks and sweaters, is interested in taking things easy, having a good time, and fostering relations with the opposite sex. He is likely to be involved in conventional life activities, participating in various school functions, athletics, and conventional work. [15]

The pot head is apt to smoke a joint when he awakens, and a second after breakfast, after he has "eaten his high away." A third cig-

[14] Herbert Blumer, Alan Sutter, Samir Ahmed, and Roger Smith, *The World of Youthful Drug Use*, Add Center Project Final Report, School of Criminology, University of California, Berkeley, January 1967.
[15] Ibid., p. 79.

arette might be used in the early afternoon and others in the evening, depending upon the social agenda. Like all youthful drug users, the pot head looks down on heroin addicts as persons who have "blown their cool."

Initiation into marijuana use by pot heads was regarded by the project researchers as something other than a fulfillment of a personality predisposition or a motivational syndrome. Various conditions were found to keep the neophyte from access to drugs, primarily conditions relating to others' estimates of his integrity and his "coolness." Many pot heads were "turned on" by older brothers, who were intent upon preventing them from "sniffing glue, drinking wine, or risking the chance of being arrested." [16]

Finally, the Oakland study team assailed standard personality theories of drug use, which they found "ridiculous." It is "primarily the defining response of associates that leads to the formation of whatever motives may be attached to drug use," it was claimed. The study evidence was said to show "overwhelmingly that the great majority of youngsters become users not to escape reality but rather as a means of embracing reality" in a setting where drug use is extensive and deeply-rooted.[17] It was the guess of the research team that most pot heads would be assimilated into conventional life as adults, though their drug experience might lead a few of them into more serious narcotics involvement.

Further light has been shed on the subsequent careers of young users of dangerous drugs by a follow-up study of a selective group consisting of 866 persons under 18 arrested for the first time on a nonopiate drug charge during 1960 and 1961 by the Los Angeles police. Subsequent arrest records of each person were examined from the date of his initial apprehension through the following five years.

Of the 866 youths, 58 percent had no subsequent recorded arrest for drug involvement. Thirty percent were subsequently arrested on marijuana and/or dangerous drug charges only (the same offense for which they had initially been apprehended). Only 12 percent of the youths were subsequently arrested for opiate involvement. These findings contradict the notion that later opiate use is necessarily a consequence of marijuana or dangerous drug involvement.[18]

[16] Ibid., p. 49.
[17] Ibid., p. 59.
[18] Dimitri Polonsky; George F. Davis; and Chester F. Roberts, Jr., *A Follow-Up Study of the Juvenile Drug Offender* (Sacramento: Institute for the Study of Crime and Delinquency, October 1967), p. ix.

Where the Grass Is Greener

Given the greater use of marijuana by the lower-classes in the past decade, it is likely that the striking recent increase in police seizures of marijuana[19] and the skyrocketing arrest rates for marijuana offenses represent in considerable measure the use of marijuana by middle- and upper-class citizens. These two groups present the major ideological challenge to marijuana laws and the major rebuff to traditional explanations of marijuana use.

A general overview of available epidemiological material by Stanley Yolles indicates that perhaps 20 percent of high school and college students have had some experience with marijuana. More men than women students report involvement, and of those students reporting use, 65 percent say they smoked marijuana fewer than ten times, with the most common response being "once or twice." It was noted as particularly interesting that fully 50 percent of the students who had tried marijuana indicated that they experience no effects from it. Four explanations were offered for the situation.

1. The agent may not have been potent.
2. Frequently effects are experienced only after repeated use.
3. The expectation of the user has a significant effect on what he experiences.
4. The social setting in which use takes place has an effect on the response.[20]

More detailed information than that supplied by Yolles may be gained from surveys of drug-use patterns among high school students on either coast of the United States. In a study at two senior high schools in Great Neck, New York, an affluent suburb with a school system considered among the best in the nation, some 207 of 2,587 students (8 percent) reported they had smoked marijuana. Fifty-five had tried LSD.[21] On the west coast, in a senior class of a high school in San Mateo County, California, more than 25 percent of 288 boys and almost ten percent of 220 girls reported that they had used

---

[19] Bulk seizures of marijuana by federal enforcement authorities totaled 5,641 kilograms in 1965, as against 1,871 kilograms in 1960. President's Commission on Law Enforcement and Adminstration of Justice, *Challenge of Crime in a Free Society* (Washington, D.C.: Government Printing Office, February 1967), p. 213.

[20] Stanley F. Yolles, "Statement on LSD, Marihuana, and Other Dangerous Drugs," statement to U.S. Senate, Committee on the Judiciary, Subcommittee on Juvenile Delinquency, March 6, 1968, pp. 14–15.

[21] United Press International, February 16, 1967.

marijuana at least once, with more than half of both groups indicating use on three or more occasions. It is interesting in this connection that the San Mateo survey made the following observations.

> There is less accurate and less medical information about marijuana than any of the other dangerous drugs or narcotics.
> Youths do not trust adults' information regarding marijuana.
> Many youths maintain that the use of marijuana is no more harmful, and probably less harmful, than the use of alcoholic beverages.[22]

It is also interesting in connection with the high school surveys that a recent Harris Poll indicates that only five percent of the nation's parents report knowing a teenager who smokes marijuana, and that the smoking of marijuana is forbidden for their own children more than any other activity, with 85 percent of the parents saying that they would forbid marijuana, compared with 84 percent who would ban LSD, 70 percent who would rule out drinking hard liquor, and 66 percent who would object to a two-week trip taken by the youngster alone.[23]

It may be, although we have no definite information on the subject as yet, that a disproportionate number of the high school drug users do not matriculate. Among the heaviest users of drugs, some may migrate to such renowned citadels as the Haight-Ashbury district in San Francisco, where research has been undertaken to gain a profile of summer transients and permanent residents. Preliminary Haight-Ashbury reports, incidentally, indicate that the largest amount of marijuana use occurs among persons regularly using methedrine. Such persons use marijuana to put themselves in a more tranquil condition after recurrent methedrine experiences or, in their own terms, at the "end of a run." In Haight-Ashbury it is the methedrine group as well that reports the highest rate of personal problems, since such problems are measured by prior contact with or referral to psychiatric services,[24] although it is possible, research logicians note, that the psychiatric experiences drove the youths to methedrine rather than that a pre-existing disordered state led both to psychiatric referral and to later drug use.

---

[22] Juvenile Justice Commission, *Narcotics Inquiry Report for San Mateo County,* November 16, 1967, p. 5.

[23] *Los Angeles Times,* March 4, 1968.

[24] David E. Smith and J. Fred E. Shick, "Marihuana and Its Relationship to Other Drug Practices," paper presented at National Marijuana Symposium, San Francisco, March 24, 1968.

The sparse data available on marijuana use in colleges also indicates a dropping off from the rates among high school seniors at the surveyed schools. One news report has indicated that, on some basis, it was decided that 15 percent of the student body at the University of Miami had had some experience with marijuana and that 8 percent of the total group had used marijuana more than ten times.[25] More useful is the result reported by William McGlothlin and Sidney Cohen of a questionnaire profile of 121 male graduate students responding to an advertisement for study subjects in January 1965. Thirteen of the respondents indicated some experience, generally of an infrequent nature, with marijuana. The advertisement, it should be noted, gave no indication that the experimenters were interested in drug issues, though it is still not unlikely that there could have been a significant under-reporting because of possible loss of the opportunity to acquire work. In either case, the current nature of our information on marijuana use by college students is clearly inadequate and obviously biased by the *New York Times*. Four years ago, write McGlothlin and Cohen, a Harvard student turned in his roommate to the authorities for smoking marijuana in order to save him. Today, "it would be embarrassing for a student to admit that he hadn't at least tried pot— just as it would be embarrassing to admit that he was a virgin."[26]

Summary: Potpourri

Our analysis suggests that early and continued use by dispossessed elements in American society may have contributed to the present legal position of marijuana, just as it suggests that shifts in use patterns may be contributing to a reexamination of that position. It has not been our intention to reargue already well-argued polemical points regarding the proper position for the law, the medical profession, or the lay public to take regarding official policies on marijuana or personal use of the drug. Rather we have attempted to marshall what concrete data exists concerning the social and epidemiological nature of marijuana use, and to let that material speak for itself. Ultimately, of course, the attitude that society chooses to take regarding marijuana must emerge from a weighing of unquantifiable

[25] Reuter's, March 18, 1968.
[26] William H. McGlothlin and Sidney Cohen, "The Use of Hallucinogenic Drugs Among College Students," *American Journal of Psychiatry* 122 (November 1965): 572–74.

values. It is only worth noting, in concluding, that that attitude itself will then become, as it has been in the past, one of the most important items shaping the epidemiological patterns and the consequences of such patterns in regard to marijuana use.

Marijuana Use Among the New Bohemians

James T. Carey, Ph.D.

The cursory look at the arrest statistics for marijuana possession and sale in most of the American states suggests that use of the drug is increasing enormously. The traditional shape of marijuana demand and distribution seems to have shifted, beginning sometime in the early 1960s. A partial explanation of the shift is that potential youthful users were no longer convinced that marijuana's effects were harmful. For decades there has been some dispute over the drug's effects. The reports published by the Federal Bureau of Narcotics described marijuana's effects as very strong, often leading to violence, often accompanied by nausea at the early stages, creating wild hallucinations, fostering wild erotic outbursts subjecting the user to a loss of moral control, resulting in a loss of will power so that any far-fetched suggestion was likely to be followed, creating vast distortions in time and space, and often causing the user to blank out—either on the scene or retrospectively, so that whatever weird behavior occurred was forgotten the following day.[1] Others reported that marijuana's effects were mild, and led to affability, high but pleasant spirits, mild distortions of time and space that were considered pleasant, increased sensitivity to taste, musical sounds, colors, and touch, and a mild release of some inhibitions.[2]

So long as the stories of marijuana's association with criminality, opiate addiction, and the like were believed, or considered distinct possibilities, the demand for marijuana remained relatively low outside specific ethnic and racial groups in low income areas. These beliefs about marijuana constantly declined in importance as more and more persons were exposed to the experience of users. In the early 1930s in the United States such exposure was limited to Mex-

"Marijuana Use Among the New Bohemians" was published in the Journal of Psychedelic Drugs 2, no. 1 (Fall 1968): 79–92. Copyright © 1968 by David E. Smith, M.D. Reprinted with minor changes by permission of the publisher and the author.

[1] See Bouquet (1944) and Munch (1966).

[2] This is the conclusion reached by the LaGuardia Report: The Mayor's Committee on Marihuana (1944).

ican-American communities, a handful of Negro ghetto areas, and a few jazz bohemian circles. In the late 1940s and early 1950s experience with marijuana seemed to spread rapidly in northern ghetto areas. Soldiers in Korea and Japan during the early 1950s were also exposed to heavy marijuana use. However, neither the knowledge of the pleasant effects of marijuana use nor the rejection of previous beliefs about it penetrated to broad numbers of the middle class until the 1960s.

The disregard of official warnings and traditional sanctions against drug use has indeed reached epidemic proportions in many communities, if one can believe official arrest and seizure figures. This is a nationwide phenomenon, though California seems ahead of the nation in this respect. The trend of drug arrests has reached a point that has numerous consequences in the style of drug use and the policies of law enforcement.

In California from 1962 to 1966, arrests for narcotics (except marijuana) and other dangerous drugs remained about equal, but marijuana arrests for adults increased from 3,291 to 14,293 and for juveniles from 248 to 3,869.

TABLE 1. California State Narcotics Arrests
(1962–June 30, 1967)

	1962	1963	Percent Annual Increase	1964	Percent Annual Increase	1965	Percent Annual Increase	1966	Percent Annual Increase	First Half of 1967
Marijuana:										
Adults	3291	4677	42%	6055	29%	8349	38%	14293	71%	11587
Juveniles	248	503	101%	1224	141%	1623	33%	3869	138%	4526
Other Narcotic or Dangerous Drugs:										
Adults	12959	12051	—	13189	9%	13095	—	14026	8%	8547*
Juveniles	1077	936	—	781	—	1068	37%	1165	9%	1209*

* Much of the rise in other narcotic and dangerous drugs for the first half of 1967 was due to the implementation of anti-LSD laws for the first time.

These enormous increases are not spread equally throughout the population but are concentrated among the young and among Caucasians.[3] This trend is also reported in many other states.[4] These sta-

[3] The average age, even of adult arrestees, is decreasing. The changes in the radical composition of arrestees are illustrated by statistics of juvenile marijuana arrests for 1964 and 1965. White arrestees increased 118 percent from 342; Mexican-American increased 15 percent from 335; and Negroes increased 41 percent from 336.

[4] New York State, in 1966, seized 1,690 pounds of marijuana, compared with approximately 100 pounds in 1960. In New York City narcotic felony arrests

tistics merely illustrate a trend that, because of its size and extent, cannot be attributed to the numerous quirks in law enforcement and in crime statistics, which often invalidate small short-term statistical changes. The statistics do not specify the extent of drug use because there is no easy way of determining what percentage of users get caught. At the present time there are no good estimates concerning rates of marijuana use. The pressure is mounting to treat use as harmless. This has the effect of making official figures even more unreliable. Courts are often reluctant to prosecute many offenders, and the police practice of freeing marijuana users as bait for bigger game raises the question of just what the arrest figures actually represent. If we assume conservatively that arrest figures represent ten percent of those who use the drugs, then the estimated number of California users in 1967 would be 320,000 persons. This is certainly considerably more than Kolb's national estimate of 5,000 users in 1962! [5]

Increasing use seems to have generated a contagion effect. The more users, the less viable the official line on marijuana and to a lesser extent on other drugs. The less respected the rationale for such sanctions, the greater the experimentation. Greater experimentation increases the number of those who use, and makes it easier for novices to obtain drugs. The more varied the user groups, the less any potential user has to change his identity to begin using. The more users, the more jobs open for drug traffickers, and the more sellers will operate among their own kind; the more they blend with their clientele, the more difficult it becomes to catch them. This leads to the perception to the seller, or pusher, of less risk, hence the greater desirability of pushing the drug. Over time the contagion effect reaches a point where serious doubt about official positions is replaced by contemptuous disregard.

Widespread use of marijuana has generated a number of different scenes. There are young and not so young scenes, lower-class and middle-class scenes, organized and free-lance scenes, calm and fran-

---

during the first 8 months of 1967 were running 44 percent above the same period in 1966. In the two counties that Long Island comprises, Nassau and Suffolk, the increase of drug arrests approximated that of California. Narcotics arrests in Nassau rose 117 percent in 1966 and through May 1967, appeared to be moving toward another 50 percent rise. The average age of arrestees decreased from 22.7 in 1966 to 20.6 during the early part of 1967. For Suffolk, narcotic arrests increased in 1967 approximately 60 percent; half the arrestees were age 16 to 21.

[5] "The reason marijuana has so little crime-producing effect in the United States as compared with alcohol is simply this: 70,000,000 of our people are alcohol drinkers, 5,000,000 are definite alcoholics, and only 5,000 are marijuana users." Kolb (1962).

tic scenes, supercool and calculatingly uncool scenes. No one knows
all the scenes or how many people are in any one scene. This poses
major problems for the social scientist interested in portraying life
styles associated with marijuana use. The simple mapping problem
involved—what are the brute landmarks of the universe we are discussing—is enormous.[6] One way sociologists have characteristically
developed information on activity that is considered deviant by the
larger community is to ask those involved in the activity what significance it has for them.[7] Hence apart from official statistics, another
source of information on marijuana use is the users themselves. The
diversity of drug scenes and the fear of public exposure usually limits these explorations. Often users may conceal information because
they do not trust the questioner or because they may know only part
of the scene in which they find themselves.

By asking people what marijuana use means to them and by observing their activity in social situations of use, one may draw attention to the settings within which the behavior occurs. This has the
result of broadening any investigation of drug use to encompass the
context of use, i.e., description of values, outlooks, and life styles
within which this particular activity fits.

At least three major marijuana-using groups among college-age
persons can be distinguished in and around Berkeley. One could be
characterized as experimenters or occasional users. The role drugs
play in their lives is very minor. If one were to list the characteristics
of this group, it might look like a description of the student body
generally. Another group can be classified as the "weekender." He is
distinguished from the experimenter by virtue of his more secure ar-
rangement with a supply source. In short, his use, though controlled,
is systematic. The weekender is likely to see himself as a radical
politically and usually has been a participant in some kind of political
action in the recent past. He tends to view marijuana and alcohol in
the same general terms. His views of marijuana are essentially an
extension of attitudes about alcohol. One takes drugs primarily for
"kicks." The third general orientation is that of the "head." He is most
easily distinguished from the weekender by the frequency and extent
of his drug use. We will examine some of the values associated with
this style of marijuana use more thoroughly in the ensuing discussion.

One starts with the assumption in this view that educational, po-

---

[6] Geis (1968) deplores the paucity of epidemiological data on marijuana use
and presents a cogent summary of what is presently known about extent of use in
various populations.

[7] This is the method employed by Lindesmith (1947), Becker (1953), and
Blumer (1967).

litical, and social structures are beyond correction. They are unresponsive to change because of their rigidity and inflexibility. What should a person's response be in the face of this diagnosis? The conclusion reached by many is that the problem of how one relates to the social order is fundamentally a moral one. The only change for which one can work is change within one's self. Massive change comes only from individual transformation. This is a precondition for improving the world.

This situation has led to the growth of what can be characterized as a *new bohemianism* among college age youth, which evidences both continuities and discontinuities with its historical antecedents. Persons involved in the movement see themselves as part of a subversive tradition that has always existed in America. Though they may not be writers, they see themselves as descendants of Emerson and Thoreau. They characteristically come from the middle class, just as previous generations of literate subversives have. Consequently, recent immigrants, second-generation persons, and minority group members are not to be found among them in substantial numbers.

The new bohemians celebrate originality in art and personal life. Authenticity is highly valued. Conventional society is rejected because originality and spontaneity are stifled. This is similar to the earlier bohemians. Voluntary poverty is also embraced, not as an absolute good but as a way of maintaining one's purity and of learning detachment from material goods. The emphasis on mutual aid and sharing points to an attempt to develop a sense of community that would be impossible to achieve in conventional society.

The new bohemians are different from previous generations of beats in their absolute numbers.[8] The message they are trying to communicate is appealing to a larger and larger group of disaffected young people. The way their values are communicated represents something novel. Values are still communicated in painting, poems, or novels of limited circulation. But a new vehicle for the dissemination of their beliefs has appeared. Rock and roll music is the framework for the new values.[9] A kind of lore is beginning to develop. It is enshrined partly in the poetry of the songs they listen to and sing. The lyrics of folk rock constitute the main body of oral tradition among the new bohemians. They have incorporated it as their own. It gives them a sense of solidarity with a wide range of people in our society. The popularity of these songs is a partial indicator of the appeal of this

---

[8] See the descriptions of earlier beat scenes by Lipton (1959), Rigney and Smith (1961), and Polsky (1961).

[9] This is one of the points made by Gleason (1967) in his essay on rock music.

new movement. There is every indication that the diffusion of this new life style is likely to increase in the future rather than decrease. Its centers are in and around colleges and universities characterized by their academic excellence.

Drugs seem to be used more frequently among these young people because of their accessibility. There is a general consensus among them that the effects of marijuana and LSD are pleasurable. Combined with this is a more discriminating attitude on the drugs' alleged evil effects. Official sanctions against them do not serve as a deterrent since the new bohemians consider the laws punitive and based on misinformation. There is also the sense that the risks in taking drugs are slight and diminishing. Drugs chosen are primarily marijuana and hallucinogens. The so-called harder drugs like heroin and amphetamines are generally rejected because their effects are thought to be desensitizing. The use of drugs in this new bohemian setting is strikingly different from previous beat scenes if for no other reason than that more drugs are available today because of scientific breakthroughs in creating new substances. What was formerly a small and isolated phenomenon among bohemians is now taking on mass proportions.

There has been some shift in the range of heroes in this new group. No longer is it the primitive alone, though the American Indian is certainly revered. The proletariat is not viewed as the only true source of values. The kinds of jobs preferred by the new bohemians suggest the change in orientation. Artistic work is still preferred above all else, but increasing acceptance has been given to low level bureaucratic jobs. The low level bureaucrat who survives and maintains his integrity has always been acceptable; now he seems to have been elevated to a heroic role. Another hero who has emerged is the one who manages to survive very well and beat the system at its own game, e.g., various rock and roll singers who flaunt society's values and make a great deal of money doing it. This indicates a shift in the value attached to voluntary poverty. Poverty is good in its demonstration that one can live without a lot of material things, that one can be detached from them. It is no longer necessary to take upon oneself the condition of the most outcast in the population to achieve truth. The other heroes are somewhat similar to those celebrated by the earlier beats. Those who exemplify by their works or life the value of existential choice, like Camus, are admired.

A most striking difference between today's bohemian and the beats of the late 1950s is in mood. The strain of pessimism or morose bohemianism is completely absent. They share with their earlier counterparts the diagnosis of society as absolutely corrupt, but the new bohemians are not despondent because of it. Rather the whole movement seems to be animated by a profound optimism. This is probably related to the discovery of the hallucinogens. The feeling is that mankind is on the verge of a major development in human consciousness and that its occurrence is inevitable. Hence the lack of interest in rearranging the social structure. The feeling is that the next stage of human development will be radically different from the present one and that it is impossible at this point to anticipate it.

An impartial look at the values associated with this new movement is difficult because so much of what is celebrated is antithetical to middle-class values. The use of certain kinds of drugs (but certainly not alcohol or cigarettes) is considered popularly to be in opposition to fundamental American values. Drug use seems to be opposed to the values of self-restraint, independence, sobriety, earned pleasure and leisure, and sexual propriety. Descriptions of young people involved in this movement have tended to distort the meaning drugs play in their lives. The significance they attach to drugs can only be ascertained within a broader context of shared values. What are some of these values?

Choice

Probably the most important value celebrated by the new bohemians is related to the choices one makes. Choice is a precondition of morality. There is likewise an emphasis on seeing a very wide range of human behavior as open to the operation of choice rather than being determined. Even in situations that appear very confining there is still room for choice. New bohemians do not see themselves as victims to whom things happen. Choice gives one the unlimited freedom to change, to make of oneself what he wants to be. This view rejects the unconscious. Man is not a plaything of the unconscious since he creates what he is. Consequently there is a rejection of psychoanalysis, psychiatry, and conventional clinical psychology as simply ways of suppressing nonconformity. One is not victimized unless he wills it. A young man who has flunked out of college will view the event, in retrospect, as an act that he willed. He did not flunk because he was in the grip of something larger than himself, but because the whole idea of "having to do something" is seen as deceitful, a way of reconciling one's behavior with an external standard and excusing it. This kind of thinking also extends to the use of the opiates. Drug addiction is seen as a matter of choice—a person in that condition chose it. If he had willed otherwise, he would either not use the drug or he would have stopped. They do not accept the view of the "junkie" as a victim in the sense that he is compelled to use drugs, but as a person who chooses to be a victim. Choices are seen as private matters, in that one is not justified in choosing for another. It is bad behavior either to try to make choices for others or to ask them to make yours.

Such choices can be interfered with in a number of ways. The demands of people to be given authority is a touchy point. On whatever grounds the demand is made—tradition, office, or charisma—these young people are reluctant to let others make up their minds, to plot courses of action, or lay down lines of discipline. Thus there is a great disrespect for tradition as a guideline for present action whether in politics, dress, or manners. There is likewise great disrespect for authority claimed on the basis of office or similar institutional attachment. Perhaps the most acceptable form of authority is that based on personal attributes—charisma.

Choices are made in the context of a benevolent universe. Mass society may be corrupt but the forces that regulate the universe are benign. There is the recognition that there are forces operative in the universe that are not visible. These forces, however, are not placated, as in the lower class, nor exploited in a coldly calculating way, as with the middle class. Rather one attunes to them. The new bohemians come from backgrounds that give them a sense of being able to control their own destiny, so there is a certain confidence attendant upon their choice. The person who exercises choice in a wide variety of situations takes risks but is not likely to be destroyed by forces over which he has no control.

The choice element is much broader than middle-class decision making. Middle-class decisions are limited to "making it" in the conventional world, to striving for mobility. This is the only way in which middle-class choice is operative. It is linked to ambition. From the new bohemian point of view, ambitious people create coercion and misery. Middle-class choice is restless, anxious, unhappy.

To the middle-class person the new bohemian seems to be one who is not decisive. This he would deny. His choice is related to searching for true values, for exploring his own mind and those of others. The passivity perceived by the middle-class person involves a choice. It is a response to the coerciveness of institutions and a decision not to collaborate with them. The major choice is made to drop out of conventional society and opt for independence in personal relationships. This is viewed not as withdrawal but as the first step in exploring those facets of the world and freeing the self from mass society.

Religious Sense

The young people involved in this new movement do not characteristically come from religious backgrounds, yet they do reveal a strong spiritual orientation. Allen Ginsberg was the first to insist on the religious character of the earlier beats; the same thing can be said of this new group.

The religious dimension in the movement is most obviously expressed in the strong attraction to certain features of Zen Buddhism, which also find their counterparts in Christianity. The Zen influence does not come directly from the Orient today any more than it did for the earlier beats.[10] What the present generation of bohemians seems to find most attractive in Zen is the idea of the holiness of the personal impulse and the dramatic role of the Zen lunatic. The lunatic is the perfect expression of the bohemian commitment to spontaneity and authenticity. His counterpart in the Christian tradition is the holy fool as depicted so forcefully by Dostoyevsky.

There is also a pronounced sense of the sacred. The world in which we live consists of a number of forces that are alien to middle-class values. These forces are by and large benevolent. We should strive to make ourselves aware of them, to open ourselves to them, to become attuned to them.

The reality perceived by these young people is different from that which is usually referred to by the term. There are two realities, both of which must be discovered: the *pseudo-reality* and *the real reality*. The pseudo-reality refers to the façade, the performance, the roles, the games, the rules, the routine. This is perceived to be a phony and superficial mode of being. More importantly, the games are restricting and prevent the individual from realizing his true self, his wholeness, or the meaning and value of life. What is important is that one discover the faces and see them for what they are—dull unconscious restrictions on the real self and impediments to the development of consciousness, of awareness of self, others, and the world. Perception of the true reality or the real reality enables one to reject material gains, middle-class status, and the institutional means for gaining these ends. These goals are replaced by a new one, the experience of really being, or having being. Having being, the experience of being in the real scene, leads to an understanding of the true meaning of existence, to the truth of life, to the real-reality.

This openness, which permits one to perceive the true reality, leads quite naturally to a deep reverence for nature and other persons. The reverence is connected with the sense that the world of men, animals, and plants—all living things—is inextricably bound together. It is almost as if all living things were part of one body.

---

[10] Tallman (1961), commenting on Kerouac's *Dharma Bums*, states that "it is an obvious attempt to adjust the practices, flavor, and the attitude of Zen to an American sensibility." P. 226.

The new bohemians seem to have a distinctive attitude toward time. The focus of interest is on the present, which is to be enjoyed, not some future good. The mind has to be really free of plans and calculations if one is to enjoy the present. Closely linked to this attitude is the disavowal of ambition. Ambition is rejected because it keeps people working for some future status and makes them ignore the present. The daily round of new bohemians is quite unscheduled. A considerable amount of time is spent just "hanging out." This may involve a search for thrills, excitement, and stimulation. It may involve engaging in interesting conversations or improvising word games. Empty time is partly filled with excitement and partly filled with waiting. Waiting for what? Waiting for the *happening*. The happening is an episode, an occurrence, or an event. It may involve conversation that reveals insight about oneself, the world, or the political order. It may entail encountering "beautiful" people, that is, persons who are spiritually attractive and loving people. It may refer to the giving and receiving of love. Nothing is likely to happen to you, you are not likely to experience a "happening," however, if you are not open to it. The language the new bohemians use reveals the importance attached to the happening. When greeting another person, rather than ask "What have you been doing lately?" as if worth were measured in terms of achievement, they ask "What has been happening to you?" or "What has been happening to your mind?"

Finally, within this evolving social movement there is a pronounced emphasis on mutual aid. This flows from the fact that identity is not developed in terms of the possessions a person has or the property he owns. Property, food, and drugs are shared. In this, of course, they are like their earlier counterparts living by the code of the small compact group faced with the problem of survival in a hostile world.[11] The response is to establish a community of love and to try to extend beauty into an ugly world. This can be done by telling people how beautiful they can be or by telling them they are basically good. Many small communes attempt to do this by passing out leaflets, buttons, or food.

---

[11] What Holmes (1960) has said about the beats can be said just as accurately about the new bohemians: ". . . their response is a return to an older, more personal, but no less rigorous code of ethics, which includes the inviolability of comradeship, the respect for confidences and an almost mystical regard for courage—all of which are the ethics of the tribe, rather than the community, the code of a small compact group living in an indifferent or hostile environment which it seeks not to conquer or change, but only to elude." P. 22.

What Does This Phenomenon Represent?

The persons involved in this new development consider themselves to be part of a general social movement. They feel it is beginning to take shape. At present there is little indication of where it is going. It tends to be unorganized; there is little official leadership or recognized membership. Progress toward whatever the goal seems to be is uneven. But of one thing these young people are sure: it represents an extraordinarily powerful force.

A new social order is presumably envisioned where honesty, authenticity and self-realization are possible. The rapidity with which this movement is spreading, if we accept increasing drug use as a sign of it, is due to the widespread dissemination of its beliefs among the many persons who are receptive to them.

Certain conditions must be present for a social movement of this sort to develop.[12] Among the most important of these conditions is the unavailability of other means to express protest or grievances among a population suffering from some kind of strain. Alternative means for reconstituting the social structure are perceived as unavailable. The age group that constitutes the recruits for this movement—those approximately between 18 and 25, despite their largely middle-class status—ranks low on wealth, power, prestige, or access to the means of communication. Their experience consequently is one of deprivation, not in any material sense, but a deprivation of participation. The disaffection springs from a sense of powerlessness in the face of inflexible political structures. This is the condition that generates the sense of disillusionment described earlier.[13]

The economic forces that set the stage for this movement are related to our advanced stage of industrialization, which has dramatically changed work practices. Old skills have become obsolescent, and reeducation in a person's career has become an imperative. This has had the effect of lengthening the time between basic schooling and desired employment among a group of persons always noted for its questioning attitudes and profoundly moral stance on social issues.

At the same time work practices are undergoing profound changes,

[12] See Smelser (1963), chapter three, for his discussion of strains that precede movements of this kind.

[13] "Such deprivations are relative to expectations. By an absolute measure, groups which are drawn into value-oriented movements may be improving . . . improvement on absolute grounds (may) involve deprivation on relative grounds; for the same group, with their new gains in one sphere (e.g., economic, cultural) is often held back in another (e.g., political)." Smelser (1963), p. 340.

the characteristics of our population and its concentration have been shifting. Internal migration and shifts in population composition generally produce strains that precede the generation of movements of this sort. The concentration of population in large cities, which is a post-World War II phenomenon, combined with the increased birth rate after the war provided the context for this new movement.[14] The increase in birth rate shifted the proportion of youths to adults significantly. The mixing of unlike populations in larger cities further contributed to the strain. One fundamental factor in the rise of religious movements is the sudden coming together of unlike elements in the population representing different stages of assimilation.[15]

The direction this movement will take depends on the response of the larger community through its agencies of social control. If consistent and firm repression is the reaction, then it is likely to be driven further underground and possibly eliminated. This does not seem a likely outcome at this point for several reasons. The resources necessary to repress the movement are more than the community is prepared to expend—in short, public opinion is not favorable to it. Firm repression does not seem likely because decision makers are too ambivalent about the movement: it is composed of their children. But finally, firm repression does not seem likely because the movement strikes responsive chords in many older people. There seems to be among all parts of our community a general vague dissatisfaction with the *quality* of our lives. This movement speaks to that.

If the agencies of social control respond to the movement with a certain amount of flexibility, then we can expect another kind of evolution. When channels are open for peaceful agitation for change and a patient and thorough hearing is given to grievances, then the larger community's response is essentially an accommodative one. This would require some initiative on the part of the agencies of social control: legislators, universities, and colleges. If we have learned anything from intergroup relations, it is that contact between community officials and the new bohemians should not be patronizing—any contact initiated must be on an equal basis and demonstrate a sympathetic regard for the values that the new bohemians hold. There is a certain urgency in doing this because of increasing disaffection of young per-

[14] Hauser (1960) points out that about 122 million people lived in urban places in 1960—some 68 percent of the total population as contrasted with 56 percent in 1950. The major shift took place during World War II and is expected to continue.

[15] Gillin (1910–11) earlier pointed out that one fundamental factor in the rise of religious movements is "the heterogeneity of the population of any social group . . . or its social unlikeness which results from the imperfect assimilation of population elements suddenly brought together. . . ." Pp. 240–41.

sons and the widening cleavage between them and adults. Any initiative exercised by community leaders requires a willingness to listen and a desire to understand. This may create the first break in the insularity of the new movement. The key theme in the young person's response to the larger community is its hypocrisy. Its hypocrisy is flagrantly announced in three areas: the Vietnam War, the unequal status of black people in the United States, and the punitive laws on marijuana. Any discussion must proceed on the assumption that the war be stopped immediately, that the larger white community demonstrate some openness to black demands for equal opportunities, and that marijuana legislation be eliminated or liberalized.

Another possible outcome, at least theoretically, is that the sources of strain that generated this movement will be eliminated. This is not likely to happen, even if we wished it, because our knowledge is inadequate to the task of reorganizing the social structure in such a way as to eliminate the sources of strain. If we were able to do it, the movement would disappear because the new world envisioned by young people in the movement would already be here.

Whatever the outcome it seems to me we shall all be the better for taking seriously the call to slow down, to live our lives instead of enduring them, to open our eyes and really see what is happening around us and in us, to respond to beauty, to humanize our large-scale social structures and yes, if you will, to love one another.

References

BECKER, H. 1953. Becoming a marihuana user. *American journal of sociology* 59:235–42.

BLUMER, H. et al. 1967. Add center project final report: the world of youthful drug use. School of Criminology, University of California, Berkeley, Cal.

BOUQUET, JR. 1944. Marihuana intoxication. *Journal of the American medical association* 124:1010–11.

GEIS, G. 1968. Social and epidemiological aspects of marijuana use. See above, pp. 78–90.

GILLIN, J. L. 1910. A contribution to the sociology of sects. *American journal of sociology* 16:236–52.

GLEASON, R. 1967. Like a Rolling Stone. *The American scholar* 36 (Autumn):555–63.

HAUSER, P. 1960. *Population perspectives*. New Brunswick, New Jersey: Rutgers University Press.

HOLMES, JR. 1960. In Krim, S., ed., *The beats: a gold medal anthology*. Greenwich, Connecticut: Fawcett Publications.

KOLB, L. 1962. *Drug addiction: a medical problem.* Springfield. Illinois: Charles Thomas.

LINDESMITH, A. R. 1947. *Opiate addiction.* Evanston, Illinois: The Principia Press of Ill.

LIPTON, L. 1959. *The holy barbarians.* New York: Julian Messner, Inc.

Mayor's committee on marihuana. 1944. *The marihuana problem in the city of New York.* Lancaster, Pennsylvania: The Jacques Cattell Press.

MUNCH, JR. 1966. Marihuana and crime. *United Nations bulletin on narcotics* 18, no. 2.

POLSKY, N. 1961. The village beat scene: summer 1960. *Dissent* 8, no. 3 (Summer):339–59.

RIGNEY, F. J., and SMITH, D. 1961. *The real bohemia: a sociological and psychological study of the beats.* New York: Basic Books Inc.

SMELSER, N. 1963. *Theory of collective behavior.* New York: The Free Press of Glencoe.

TALLMAN, T. 1961. In Parkinson, T., ed., *Casebook on the beats.* New York: Thomas Y. Crowell.

U. S. Marijuana Legislation and the Creation of a Social Problem

Roger C. Smith, M.S.

The possession, sale, or use of marijuana in the United States today is considered serious deviant behavior, both legally and socially, and the penal sanctions that may be imposed on a convicted marijuana offender are among the most severe in both the federal and state penal codes. The threat of arrest and conviction is currently the most persuasive argument advanced to young people when attempting to dissuade them from the use of the drug. Simple logic would suggest to us that there must be more to our proscription of marijuana than meets the eye; in order to merit such severe legal penalties, marijuana surely must pose a major threat to the fabric of our society, in the same way that society is threatened by acts of murder, arson or burglary—criminal acts that carry similar stiff penal sanctions.

Although the professional literature reveals conflicting data regarding the pharmacological, psychological, and social effects of marijuana use, there is nowhere presented fact or research data that would justify our current legal attitude toward the drug. It is for this reason that we seek, in this paper, to examine some of the less tangible aspects of attempts to control marijuana use in this country, as well as to review some of the highlights of such legislation historically. Because the history of marijuana legislation has been extensively reported in both the professional and lay literature, a certain familiarity with the content and implications of that specific legislation is assumed, although reference will be made to it when it is of some particular value or interest.

"U. S. Marijuana Legislation and the Creation of a Social Problem" was published in the Journal of Psychedelic Drugs 2, no. 1 (Fall 1968): 93–103. Copyright © 1968 by David E. Smith, M.D. Reprinted with minor changes by permission of the publisher and the author.

The Historical Background

In the years that preceded the passage of the Marijuana Tax Act, the specter of "demon rum" was still quite clear in the minds of the moral entrepreneurs of this nation, when a new menace, the "killer weed" raised its ugly head.[1] Like alcohol, it was an intoxicant sought after primarily because of the pleasure it gave the user, but unlike alcohol, it did not provide the spiritually redeeming morning-after hangover. Its use, like that of alcohol, is a pleasurable, hedonistic, nonproductive, and above all, a sinful practice. As a pharmacological entity, marijuana can be regarded as a relatively innocuous and insignificant weed, but as a social, legal, and philosophical entity, it has assumed menacing proportions. Just why this has happened requires a close examination of the images that were drawn of the marijuana smoker and the methods employed to arouse a generally apathetic and unaware public to this new menace.

It is somewhat difficult to understand where the impetus for such an energetic anti-marijuana campaign on the national level arose. In the late 1920s marijuana was used primarily in the south and southwest parts of the country, where the majority of the habituates were of Mexican descent, although the practice had slowly spread to the urban centers in the north, where marijuana smoking was practiced by musicians and other "bohemian" groups.

One of the earliest and most forceful of the anti-marijuana crusaders was Earle Albert Towell, who was convinced that he had discovered the ultimate aim of the tobacco industry, namely, turning everyone on to marijuana, which, in his opinion, would lead ultimately to the destruction of the morals and health of the nation. In his popular book *On the Trail of Marijuana, The Weed of Madness,* Towell clearly outlines the potential of this new drug.

1. Destroys will power and makes a jellyfish of the user. He cannot say no.
2. Eliminates the line between right and wrong, and substitutes one's own warped desires or the base suggestions of others as the standard of right.
3. Above all, causes crime; fills the victims with an irrepressible urge to violence.

---

[1] For a detailed description of the Marijuana Tax Act of 1937 and the testimony of the key witnesses, see Alfred R. Lindesmith, *The Addict and the Law* (Bloomington: Indiana University Press, 1963); the David Solomon, ed., *Marijuana Papers* (Indianapolis: Bobbs-Merrill, 1966); Edwin M. Schur, *Crimes Without Victims* (Englewood Cliffs, N.J.: Prentice-Hall, Inc., 1965).

4. Incites to revolting immoralities, including rape and murder.
5. Causes many accidents, both industrial and automobile.
6. Ruins careers forever.
7. Causes insanity as its specialty.
8. Either in self-defense or as a means of revenue, users make smokers of others, thus perpetuating evil.[2]

The Federal Bureau of Narcotics, formed in 1930 and staffed largely by former prohibition agents, was apparently not particularly concerned with the national control of marijuana until the middle 1930s. By 1930 some 16 states had passed legislation restricting the sale or use of marijuana in some way, although these laws were not vigorously enforced for the most part. In 1932 the Federal Bureau of Narcotics (FBN) was an interested observer at the National Conference of Commissioners on Uniform State Laws, which touched on the matter of marijuana legislation on the state level. It was about this time that a rash of lurid articles and stories began to appear in the popular press concerning marijuana, most of which were outrageous enough to prompt the FBN to minimize publicly the importance of the "marijuana menace." [3] At this time they apparently saw marijuana control as properly the bailiwick of the states.

Despite the fact that following the Uniform State Laws conference in 1932 several additional states enacted legislation prohibiting the manufacture, sale, or possession of marijuana, the FBN became increasingly insistent that the states were not doing enough and that if they did not step up their efforts, the FBN would be forced to seek legal controls at the federal level. By 1936 the FBN, and particularly Commissioner Harry J. Anslinger, was deeply involved in a campaign to alert the public to the menace of marijuana. There is an interesting parallel between their efforts to shape policy with regard to marijuana and their previous campaign to impose their will on the administration of various pieces of legislation intended to control the distribution and use of the "hard" narcotics, principally the opiates and cocaine.

The opiate addict at the turn of the century was regarded as an unfortunate victim of ignorance, who had become addicted to drugs that he had initially used for alleviating pain, and not simply for the pleasurable feelings that accompanied its use. The majority of addicts at this time were women; most were Protestants, white, and from rural areas. With the passage of the 1906 Pure Food and Drug Act, the patent medicines loaded with opiates were taken off the market, and

---

[2] For a detailed description of Towell's activities, see Alfred Lindesmith, *The Addict and the Law*, pp. 222–42.

[3] Howard Becher, *The Outsider* (Glencoe: Free Press, 1963), p. 138.

the Harrison Act of 1914 curbed the indiscriminate sale of opiates across the counter. The Harrison Act, like the Marijuana Tax Act, is a revenue act, and is enforced by agencies within the Treasury Department. The original law made no mention of addicts or addiction and reflected a growing concern about the widespread use of narcotics for the self-treatment of a variety of complaints. The legislation came at a time when the medical profession was becoming aware of the potential dangers of such drugs and sought to curtail sharply their use.

Those who were addicted to narcotics immediately after the passage of the Harrison Act had little difficulty in receiving proper medical care until a series of court interpretations of the act made it impossible for the addict to obtain drugs from any source other than the black market. Thus many cities opened up ambulatory drug clinics, the first being in New York City in 1919, with hopes for rehabilitating the addict and preventing his involvement with criminal drug distributors. Later, other cities began opening drug clinics; there were soon a total of 44 throughout the United States.

The clinic experience was the critical period insofar as the development of our current punitive policy toward drugs is concerned. The addict was publicly characterized as an individual in need of medical help and assistance when the clinics opened in 1919. Narcotics addiction was regarded as an unfortunate occurrence, but not really the fault of the individual. The public was receptive to treating him as such. By 1923 all of the clinics had closed their doors, the addict was left with only the criminal underworld as his source of supply, and he had come to be regarded by the lay public as a willfully indulgent criminal, unwilling to respond to humane medical treatment, and fully deserving of society's moral and penal sanctions. It was only after this radical transformation of the addict's image that the increasingly punitive approach advocated by the Federal Bureau of Narcotics could become official policy. It is of significance that nowhere in the discussions of the ambulatory clinics does one find a critical analysis of the treatment methodology. The FBN was instrumental in exposing the weaknesses of the clinics, and the press had a field day with them.

As the public became more aroused and outraged by the activities of narcotics addicts as described to them in the press, they became less receptive to pleas for moderation or rationality, and insisted on the strongest possible punitive measures. The addict was no longer a victim, but a threat, a transformation that took but four years to accomplish.[4]

[4] For a discussion of the clinic experiment and the reversal of the imagery surrounding the addict, see Roger Smith, "Status Politics and the Image of the Addict,"

In order to set the stage for federal legislation controlling marijuana use, the FBN set about to promote the notion that the marijuana smoker was a serious threat and responsible for an increasing number of crimes, particularly crimes of violence. To this end, they widely publicized several "examples" of heinous crimes, which they claimed were directly related to the use of marijuana. For example:

In 1935, a 30-year-old male assaulted a 10-year-old girl, admitted being under the influence of marijuana, so "crazy," convicted in court trial. Hanged.

1936, in San Antonio, Texas. Two women arrested for possession of marijuana violently attacked Officer C. Cullen. Arrested.

1921, male 30, beat to death with rock T. Bernhardt, boy, 14, while herding cattle in pasture; accused boy of polluting his water supply. Boy's head crushed, one eye gouged out, and missing. Arrested several hours later, he screamed and tore jail furnishings. Smoking marijuana at the time; claimed insane, found to be sane. Hanged.

1933, Tampa, Florida. A boy murdered his father, mother, sister, and two brothers with an axe while under the influence of marijuana. Didn't know of all this until next morning. Arrested.[5]

Although few people in this country objected to statements linking marijuana use and crime, it is clear that in the numerous cases previously cited, the "causal relationship" between marijuana and crime was tenuous, at best, and in some cases, outright fabrication. Thus we turned to other sources for confirmation of the dangerous qualities inherent in the drug. Longitudinal studies on users in this country were impossible because it had not been a drug problem for an adequate length of time and no research had been done on long-term effects. Thus we looked to the experiences of other cultures. One of the more popular stories about marijuana was that of the "assassins," in which we discover that the use of hashish by members of a certain Persian religious sect led directly to the commission of political assasinations by individuals who were in no way predisposed to such violence. In another variation of the same story, FBN officials related stories about how warriors would become fearless fanatics on the battlefield under the influence of the drug. They failed to explain how

Issues in Criminology 2 (Fall 1966), School of Criminology, University of California, Berkeley.
[5] James C. Munch, "Marijuana and Crime," reprinted from *United Nations Bulletin on Narcotics*, vol. 18, no. 2 (April–June, 1966). Munch is a member of the advisory committee of the U.S. Bureau of Narcotics.

in the first instance hashish made one a stealthy cunning assassin, and
in the latter, a screaming fanatic.

Few have called into question this particular bit of folklore from
another culture, and in fact many law enforcement officials still use
this story to underscore their contention that marijuana can lead to
acts of violence. Jerry Mandel's analysis of this story would suggest
that it has been grossly distorted and that indeed hashish was a reward for certain kinds of behavior, not the cause of it.[6]

As the campaign against marijuana was stepped up, an increasing
number of sensational horror stories were related in magazines and
newspapers that deplored the juicy sex and violence attributed to
marijuana smoking. Some enterprising attorneys attempted unsuccessfully to introduce marijuana intoxication as a defense in capital cases.

By the time the Treasury Department went to Congress with the
proposed Marijuana Tax Act, the fervor had reached a high pitch. The
hearings before the House Committee on Ways and Means lasted five
days. There was little doubt in anybody's mind that the legislation
would be enacted. Rather, the primary function of the hearing was to
titillate the legislators with horror stories. They were assured that the
act had the blessings of the newspapers. The Hashish-assassin story
was related. The various crimes that the FBN linked directly to marijuana were related, including the tale of the youngster who murdered
his family while under the influence of the drug, and could not recall
having done it the following day. A district attorney told the committee that marijuana was used as an aphrodisiac, but that prolonged
use led to impotence. A pharmacologist who had done research on
doped race horses testified that marijuana produced mental and
physical deterioration when administered to dogs. Though he admitted
that he had done no work with humans, he stated unequivocally that
the drug was dangerous because it produced degeneracy of the brain.
A district attorney from New Orleans related that several individuals
who had been prosecuted through his office had claimed that they
were not criminally responsible for their acts because they were under
the influence of marijuana at the time the crime was committed.

The dissenting witnesses before the committee were limited. The
birdseed industry feared that the new law would inhibit their use of
hempseed. The committee quickly amended its bill to allow the industry to continue its production unhindered.

The last remaining witness, Dr. William C. Woodward, the legislative counsel for the American Medical Association and himself an attorney, opposed the bill on a number of counts. He felt that the state

[6] Jerry Mandel, "Hashish, Assassins, and the Love of God," *Issues in Criminology*, pp. 149–56.

legislation was sufficient to meet the problem and that previous testimony was based primarily on hearsay evidence. The passage of this act, he added prophetically, would inhibit further research into its pharmacology and would rule out further investigation into the medical possibilities of the drug. He cited its use in medicine as a sedative and muscle relaxant.

Dr. Woodward's testimony aroused the ire of the committee, which apparently had anticipated little opposition to its efforts. In response to Woodward's testimony, committee members challenged his credentials, which turned out to be impeccable, and criticized him for not cooperating. The members assured themselves that they were doing the right thing by reminding the doctor of the tales of horror that had been previously related. In their parting shot, they rebuked the doctor with the following sentence: "If you want to advise us on legislation, you ought to come here with some constructive proposals, rather than criticism, rather than trying to throw obstacles in the way of something the Federal Government is trying to do."[7]

The Marijuana Tax Act quickly passed the House of Representatives and shortly thereafter, the Senate. There was little debate during the Senate hearings. The star witness was again Commissioner Harry J. Anslinger, who reiterated the numerous crimes that he felt were committed by individuals under the influence of marijuana.

The Marijuana Tax Act, now a part of the Internal Revenue Code, provides "a graduated occupational tax by all persons who import, manufacture, produce, compound, sell, deal in, dispense, prescribe, administer, or give away marijuana. A tax is also imposed upon all transfers of marijuana at the rate of $1 per ounce or fraction thereof, if the transfer is made to a taxpayer registered under the Act, or at the rate of $100 per ounce, if the transfer is made to a person who is not a taxpayer registered under the act."[8] Obviously, the Act has not produced significant tax revenue, since few Marijuana Tax Stamps have been issued, although the Internal Revenue Service still attempts to collect $100 per ounce of illegally possessed marijuana from those convicted of violating the act. In many cases this tax is collected from an individual upon his release from prison on parole, a time when the individual finds himself in a most difficult position financially.

The obvious intent of this legislation was to impose federal police powers in the area of marijuana enforcement. The original act pro-

[7] Joseph Oteri and Harvey Silverglate, "In the Marketplace of Free Ideas: A Look at the Passage of the Marijuana Tax Act," *Marijuana Myths and Realities* J. L. Simmons, ed. (North Hollywood, California: Brandon House, 1967), p. 152.
[8] *Narcotic Drug Addiction Problem,* Proceedings of the Symposium on the History of Narcotic Drug Addiction Problems, Bethesda, Maryland (March 27–28), p. 50.

vided for a maximum penalty of $2,000 fine and/or five years in prison, with probation or suspended sentence possible.

By the time that the Marijuana Tax Act had passed the Congress, most states had outlawed marijuana under the Uniform Narcotic Drug Act, an act that grouped marijuana with the opiates. This system of classification posed no problem for Donald Miller, chief counsel for the United States Bureau of Narcotics, who stated in a recent speech:

> Legally, marijuana is not considered a narcotic drug under the federal law, but it is considered a narcotic under the state laws. I do not consider these differences to be significant, since both laws are designed to control a substance which is socially unacceptable. It is less important that the controls fit like some finely balanced formula under either the taxing clause or the commerce clause of the Constitution, or in a category according to its similarity with other dangerous drugs. In fact, the Supreme Court of Colorado has ruled it is perfectly permissible to define marijuana as a narcotic drug.[9]

With a reported upswing in the number of young people addicted to heroin a few years after World War II, increasing pressure was brought to bear by the FBN for increased penalty provisions, both on the state and federal level. By this time, however, there were grave doubts in even the most conservative minds about the relationship between marijuana smoking and insanity or violence. Hence a new theme emerged that persists to this date, despite data to the contrary. In testimony before the Senate subcommittee investigating drug abuse in 1955, Commissioner Anslinger, in response to a question regarding the relationship between marijuana and heroin addiction, stated: ". . . our great concern about the use of marijuana . . . [is] that eventually, if used over a long period, it does lead to heroin addiction." However, on the relationship between marijuana smoking and crimes of violence, he has taken a new tack: "It does not follow that all crime can be traced to marijuana. There have been many brutal crimes traced to marijuana, but I would not say that it is a controlling factor in the commission of crimes." [10]

Convinced that the answer to the problems of drug use and sale was heavier penalties, the Congress authorized minimum mandatory

[9] Narcotic Drugs and Marijuana Controls, a paper presented by Donald E. Miller at the National Association of Student Personnel Administration Drug Education Conference, Washington, D.C., November 7–8, 1966.

[10] For a detailed description of Anslinger's testimony, see Alfred Lindesmith, *The Addict and the Law*, p. 230.

sentences, with no chance for probation, suspended sentence or parole, and an optional fine of up to $20,000 for individuals convicted of selling narcotics, including marijuana. For first offenders convicted of possession, the penalties were increased to 2 to 10 years, an optional fine of up to $20,000, and the possibility of probation, suspended sentence, or parole.

Following the lead of the federal government, many states enacted new legislation that increased the penalty provisions in their narcotic laws, which by definition included marijuana. In several states a person convicted of selling marijuana to a minor could be subjected to death or life imprisonment.

The FBN is dedicated to the notion that increasing penalties is the only way to limit the traffic in narcotics. One of its initial fears upon passage of the Narcotic Control Act of 1956 was that judges would be hesitant about convicting an individual in a case that carried a minimum mandatory sentence.

In testimony before a House subcommittee in 1960, Commissioner Anslinger expressed great satisfaction with the sentences that had been handed down by federal judges since the 1956 legislation, but expressed concern about the traffic in marijuana. The solution, as he saw it, lay in increasing the penalties. In response to the question as to whether marijuana led to heroin addiction, Anslinger replied: "Yes, Sir. That is the beginning, especially in the New York and Los Angeles areas. They start on marijuana and get sort of a jaded appetite and want to get to something real. Well, they switch to heroin, and that is when the trouble starts." [11]

What we have seen then, in less than 30 years from the passage of the Marijuana Tax Act, is a dramatic transformation in the qualities of a drug, from a substance that produces moral degeneration and is the cause of crimes of violence, to a drug that has only a tenuous causal relationship to crimes of violence, but is directly responsible for progression to harder narcotics. This transformation took place without benefit of even minimal research into the actual properties of the drug, which was severely restricted because of the limitations imposed on legitimate researchers.

If the assumptions of the commissioner and law enforcement officials in general are correct, we might assume that with increased penalties for possession and sale of marijuana since 1956, the practice by 1968 would be almost totally eradicated. This apparently not being the case, we are forced to look at the implications of existing laws and how they have shaped the contemporary scene.

[11] Hearings before the Subcommittee of the Committee on Appropriations, House of Representatives, January 26, 1960, p. 182.

The Current Scene

Marijuana smoking is no longer confined to the southwest part of this country, nor are its users primarily from the lower socioeconomic classes. Attorney General Thomas Lynch has characterized the current drug offender in California as being "young, white, urban, and without previous arrest record." It is perhaps this fact, more than any other, that accounts for the reexamination of our current laws that is being undertaken on all levels of government. During the White House Conference on Narcotic and Drug Abuse in September of 1962, doubts were voiced by many individuals who had pressed for severe penalties in 1956. Senator Thomas Dodd, in a very forceful presentation to the conference, gave the following example of the implications of the minimum mandatory sentences by quoting from a United States District Judge:

> The mandatory sentence can work extreme injustice. I was compelled to impose a five-year sentence on a Marine veteran of the Korean campaign who was found with three or four marijuana cigarettes. He had been drinking in Tijuana and was arrested at the border. Obviously, three or four cigarettes did not make him a peddler and these were not commercial amounts. He had a spotless civilian record and an excellent military career. He had received a Purple Heart and had been wounded in action and had a wife and children. I held up sentencing 60 days with the defendant's consent, to attempt to get the U.S. attorney to file a tax consent on a smuggling charge which would not have carried at least a 5 years sentence. I was unsuccessful. I sentenced the man to 5 years in the penitentiary without parole.[12]

That conference suggested that ". . . the hazards of marijuana per se have been exaggerated and that long criminal sentences imposed on an occasional user or possessor of the drug are in poor social perspective."[13] The recent report of the President's Commission on Law Enforcement and the Administration of Justice also recommends differentiating between narcotic and marijuana offenders by allowing more discretion in the sentencing of marijuana offenders to the courts or to correctional institutions.[14]

[12] Proceedings of the White House Conference on Narcotic and Drug Abuse, Washington, D.C., September 27–28, 1963, p. 231.

[13] Ibid., p. 286.

[14] *Challenge of Crime in a Free Society,* Report by the President's Commission on Law Enforcement and Administration of Justice, Washington, D.C., February 1967, pp. 211–31.

We should have learned something as a result of our national experience with marijuana. We did not. Congress has been considering legislation that would make possession or sale of LSD a criminal offense and carry with it long prison terms, despite the fact that there appears to be a tapering off in the extent of LSD use, prompted not so much by the fear of arrest, but because medical research has suggested the possibility of real harm resulting from its use under certain conditions. The information that was made public was not in the nature of bizarre claims or unfounded rumors offered by ill-informed enforcement officials, but rather, by medical research. We as a nation seem obsessed with the notion that the threat of punishment will deter people from doing things that they enjoy.

In demanding new legislation, the legislators both on the state and federal level are assured that the real intent of the legislation is to control traffic and to arrest and imprison the criminal offender, not the so-called victim. As a practical matter, however, few of the major traffickers in drugs are arrested; it is the user or dealer in the street who is arrested and imprisoned.

Let us examine some of the practical effects of our current position on marijuana. The obvious fact is that police activity is at an all time high. We witness the spectacle of police invading the high schools and grilling students about their use of drugs and that of their friends. Convinced that early detection is the only answer to later addiction, parents are bringing their teenaged sons and daughters to the police station for arrest. Local police departments author ludicrous pamphlets for distribution in the schools, which are an affront to even the novice. Telling lies to a youngster who has read scientific data on the pharmacology of marijuana in one of the many paperback books readily available in every magazine rack is hardly the way to develop respect for law enforcement. Nor does it pave the way to a receptive mind when an informed person urges individual restraint and caution with regard to other more harmful substances.

Marijuana smoking among the majority of teenagers is interwoven into their daily round of activities. It is but one facet of an adolescent style that emphasizes clothes, music, friendship, sexuality, freedom from restraint, and nonviolence. It is a drug that makes a small gathering in some homes more convivial.

Heroin addicts are regarded by most as relics of the past; as weak minded individuals who are untrustworthy and incapable of relating to other people. It would seem that this assessment is generally correct. The heroin addict of today is little different from the addict of ten or twenty years ago. He is still a product of a slum environment, he is still a dependent inadequate individual, unable to cope with the challenges of everyday life. The pressure in most adolescent groups is away from the use of addictive drugs, contrary to popular opinion. Street gang workers in New York and other cities have noticed a trend away from violence and toward "coolness." One group, formerly called the Assassins, is typical of this change. Several years ago they were one of the most violent gangs in Manhattan. Today the overwhelming majority of the gang smokes marijuana, and the club has been renamed the Socializers.[15] This is not to suggest that we have found the answer to gang violence, but merely to emphasize that the culture has built-in mechanisms of control that restrict the use of drugs by all but the most disturbed youngsters in a way that is infinitely more effective than the threat of arrest and detention.

What of the youngsters who are arrested? Have we indeed saved them from a life of degeneration and crime as an addict? It is difficult to understand how being excluded from school as a menace to other youngsters contributed to the alleged "rehabilitative" process. The felony conviction of youngsters over 18 certainly poses major problems in terms of their educational or vocational plans.

Incarceration, although a decreasing probability for most persons convicted of marijuana offenses, is perhaps one of the best ways to assure continued drug use on a larger scale upon release. It is within criminal subcultures, not groups of pot heads, that the peer sanctions against the use of addictive drugs are lowered. It would thus seem that the notion that there is a single line of progression from a mild drug to the addictive drugs leaves out the most important variables, namely, the individual's public and personal image and the cultural controls against certain forms of deviant behavior, including narcotic drug use.

Perhaps the most ludicrous expressions of our popular conception relating marijuana use to hard narcotics is the use of the Nalline clinic for marijuana offenders. The purpose of this testing, authorized by legislation in 1957, was to "discourage" the individual from progressing to harder drugs. Although this program might do much to discourage some from returning to heroin, we might speculate upon the implications of such a program in a larger urban area, where the majority of individuals taking Nalline shots are heroin addicts. The weekly meetings are very convivial events, with each person being required to wait in a reception room from 20 minutes to half an hour following the injection of Nalline before being examined. The associations that might be made in such a setting are obvious.

In reviewing the merits of this legislation, we must ask ourselves a question that as a nation we were forced to ask during prohibition:

---

[15] Gilbert Geis, *Juvenile Gangs,* President's Committee on Juvenile Delinquency and Youth Crime, Washington, D.C., June 1965, p. 49.

does the legislation restricting behavior that we have decided is harmful to our society cause more harm in its enforcement than the original harm we set out to control? In the case of our current marijuana legislation, we must answer in the affirmative.

References

DAVIS, F.; and MUNOZ, L. 1968. Heads and freaks: patterns and meanings of drug use among hippies. *Journal of Health and Social Behavior* 9: 156–64.

McGLOTHLIN, W. H. 1964. Hallucinogenic drugs: a perspective with special reference to peyote and cannabis. RAND Corporation pamphlet.

MEYERS, F. H. 1968. The pharmacological effects of marijuana. *Journal of Psychedelic Drugs* 2, no. 1: 31–36 [see above, pp. 35–40].

MEYERS, F. H.; ROSE, A. J.; SMITH, D. E. 1967. Incidents involving the Haight-Ashbury population and some uncommonly used drugs. *Journal of Psychedelic Drugs* 1: 136–46.

SMITH, D. E. 1967. LSD: an historical perspective. *Journal of Psychedelic Drugs* 1: 3–7.

SMITH, D. E.; ROSE, A. J. 1967. LSD: its use, abuse, and suggested treatment. *Journal of Psychedelic Drugs* 1: 117–23.

Privacy and the Marijuana Laws

Michael A. Town, LL.M.

The Contemporary Setting

The criminal sanctions governing use and possession of marijuana
are considered in this article in light of the concept of personal privacy
as a constitutional guarantee and as a general value in American life.
Although the wisdom and constitutionality of the marijuana laws are
fairly recent themes with relatively little legal literature treating the
subject,[1] the general issue of law and drugs has been hotly disputed
over the years in many contexts.[2] Not only has the legislative wisdom
behind the marijuana laws been recently questioned in many quarters,
but the characterization of the problem as a crime, sin, disease, vice,
recreation or merely another form of social behavior in a pluralistic
society has come into dispute as a special case of drug usage.[3]

"Privacy and the Marijuana Laws" was published in the Journal of Psychedelic
Drugs *2, no. 1 (Fall 1968): 105–47. Copyright © 1968 by David E. Smith, M.D.
Revised by the author for this volume and reprinted by permission of the pub-
lisher and the author.*

[1] The seminal legal articles dealing with the current marijuana laws are Boyko
& Rotberg, "Constitutional Objections to California's Marijuana Possession Statute," 14 U.C.L.A.L. Rev. 773 (1967) and Laughlin, "LSD-25 and Other Hallucinogens: A Pre-Reform Proposal," 36 Geo. Wash. L. Rev. 23 (1967).

Many of the articles in the following two symposia deal with marijuana: "Symposium Drugs and the Law," 56 Calif. L. Rev. 1 (1968); "Symposium: Narcotic
and Hallucinogenic Drugs," 19 Hastings L. Rev. 601 (1968). Student notes and
comments have been on the increase. *E.g.,* "Marijuana and the Law: The Constitutional Challenge to Marijuana Laws in Light of the Social Aspects of Marijuana
Use," 13 Villanova L. Rev. 851 (1968); "Legalization of Marijuana," 21 Vand.
L. Rev. 517 (1968); "Hallucinogens," 68 Colum. L. Rev. 521 (1968); "Constitutional Law: (Freedom of Religion)/(LSD) = (Psychedelic Dilemma)," 41 Tem-
ple L. Q. 52 (1967); "Constitutional Law—Freedom of Religion—Use of Drugs,"
20 Case W. Res. L. Rev. 251 (1968); "Marijuana Laws: A Need for Reform,"
22 Ark. L. Rev. 359 (1968); "Substantive Due Process and Felony Treatment
of Pot Smokers: The Current Conflict," 2 Ga. L. Rev. 247 (1968); "Marijuana
and the Law: Problem of Education or Enforcement," 1 U.S.F.V.L. Rev. 139
(1968).

[2] *See generally,* W. Eldridge, Narcotics and the Law (2d ed. 1967); A. Lindesmith, The Addict and the Law (1965); E. Schur, Drug Addiction in Britain and
America: The Impact on Public Policy (1962); Symposia, *supra* note 1.

[3] On the medical-legal characterizations of deviance, see T. Szasz, Law, Liberty and Psychiatry (1963). On the sociology of deviance dealing with marijuana
use, see H. Becker, Outsiders: Studies in the Sociology of Deviance, 41–78 (1963).

Tough questions are raised in considering the philosophical, socio-logical, and medical aspects of marijuana use; yet even as the debate rages, there are very real costs to society in maintaining the legal strictures against use and possession of marijuana. Thousands of people, many of them quite young and for the first time, experience the criminal process involving arrest, prosecution, conviction and possible sentences of great duration with the attendant difficulties of re-entering society.[4] Limited law enforcement resources that might well be used elsewhere are allocated to handle this particular problem. Methods of detection are employed that, because of the lack of a complainant or "victim," approach the gray areas of the law of arrest and search and seizure.[5] Subcultures arise that go to great lengths to continue covert usage in spite of heavy penalties.[6] This article will con-

---

The "morality" of marijuana use is reflected in the writings of H. Anslinger & W. Tompkins, The Traffic in Narcotics (1953); W. Oursler, Marijuana, The Facts, The Truth (1968). Rowell & Rowell, On the Trail of Marijuana, the Weed of Madness, 33 (1939) states: "We know that marijuana—1. Destroys will power making a jellyfish of the user. . . . Incites to revolting immoralities, including rape and murder. . . . Ruins careers forever. . . . Causes insanity as its specialty."

Marijuana use along with other drug use has been considered as another form of recreation. *See* Symposium on Recreational Drug Use, 9 J. of Health and Soc'l Behavior 99 (1968). *See also* How to Use Pot; course description from the Bulletin of Mid-Peninsula Free University, Stanford, Calif., 51 Sat. Review 62 (Sept. 21, 1968).

[4] Bureau of Criminal Statistics, Drug Arrests and Dispositions in California 1964, at 51, shows that arrests for possession of marijuana have tripled since 1960. The report also indicates that *juvenile* arrests for marijuana possession have increased over 500% since 1960 *Id.* at 88.

In 1966 65.3% of those adults arrested for possession of marijuana had no prior record, and 22.1% had only a record for minor offenses. Bureau of Criminal Statistics, Drug Arrests and Dispositions in California 1966 at 63.

[5] Recent developments in constitutional law have limited some deceptive and secretive police techniques and upheld others. Katz v. U.S., 389 U.S. 347 (1967) [warrant required for bugging device]; Lee v. Florida, 392 U.S. 378, 88 S.Ct. 2096 (1968) [wiretap in violation of federal law inadmissible in state court]. Hoffa v. U.S., 385 U.S. 293 (1966); Osborn v. U.S., 385 U.S. 323 (1966); and Lewis v. U.S., 385 U.S. 206 (1966) [upholding the propriety of police spies]. Police "encouragement" of crime is permissible where "entrapment" is not. Sherman v. U.S. 356 U.S. 369 (1958); Sorrels v. U.S., 287 U.S. 435 (1932). *See generally,* Donnelly, Judicial Control of Informants, Spies, Stool Pigeons, and Agent Provocateurs, 60 Yale L. J. 1091 (1951); Note "Judicial Control of Secret Agents," 76 Yale L. J. 994 (1967).

It is interesting to note that the Wickersham Report on the Prohibition Laws noted many of the same "costs" to society in enforcing that law. National Commission on Law Observance and Enforcement, Report on the Enforcement of the Prohibition Laws of the United States (Wickersham Report) 91, 97, 99–105 (1931).

[6] Becker, *supra* note 3, at 59–78. Fiddle, "The Addict Culture and Movement

sider the claim that a valuable and fundamental right—the right to personal privacy—has been abridged by the existence of such laws.

Some of these costs to society mentioned above are peculiar to the marijuana laws; some apply to any law where there is no victim, such as the laws prohibiting gambling, prostitution, or homosexuality; and some such costs are necessary when any law is promulgated and enforced. To assure ourselves that the benefits realized by the marijuana laws are such that they outweigh these costs, serious reconsideration of the legal proscriptions on marijuana use and possession is in order.

In considering the value of privacy as an objection to the criminal regulation of marijuana use and possession, use will be made of the California law prohibiting use and possession of the drug as an example. Not only is this law representative of those in effect across the country, but California is involved in a serious reconsideration of the marijuana laws through legislative and judicial channels. There are consequently enough statistics, legislative materials, and cases involving marijuana to make such a particularized examination useful as illustrative of the general problem.

Under California law, "Every person who possesses any marijuana, except as otherwise provided by law, shall be punished in the county jail for not more than one year, or in the state prison for not less than one year nor more than 10 years." [7] The statute goes on to provide for a 2- to 20-year sentence for a second offense, and 5 years to life imprisonment for a third offense.

The severity of punishment for possession of marijuana may be compared with the same penalty assessed for possession of LSD (lysergic acid diethylamide).[8] If the drug possessed is one of the "hard" narcotics such as heroin, morphine, or cocaine, which are recognized as physically addictive where marijuana is not,[9] the punishment is quite similar to the penalties for marijuana possession. The statute assesses penalties of 2 to 10 years for a first conviction, 5 to 20 years for a second conviction, and 15 years to life imprisonment for a third conviction.[10]

---

into and out of Hospitals," U.S. Senate Committee on the Judiciary, Subcommittee to Investigate Juvenile Delinquency. *Hearings* part 13 at 3156 (1963).

A subculture really redefines for itself a new type of privacy by its (1) ideology of justification, (2) reproductive cycle (proselytism), (3) defensive communications, (4) neighborhood warning systems, (5) ritualistic, magical, and cyclical patterns, and (6) attractiveness of personal relations. Fiddle, *supra* at 3157–60.

[7] Cal. Health & Safety Code § 11530.

[8] Cal. Health & Safety Code § 11910.

[9] Cal. Welf. & Inst'ns Code § 3009 states: "A 'narcotic addict' as used in this subdivision refers to any person . . . who is addicted to the unlawful use of any narcotic . . . *except marijuana.*" (emphasis added).

[10] Cal. Health & Safety Code § 11500.

As a further contrast, it is noted that there is no law against the mere private possession of alcoholic beverages in spite of the well-known dangers of this intoxicant.[11] Criminal penalties are imposed only when alcohol is used in some *abusive* manner, such as when a person is intoxicated in public[12] or operates a motor vehicle while under the influence of alcohol.[13]

The legislative history of marijuana regulation in California shows a trend of increasingly severe penalties for its possession. In 1907 marijuana was first regulated by the California Legislature when the drug was included within the class of substances which had to be labeled as "poison." [14] Possession of marijuana was lawful until 1915, when possession, unless prescribed by a physician, was prohibited.[15] In 1929 the legislature passed the State Narcotics Act which regulated the possession of marijuana by including it among habit forming, narcotic and other dangerous drugs and substances.[16] Thus marijuana was at this time first included among the "hard" narcotics such as heroin, morphine, and cocaine.

In 1939 the State Narcotics Act was incorporated into the California Health and Safety Code[17] along with the same illicit narcotics grouped together in 1929.[18] Marijuana possession and the planting provisions were placed in section 11530 of that code, a separate section in 1959.[19] Mandatory felony sentences were imposed as part of a scheme by which longer sentences for possession of all narcotics were required in 1961.[20] Prior to 1961 the punishment for marijuana possession was

---

[11] Where possession by certain groups likely to misuse alcohol is discouraged, the method of control is to restrict the sale of alcoholic beverages to them. *E.g.*, Cal. Bus. & Prof. Code § 25658 (a) makes sale of alcoholic beverages to a minor a misdemeanor, and Cal. Pen. Code § 397 makes the sale of alcoholic beverages to any habitual drunk a misdemeanor.

It has been suggested that the difference between the drug and alcohol laws might reflect fundamental differences in societal attitudes based upon the puritan work ethic and its intolerance of inaction. See Murphy, "The Cannabis Habit: A Review of Recent Psychiatric Literature," 15 U.N. Bull. on Narcotics 20 (1963); Eldridge, *supra* note 2; Watts, "Psychedelics and Religious Experience," 56 Calif. L. Rev. 74, 79–85 (1968).

[12] Cal. Pen. Code § 647(f) punishes as a misdemeanant one "[w]ho is found in any public place under the influence of intoxicating liquor. . . ."

[13] Cal. Vehicle Code §§ 23101–02.

[14] Cal. Stats. 1907, ch. 102 §§ 1–10, at 124–26 (Indian hemp, another name for marijuana, is used in the statute).

[15] Cal. Stats. 1915, ch. 604, § 2, at 1067–71 (Loco weed, another name for marijuana is used in the statute).

[16] Cal. Stats. 1929, ch. 216, § 1, at 380–83.

[17] Cal. Stats. 1939, ch. 60 §§ 11000–797, at 755–76.

[18] Cal. Stats. 1939, ch. 60, § 11712, at 771.

[19] Cal. Stats. 1959, ch. 1112, § 7, at 3194–95.

[20] Cal. Stats. 1961, ch. 274, § 7, at 1305.

in the alternative so that the trial judge at his discretion could make the offense either a misdemeanor or a felony depending on the length of the sentence imposed and the institution in which it was to be served.[21] An amendment in 1968 restored alternative sentencing.[22]

Clearly the development of legal sanctions against possession of marijuana has been one of increasing severity. As a felony possession falls within a class of crimes that our society regards with special opprobium.[23] Yet as more offenders are arrested each year and the number of users continue to multiply, the question of the propriety and constitutionality of the law should be more sharply focused. While only a few cases have raised constitutional objections to marijuana possession statutes in the past, their number is increasing.[24] Without legislative action to modify substantially or abolish the possession statutes, such constitutional objections will be raised with greater frequency and, perhaps, with no greater success.

Constitutional Objections to Marijuana Possession Statutes

Although this article is concerned with the notion of privacy as an objection to marijuana possession statutes, it should be emphasized that other constitutional questions can be raised as well. The right to free expression of religious beliefs as guaranteed by the First Amendment might be used to carve out an exception to the statute. This was done in *People v. Woody*,[25] where a California statute prohibiting the possession of peyote was under consideration.[26] The right of religious expression would be applicable to the marijuana possession statute if a user could show that his use of marijuana was essential to his religious beliefs or practices and if he could show

---

[21] Cal. Stats. 1959, ch. 1112, §7, at 3194–95.

[22] Cal. Stats. 1968, ch. 1465, § 1, at ——.

[23] R. Perkins, Criminal Law 8–21 (1957).

[24] On the establishment and free exercise of religion: see U.S. v. Kuch, 288 F.Supp. 439 (D.D.C. 1968); Leary v. U.S., 383 F.2d 851. (5th Cir. 1967) *cert. granted on other grounds,* 392 U.S. 903 (June 10, 1968); People v. Mitchell, 244 Cal. App.2d 176, 52 Cal. Rptr. 884 (1966); State v. Bullard, 267 N.C. 599, 148 S.E.2d 565 (1966).

On due process and equal protection: People v. Aguiar, 257 Cal. App.2d 597, 65 Cal. Rptr. 171 (1968); People v. Glaser, 238 Cal. App.2d 819, 48 Cal. Rptr. 427 (1965); People v. Mistriel, 110 Cal. App.2d 110, 241 P.2d 1050 (1952); People v. Stark, 157 Colo. 59, 400 P.2d 923 (1965); Normand v. People, —— Colo. ——, 440 P.2d 282 (1968) [not cruel and unusual punishment].

[25] 61 Cal. 2d 716, 394 P.2d 813, 40 Cal. Rptr. 69 (1964).

[26] Cal. Health & Safety Code § 11500.

his sincerity in those beliefs.[27] In two recent federal cases, *Leary vs. United States*[28] and *United States vs. Kuch*,[29] defendants failed to do this. If the free exercise clause were applied to the use of marijuana, the user could not be successfully prosecuted without the state's demonstrating a compelling interest, narrowly drawn, why that personal right should be infringed upon.

It might also be argued that a marijuana possession statute violates the constitutional guarantee against cruel and unusual punishment found in the Eighth Amendment. The statute might be invalidated if the possession of marijuana is conduct that the court would consider not within the legislative power to punish as a felony. This of course would depend upon the legislative justifications for making possession a criminal act, since it is the discrepancy between the conduct and the punishment that makes the punishment cruel and unusual under the United States Supreme Court ruling of *Robinson vs. California*.[30] By making possession of marijuana a felony, thus equating such arguably harmless conduct with the whole spectrum of common law felonies such as rape, arson, larceny and murder, the statute might be construed as imposing cruel and unusual punishment. A California court has taken judicial notice that respected medical authorities are of the opinion that marijuana is harmless, but a recent Colorado case flatly

---

[27] This was a major point in People v. Woody, 61 Cal. 2d at 720–22, 394 P.2d at 817–18, 40 Cal. Rptr. at 73–74 (1964). In another case the California Supreme Court granted habeas corpus to a defendant convicted of peyote possession and remanded to the trial court on the question of whether defendant's belief that the use of peyote for religious purposes was honest and bona fide. *In re* Grady, 61 Cal. 2d 887, 394 P.2d 728, 39 Cal. Rptr. 912 (1964).

[28] 383 F.2d 851 (5th Cir. 1967) rev'd on other grounds 394 U.S. ——, 37 U.S.L.W. 4397 (1969). For an interesting article by Dr. Leary's counsel which includes the brief to the Fifth Circuit in that case, see Finer, "Psychedelics and Religious Freedom," 19 Hastings L. J. 667 (1968). With respect to the essentiality of marijuana to Dr. Leary's practice of Hinduism, the Fifth Circuit said at 860: "There is no evidence in this case that the use of marijuana is a formal requisite of the practices of Hinduism. . . . At most, the evidence shows that it is *considered by some as being an aid to attaining consciousness expansion by which an individual can more easily meditate or commune with his god.*" (Emphasis added.)

[29] 288 F. Supp. 439 (D.D.C. 1968).

[30] 370 U.S. 660 (1962). The case struck down as unconstitutional a California statute making criminal the status of being "addicted to the use of narcotics." Justice Douglas in a concurring opinion, *id.* at 676, said: "A punishment all out of proportion to the offense may bring it within the ban against 'cruel and unusual punishments.'" *Compare* Driver v. Hinnat, 356 F.2d 761 (4th Cir. 1961) and Easter v. Dist. of Columbia, 361 F.2d 50 (D.C. Cir. 1966), where the cruel and usual punishment argument was successfully applied to drunkenness prosecutions of alcoholics under local statutes, *with* Powell v. Texas, 392 U.S. 514, (1968) [4:1:4 split on the offense of being found intoxicated in a *public place*].

rejected the defense in light of the legislative decision that *some* harm existed.[31]

There is also an argument that the classification of marijuana as a narcotic and the prohibition of possession violate the equal protection clause of the Fourteenth Amendment. In order to satisfy the equal protection guarantee, a law, in pursuing its legitimate goals, must not invidiously discriminate against any particular group. Making possession of marijuana illegal, while excluding other euphorics such as alcohol, might be considered a violation of the guarantee of equal protection by such a test. This argument was unsuccessfully tried in the California case of *People vs. Aguiar*.[32] It would be necessary, therefore, to bring marijuana within a "suspect classification," which includes personal rights protected by the constitution. Such suspect classifications are subject to closer judicial scrutiny, where the courts will engage in weighing fact-finding studies, unlike the usual type of equal protection case where any rational distinction is accepted.[33]

Privacy as a Constitutional Concept

GRISWOLD *v.* CONNECTICUT

Privacy would seem to be a commonly accepted value in America.[34] Yet, as such a vague concept, privacy is only useful when the cir-

[31] *Compare* People v. Aguiar, 257 Cal. App. 2d 597, 603, 65 Cal. Rptr. 171, 174 (1968) *with* Normand v. People, —— Colo ——, 440 P.2d 282 (1968). *cf.* Fenster v. Leary, 20 N.Y.2d 309, 229 N.E.2d 426, 282 N.Y.S.2d 739 (1967) [vagrancy statute overturned]. *See generally,* Packer, "Making the Punishment Fit the Crime," 77 Harv. L. Rev. 1071 (1964).

[32] 257 Cal. App.2d 597, 65 Cal. Rptr. 171 (1968). The court quite properly refused to second-guess the legislature where some harm was possible and no constitutionally protected rights were infringed upon. *Accord.* People v. Stark, 157 Colo. 59, 400 P.2d 923 (1965).

[33] Loving v. Va., 388 U.S. 1 (1967) [race; Levy v. Louisiana, 391 U.S. 68 (1968) [Mother-child status]; McLaughlin v. Fla., 379 U.S. 184 (1964 [race]; Skinner v. Okla., 316 U.S. 535 (1942) [procreation]. *See generally* Tussman & Tenbroeck, "The Equal Protection of the Laws," 37 Calif. L. Rev. 341 (1949).

[34] The philosophical and empirical bases for this rather bald assertion have been discussed extensively. A. Westin, Privacy and Freedom, 3–63 (1967); Fried, "Privacy," 77 Yale L.J. 475 (1968); Gross, "The Concept of Privacy," 42 N.Y.U.L. Rev. 34 (1967); Beaney, "The Griswold Case and the Expanding Right to Privacy," 1966 Wis. L. Rev. 979 (1966); Griswold, "The Right to be Let Alone," 55 Nw L. Rev. 216 (1960); Warren & Brandeis, "The Right to Privacy," 4 Harv. L. Rev. 193 (1890); Prosser, "Privacy," 48 Calif. L. Rev. 383 (1960); Bloustein, "Privacy as an Aspect of Human Dignity: An Answer to Dean Prosser," 39 N.Y.U.L. Rev. 962 (1964); Symposium, on the Griswold Case and the Right of Privacy, 64 Mich. L. Rev. 197–288 (1966); Symposium, Privacy,

cumstances which give rise to expectations of privacy are considered. People have expectations of *associational privacy* when various types of personal relationships are formed.[35] Such relationships may range from marriage to friendships to business partnerships. Expectations of confidence and trust are present in varying degrees in many such interpersonal relationships and are often enforced by law as fiduciary obligations and recognized as constitutional rights.[36]

Certain types of what can be called *situational privacy* are also accepted and protected.[37] Situations or areas regarded as private might include any place where diverse sorts of privacy can be reasonably expected such as one's home, a car, a telephone booth, or a city street, depending upon the particular activity.[38] Invasions of this kind of privacy are limited by the Fourth Amendment of the Constitution to "reasonable" invasions where there is "probable cause."

To be distinguished from a relationship with another person or a place where privacy is reasonably expected is what can be called *personal privacy*. This type of privacy would include conduct that in and of itself is regarded as related solely to the individual and his "life style." It is essentially one's right to personal autonomy.[39] As a matter of social practice where there is any intrusion into this realm of personal privacy, an explanation or justification is demanded and usually the consent of the individual is required.

The fact that the conduct is private does not necessarily mean that personal privacy is involved since almost any activity can be conducted in private. It is the *personal* aspect that is most significant here.[40] What one eats, wears, or thinks is generally considered no one

---

31 Law & Contemp. Prob. 251 (1966); Note, "Right to Privacy: Social Interest and Legal Right," 51 Minn. L. Rev. 531 (1967).

[35] Westin, *supra* note 34, at 25–28, 42–51, 350.

[36] The right of association is constitutionally recognized and protected. United Mine Workers v. Ill. Bar Ass'n 389 U.S. 217 (1967); Brotherhood of Railroad Trainmen v. Va., 377 U.S. 1 (1964); NAACP v. Button, 371 U.S. 415 (1963).

[37] Westin, *supra* note 34, at 356–64.

[38] In Katz v. U.S., 389 U.S. 347 (1967), overruling in effect Olmstead v. U.S., 277 U.S. 438 (1928) and Goldman v. U.S., 316 U.S. 129 (1942), the Court held that the fourth amendment protects *persons not places* thus freeing it of prior conceptual limitations of property law. *Compare* Silverman v. U.S., 365 U.S. 505 (1961) and Clinton v. Va., 377 U.S. 158 (1964) *with* Olmstead v. U.S., *supra*, and Goldman v. U.S., *supra*.
See also Carroll v. U.S., 267 U.S. 132 (1925) [car]; Katz v. U.S., *supra* (telephone booth); Terry v. Ohio, 399 U.S. 1 (1968) [public stop and frisk].

[39] Westin, *supra* note 34, at 33–34.

[40] Lord Devlin in The Enforcement of Morals 7 (1965) and Basil Mitchell in Law, Morality, and Religion in a Secular Society 5 (1967) confuse the personal and private elements. Euthanasia, duelling, abortion, bigamy and incest are not wholly personal acts as they by definition involve two or more persons. The

else's decision. These and other parts of one's personal life are regarded as relatively immune from outside interference. Any regulatory attempt by outsiders raises the specter of Orwellian fantasy.

Although privacy may be an important and fundamental aspect of life in any society, it is not specifically enumerated as such in the Constitution of the United States. This presents a serious problem because it is through the Constitution that our most basic personal rights are protected. Until the case of *Griswold vs. Connecticut*[41] privacy as a substantive constitutional right, immune from legal invasion, was unknown. Certain attempts had been made in the past to articulate the concept in other legal contexts, however. The right of privacy as the "right to be let alone" was eloquently sketched by Justice Brandeis in 1928 in his oft-quoted dissent in *Olmstead v. United States*,[42] a wire tapping case.

> The makers of our Constitution undertook to secure conditions favorable to the pursuit of happiness. They recognized the significance of man's spiritual nature, of his feelings and of his intellect. They knew that only a part of the pain, pleasure and satisfactions of life are to be found in material things. They sought to protect Americans in their beliefs, their thoughts, their emotions and their sensations. They conferred as against the Government, the *right to be let alone*—the most comprehensive of rights and the right most valued by civilized men.

Although while Justice Brandeis was specifically concerned in *Olmstead* with the guarantees of the Fourth Amendment against unreasonable searches and seizures (what was called situational privacy), as a general theme it rings true. A similar "right to be let alone" has been developed in the law of torts under the rubric of privacy as a basis for civil liability; this is also due to the persuasive writing of Justice Brandeis prior to his appointment to the Supreme Court.[43] In spite of the novelty of privacy as a substantive constitutional right, it is clear that as a general concept privacy is not foreign to the law.

As noted, the leading case supporting the existence of a substantive right of privacy is *Griswold vs. Connecticut*. Consequently, a thorough understanding of the *Griswold* decision is necessary before considering what use might be made of its teachings in dealing with a mari-

---

fact they can be performed in private is not really helpful unless that refers to their consensual nature.

[41] 381 U.S. 479 (1965).

[42] 277 U.S. 438, 478 (1928). See cases cited note 38 *supra* for a breakdown of areas protected by the fourth amendment.

[43] Warren & Brandeis, *supra* note 34; *see generally* W. Prosser, Torts § 112, at 829–51 (3rd ed., 1964); Prosser, *supra* note 34; Bloustein, *supra* note 34.

juana possession statute. The Court in *Griswold* overturned the Connecticut anti-birth control statute.[44] This "uncommonly silly law" as it was called by Justice Stewart,[45] was an antiquated, rarely invoked statute making it a criminal offense to use birth control devices for the purpose of preventing conception. It was no surprise that the law was held unconstitutional but the importance of the case lies in the way in which the Court arrived at this decision.

Privacy was the basis for the Court's decision and, as a substantive right, privacy was raised as a defense to any application of the Connecticut statute. As mentioned earlier, this right of privacy is not the procedural or "situational" right of privacy that protects an individual from unreasonable searches and seizures employed in enforcing *constitutionally valid* statutes.[46] The right of privacy recognized in *Griswold* must also be distinguished from that right of privacy found in the law of torts.[47] In *Griswold* the Court held that the statute infringed on the zone of privacy that a married couple possessed. Within this zone the couple was free to decide whether or not they would use contraceptive devices;[48] this was characterized above as "associational privacy" of a special kind, marital privacy.[49]

Support for this right of privacy was found by looking to the "specific guarantees in the Bill of Rights having penumbras, formed by emanations from those guarantees that help give them life and substance."[50] The court found that the right of privacy protected in *Griswold* was created by several fundamental constitutional guarantees; it based its decision on five of these guarantees contained in the Bill of Rights:

> Various guarantees create zones of privacy. The right of association contained in the penumbra of the First Amendment is one. . . . The Third Amendment in its prohibition against the quartering of soldiers "in any house" in time of peace without the consent of the owner is another facet of that privacy. The Fourth Amendment explicitly affirms the "right of the people to be secure in their persons, houses,

[44] Conn. Gen. Stat. Rev. §§ 32–33 (1958). "Any person who uses any drug, medicinal article or instrument for the purpose of preventing conception shall be fined not less than fifty dollars or imprisoned not less than sixty days nor more than one year or be both fined and imprisoned."

[45] 381 U.S. at 527 (dissenting opinion).

[46] See text accompanying notes 34–40 *supra.*

[47] See note 43 *supra.*

[48] 381 U.S. at 485.

[49] The Supreme Court has been particularly solicitious of the institution of marriage over the years. *See* Reynolds v. U.S., 98 U.S. 145 (1878); Musser v. Utah, 333 U.S. 95 (1948) [bigamy convictions upheld]; Loving v. Va., 388 U.S. 1 (1967) [miscegenation statute overturned].

[50] 381 U.S. at 484.

papers, and effects, against unreasonable searches and seizures." The Fifth Amendment in its Self-incrimination Clause enables the citizen to create a zone of privacy which government may not force him to surrender to his detriment. The Ninth Amendment provides: "The enumeration in the Constitution, of certain rights, shall not be construed to deny or disparage others retained by the people." [51]

The Court reinforced its argument that penumbral zones of privacy existed by showing that past decisions had found fundamental constitutional rights not specifically mentioned in the Constitution. Rights such as freedom of inquiry, freedom of thought, and freedom to teach were considered essential because "without those peripheral rights the specific rights would be less secure." [52]

Although the language of *Griswold* is broad, the holding itself is narrow; only marital privacy is protected. The case is significant in that six Supreme Court Justices found a right of privacy within the Constitution.[53] Of greater importance than the holding is the reasoning of the court that the peripheral rights do exist and are essential to the specific rights. Nevertheless, privacy as a substantive constitutional right is still in its embryonic stages.

It is possible that *Griswold* will be treated as an aberration limited by a plurality opinion and the special facts that are said to reduce its significance as a source of newer kinds of personal privacy.[54] But the converse would appear to be true. The case is cited for a variety of purposes and has become a judicial warrant for many innovations in constitutional law.[55] But this in itself may prove to discredit the

---

[51] *Id.*

[52] *Id.* at 482. *See* Weiman v. Updegraff, 344 U.S. 183, 195 (1952).

[53] Although six justices found privacy, they did not all find it in the same place in the Constitution. Justices Goldberg, Brennan, and Chief Justice Warren joined with Justice Douglas in finding privacy supported by fundamental personal rights found in the penumbra of the Bill of Rights. *Id.* at 486.

Justice Goldberg, Brennan and Chief Justice Warren went on to use the ninth amendment as authority for the right of privacy. *Id.* at 488.

Justice Harlan found support for privacy in the due process clause of the fourteenth amendment. "The Due Process Clause of the Fourteenth Amendment stands . . . on its own bottom." *Id.* at 500.

Justice White also relied on the fourteenth amendment as the Connecticut statute deprived married couples of liberty without due process of law. *Id.* at 502.

[54] The Griswold decision has been criticized as ill-founded and vague. See for example, the dissent of Justice Black in Griswold, 381 U.S. at 507; Kauper, "Penumbras, Peripheries, Emanations, Things Fundamental and Things Forgotten: The Griswold Case," 64 Mich. L. Rev. 235, 244, 252 (1965).

[55] *E.g.*, State v. Abellano, 50 Haw. ——, 441 P.2d 333, 335 (1968) [concurring opinion] recognizing a "right to movement" in the ninth amendment. Finot v. Pasadena City Bd. of Educ., 250 Cal. App.2d 189, 58 Cal. Rptr. 520 (1967)

Griswold decision since ready use of the decision for a multitude of purposes may dilute its persuasive value. Consequently, a tighter definition of privacy or the "peripheral right" to be protected would be in order whenever any right differing appreciably from marital or associational privacy is in issue. In approaching the concept to be considered in the context of marijuana use and possession—personal privacy—it is instructive to see how other courts have treated *Griswold* and the right to privacy.

GRISWOLD'S PROGENY

If the use and possession of marijuana is to be given constitutional protection by reference to a right of personal privacy, two approaches must be considered. One is the frank advocacy of a general right of personal privacy with respect to inherently private and personal conduct in spite of the difficulties involved in making the step from the "sacred precincts of marital bedrooms"[56] to the residence of an individual who purposefully induces a mild hallucinatory condition through the use of marijuana. Just as the individual may express himself graphically,[57] verbally,[58] and physically[59] in certain constitutionally protected ways, it can be argued that there is a zone of privacy in which one can express himself mentally or inwardly by using marijuana. This may be for spiritual purposes, as was the case in *People vs. Woody* with peyote,[60] or for the mere enjoyment of the experience, as might also be the case.

Certainly the actual use of marijuana involves no one other than the user. There is no doubt, however, that the user is affected. In the words of a leading authority on the subject: "Marijuana is taken for

---

[right to wear a beard within first amendment]; American Motorcycle Ass'n v. Davids, 11 Mich. App. 351, 158 N.W.2d 72 (1968) [dictum] *noted*, 82 Harv. L. Rev. 469 (1968) [statute requiring motorcycle helmet not within police power].

[56] 381 U.S. at 485.

[57] *E.g.*, Memoirs v. Mass. 383 U.S. 413 (1966) [obscenity defined]; Curtis Publishing Co. v. Butts, 388 U.S. 130 (1967) [libel protected under "public figure" doctrine].

[58] *E.g.*, Saia v. N.Y., 334 U.S. 558 (1948) [loudspeaker allowed]; Kunz v. N.Y., 340 U.S. 290 (1951); Cantwell v. Conn. 310 U.S. 296 (1940) [religious advocates].

[59] DeJonge v. Ore., 229 U.S. 353 (1937). *Compare* Brown v. La, 383 U.S. 131 (1966); Cox v. La, 379 U.S. 536 (1965); Edwards v. S. C., 372 U.S. 229 (1963) *with* Adderly v. Fla., 385 U.S. 39 (1966) and U.S. v. O'Brien, 391 U.S. 367 (1968). *See generally* Kalven, "The Concept of the Public Forum: Cox v. Louisiana," 1965 Sup. Ct. Rev. 1 (1965).

[60] 61 Cal.2d 716, 394 P.2d 813, 40 Cal. Rptr. 69 (1964).

euphoria, reduction of fatigue, and relief of tension. . . . Small to moderate doses also increase appetite, distort the time sense, increase self-confidence and, like alcohol, can relax some inhibitions." [61] Philosopher-theologian Alan Watts would classify the characteristic effects of marijuana as giving the user

1. a concentration in the present which disregards future considerations and anxieties,
2. heightened awareness of polarity in interdependent relationships,
3. heightened awareness of relativity between man and his total environment, and
4. an awareness of eternal energy.[62]

In short, marijuana is used for the experience and insight it provides the user, be it characterized as religious, philosophical, emotional, or self-gratifying. As an experience dealing solely with the mind, it is the most personal and private sort of experience possible. Based on this it could be argued that possession of marijuana, as a necessary incident to its use, could be brought within a zone of personal privacy using *Griswold* as authority.

Although this approach may have both logic and candor to recommend it, other ways of raising the issue of personal privacy may be preferred for reasons of strategy and constitutional theory. Except for marital privacy as laid down by *Griswold,* the courts generally have not accepted the right of privacy as an independent substantive right.[63] Not only is the concept of privacy so overwhelming and ill-defined that it may threaten to sweep many forms of human endeavor within it, but its absence from the constitution as a specific guarantee makes its acceptance a very sensitive judicial judgment. Where a court is given the choice, it would appear obvious that it will opt for an historically protected and more specifically articulated right such as freedom of expression rather than the recently enunciated right of privacy. Privacy would then be an alternative holding or a right which is tucked into one of the more specific and established rights.

In 1969, a decision of the United States Supreme Court has pro-

[61] Fort, "Social and Legal Response to Pleasure-Giving Drugs," The Utopiates 213–14 (Blum ed. 1964).

[62] Watts, "Psychedelics and Religious Experience," 56 Calif. L. Rev. 74, 76–79 (1968).

[63] *E.g.,* Davis v. Firment, 269 F. Supp. 524 (D.La. 1967) [right to wear long hair not within ninth amendment or right to privacy]; Finot v. Pasadena City Bd. of Educ., 250 Cal. App.2d 189, 58 Cal. Rptr. 520 (1967) [beard not within right to privacy but is protected by first amendment]; *But see* State v. Abellano, —— Haw. ——, 441 P.2d 333, 335 (1968) [concurring opinion].

vided a perfect illustration of this kind of judicial approach, linking together the First Amendment and personal privacy. In *Stanley vs. Georgia* the court held that mere possession of obscene matter cannot constitutionally be made a crime and reversed the conviction of Mr. Stanley, who was arrested in his own home in possession of obscene films.[64] In an opinion by Mr. Justice Thurgood Marshall the court reasoned that the right of free expression necessarily protects the right to receive information and ideas regardless of their social worth. Indeed, the line between useful ideas and mere entertainment was found to be too elusive a distinction to make. An "added dimension" was the fact that the defendant was arrested for possession of obscene film in his own home. For the proposition that there is a fundamental right against unwanted intrusions into one's privacy, the court found it appropriate to cite the famous Brandeis dissent in *Olmstead vs. United States* and *Griswold vs. Connecticut*.[65] In short, the court said the defendant "is asserting the right to read or observe what he pleases—the right to satisfy his intellectual and emotional needs in the privacy of his own home." [66] Justice Marshall further asserted that "our whole constitutional heritage rebels at the thought of giving government the power to control men's minds." [67]

What is quite obvious is that those laws restricting the possession of marijuana for personal use do control an individual's options for self-expression. New sources of knowledge and experience, even if "mere entertainment," are denied the individual who chooses not to violate the law. The state, in effect, limits a potentially vast source of information that may be revealed or elicited through the use of marijuana.

The sort of conduct referred to in *Stanley* must be distinguished from so-called mixed speech and conduct, where subsequent to the formulation of an idea, conduct is essential to communicate that idea.[68] Mere possession of the film would be conduct *antecedent* to the speech, not *subsequent* to it. In this sense, the conduct in issue in *Stanley* relates only to control over the options available for later public exposure or attention. The decision to divulge or disseminate the information exposes such an act to legal sanctions. Until such divulgence is made, the possessor of obscene photographs, like the possessor of seditious, homicidal, or defamatory thoughts, is protected. As part of the process of free expression, the rights, antecedent to

---

[64] 394 U.S. 557 (1969).
[65] Id. at 564. The Olmstead dissent is quoted in the text of this article accompanying footnote 42.
[66] 394 U.S. at 565.
[67] Id.
[68] Cases cited note 59 *supra.*

speech might fall within what Professor Emerson would call "freedom of belief" or might better be phrased as a "right of self-expression" when some conduct is necessary in gathering or facilitating the information.[69]

The specific guarantees of free speech and expression would lose much of their substance and impact if control of the *preconditions to speech and expression* were such that only harmless or proper alternatives were allowed to be considered. Any attempt to control an individual's beliefs or self-expression "invades the innermost privacy of the individual and cuts off the right of expression at its source." [70] Speaking of the function of the First Amendment Judge Learned Hand has said, "it presupposes that right conclusions are more likely to be gathered out of a multitude of tongues, than through any kind of authoritative selection." [71] This would apply with even greater strength to the methods of formulating expression as well.

Finot vs. Pasadena City Board of Education is a case that finds protected personal rights in the periphery of the First Amendment with respect to an individual's physical appearance.[72] In *Finot* the California Court of Appeal held that a high school teacher could wear a beard without losing his job using *Griswold* as authority. This right to wear a beard was brought within the periphery of the First Amendment's right of free speech as "expression" through non-verbal conduct. The court in *Finot* emphasized this point saying:

> It seems to us that the wearing of a beard is a form of expression of an individual's personality and that such a right of expression, although probably not within the literal scope of the First Amendment itself, is as much entitled to its peripheral protection as the personal rights established . . . with respect to the right of parents to educate their children as they see fit.[73]

It is not clear from the opinion on which side of the First Amendment the expression lies. If the wearing of a beard, although a "symbol" to some, is not intended to communicate anything, it too might be considered conduct antecedent to expression thereby falling within the realms of "self-expression." The court in *Finot* recognized this and chose not to inquire into the appellant's reasons for wearing a beard.[74]

---

[69] T. Emerson, Toward a General Theory of the First Amendment, 64 (1967).
[70] *Id.*
[71] U.S. v. Associated Press, 52 F. Supp. 362, 372 (1943) quoted by Justice Frankfurter concurring in the same case on appeal, 326 U.S. 1, 28 (1944).
[72] 250 Cal. App.2d 189, 58 Cal. Rptr. 520 (1967).
[73] *Id.* at 198, 58 Cal. Rptr. at 527.
[74] *Id.* at 201, 58 Cal. Rptr. at 228–29.

The reasoning of *Stanley vs. Georgia* with respect to obscenity, supplemented by the kind of argument that the California court made in *Finot* with respect to personal appearances, will undoubtedly be used as starting points for an attack on the marijuana possession statutes across the country. However, in *Stanley* there appears a rather cryptic footnote inserted possibly to forestall just such attacks.[75]

> What we have said in no way infringes upon the power of the State or Federal Government to make possession of other items, such as narcotics, firearms, or stolen goods, a crime. Our holding in the present case turns upon the Georgia statute's infringement of fundamental liberties protected by the First and Fourteenth Amendments. No First Amendment rights are involved in most statutes making mere possession criminal.

Such a statement, while mere dictum and not necessary to the case, may signal the court's attitude towards such future cases involving narcotics possession laws or may have simply been necessary to gain a majority of the justices to adhere to the majority opinion in *Stanley*. Justices White and Brennan concurred in a separate opinion written by Justice Stewart on the basis that the search warrant used to gain access to the defendant's home was faulty and on that basis alone the conviction should have been reversed.[76]

In considering the constitutional dimensions of marijuana possession, the question squarely presented is whether possession incident to private use can be brought within a First Amendment right of personal privacy or self-expression, contrary to the footnote in *Stanley* that narcotics statutes are excluded. By analyzing the nature of the drug (affecting one's consciousness),[77] the reasons for its use (clearly for personal expression),[78] and the conduct at issue (possession for private use), the scope of self-expression would appear to comprehend such conduct. Unless a person has certain freedoms to formulate his thoughts (free from coerced beliefs[79] and free to choose the educational institutions he will attend),[80] to prepare what he will say or do with complete license (unedited obscenity[81] or defamation), to inspire himself in less than conventional fashions (meditation, fasting, hair-

---

[75] 394 U.S. at 568 n 11.

[76] Id. at 569.

[77] See text accompanying notes 61–62 *supra*.

[78] *Id.*

[79] West Va. State Bd. of Educ. v. Barnette, 319 U.S. 624 (1943).

[80] Pierce v. Soc'y of Sisters, 268 U.S. 510 (1925); Meyer v. Neb., 262 U.S. 390 (1923).

[81] Stanley v. Georgia, 394 U.S. 557 (1969); in re Klor, 64 Cal. 2d 816, 415 P.2d 791, 51 Cal. Rptr. 903 (1966).

shirts, drugs),[82] to alter his surroundings to suit his needs (travel,[83] associations),[84] or to assume different modes of personal habits and physical appearances (hair; beard, clothes),[85] the guarantees of free speech and the pluralistic quality of American life would lose much of their substance and impact.

The United States Supreme Court in *Pierce vs. Society of Sisters*[86] protected a student's right to attend a private school when the state law would have compelled only public school attendance. Likewise in *Meyer vs. Nebraska*[87] the content of the curriculum at a private school was protected from arbitrary state regulation. These cases, although old are still good law and can be considered First Amendment guarantees of a person's right to self-expression, whereby he may develop and direct his thinking as he sees fit.[88] By this analysis they can be

[82] The court in People v. Woody, 61 Cal. 2d at 727–28, 394 P.2d at 821–22, 40 Cal. Rptr. at 77–78, recognized this inspirational function when it said: "In a mass society which presses at every point toward conformity, the *protection of self-expression*, however unique, of the individual and the group becomes ever more important. The varying currents of the subcultures that flow into the mainstream of our national life give it depth and beauty. We preserve a greater value than an ancient tradition when we protect the rights of the Indians who honestly practiced an old religion in using peyote one night at a meeting in a desert hogan. . . ." [emphasis added].

The Fifth circuit in denying Dr. Leary a religious exemption from the federal marijuana statute also saw this: "At most, the evidence shows that it is considered by some as being an aid to attaining *consciousness expansion* by which an individual can more easily meditate or commune with his god." Leary v. U.S., 383 U.S. 851, 860 (5th Cir. 1967). [emphasis added].

[88] International. Kent v. Dulles, 357 U.S. 116, 125–27 (1958); Aptheker v. Sec. of State, 378 U.S. 500 (1964). *Compare* Zemel v. Rusk, 380 U.S. 1 (1965) *with* U.S. v. Laub, 385 U.S. 475 (1967) [area restrictions valid under Zemel not criminally enforceable].

Domestic. Edwards v. Calif., 314 U.S. 160 (1941); Shapiro v. Thompson, 394 U.S. 615 (1969).

[84] Cases cited note 36 *supra*.

[85] These kinds of issues usually arise in the context of deprivation of governmental benefits, not as criminal statutes. While adults appear to have the right to a physical appearance, students have consistently been denied these rights during their formative years. *Compare* Finot v. Pasadena City Bd. of Educ., 250 Cal. App. 2d 189, 58 Cal. Rptr. 520 (1967) *with* Akin v. Bd. of Educ. 262 Cal. App. 2d ——, 68 Cal. Rptr. 557 (1968) [student denied right to wear beard while teacher was not]. *See also* Ferrell v. Dallas Independent School Dist., 392 F.2d 697 (1968) *cert. den.* 37 U.S.L.W. 3135 (U.S. Oct. 15, 1968) [Douglas, J. dissenting]; David v. Firment, 269 F. Supp. 524 (D. La. 1967); Leonard v. School Comm. of Attleboro, 349 Mass. 704, 212 N.E.2d 468, 14 A.L.R.3d 1192 (1965). Students' *political rights* are protected however. Tinker v. DesMoines Independent Community School Dist., 393 U.S. ——, 37 U.S.L.W. 4121 (Feb. 24, 1969).

[86] 268 U.S. 510 (1925).

[87] 262 U.S. 390 (1923); *see also* Bartels v. Utah, 262 U.S. 404 (1923).

[88] In Tinker v. DesMoines Independent School Dist., 393 U.S. ——, 37 U.S.L.W.

considered privacy cases in both the associational and personal sense. In *Griswold*, Justice Douglas referred to these cases among others as maintaining that "the State may not, consistently with the spirit of the First Amendment, *contract the spectrum of available knowledge*." [89]

In the same sense that freedom of association enhances "effective advocacy of both public and private points of view," [90] the judicially recognized right to travel within and without the United States might be considered a guarantee antecedent and essential to freedom of expression.[91] Although travel could be said to be a general liberty as was the case in *Kent vs. Dulles*,[92] mobility and personal encounters are crucial to the acquisition and dissemination of ideas. The federal Riot Control Act of 1968, making criminal interstate travel to incite riots, clearly recognized this.[93] In *Kent* the Supreme Court said that "travel may be as close to the heart of the individual as the choice of what he *eats, or wears or reads*." [94]

One difficulty with the extension of the First Amendment's protection into the area of purely personal conduct as in the case of drug use is that such a principle might comprehend too much to be judicially acceptable. Almost any personal conduct could be subsumed into a broad concept based upon the freedom of expression. The result is a general right of personal privacy. Yet as a matter of policy and preference, the courts have a tendency to resolve all doubts in favor of First Amendment protection. The United States Supreme Court has displayed this propensity with respect to the First Amendment while limiting the use of the due process clause of the Fifth and Fourteenth Amendments as sources of personal liberties.[95] The use of the First Amendment would therefore be impelled by expediency as well as principle.

Any extension of the First Amendment would obviously be limited

---

4121, 4122 (Feb. 24, 1969) the Court cited *Meyer* and *Pierce* as first amendment cases.

[89] 381 U.S. at 482 [emphasis added].

[90] NAACP v. Ala., 357 U.S. 449, 460 (1958).

[91] On the right to travel see cases cited note 81 *supra*.

[92] 357 U.S. 116, 125 (1958).

[93] 18 U.S.C. §§ 2101–02 (1968 Supp.).

[94] 357 U.S. at 126.

[95] A number of rights not squarely within the letter of the first amendment's protection of speech, press and assembly have nevertheless been recognized. Right of association, cases cited note 36 *supra*; right of inquiry and thought, Wieman v. Updegraff, 344 U.S. 183, 195 (1952) [Frankfurter, J., concurring]; right to distribute, read and receive literature or information, Martin v. Struthers, 319 U.S. 141 (1943). *See generally* M. Shapiro, Freedom of Speech, The Supreme Court and Judicial Review 34–39, 111–115 (1966).

by the reasons for the liberalization: (1) that the conduct to be protected is purely personal and (2) involves an activity related to expression. By definition possession of marijuana for one's own use is personal; while the fact that marijuana is an euphoric drug which clearly affects one's consciousness gives it a claim of self-expression derived from the nature of the drug and the reasons for its use.[96]

Whether or not the constitutional arguments with respect to the use and possession of marijuana are accepted, the privacy value remains one that a legislature should consider in formulating the drug laws. Not only are values of personal privacy infringed upon but the attendant supplementary statutes prohibiting the presence of a person in a place where marijuana is used[97] limits one's freedom of movement and restricts one's associational privacy broadly construed. At least one state has held this kind of statute unconstitutional.[98] Furthermore, the technique of police detection required to enforce this kind of consensual law with no "victim" or complainant strains the protections of the fourth amendment's guarantees of situational privacy. Dogs trained to detect the odor of drugs, undercover agents, "no knock" search warrants, and official "encouragement" to commit the crimes are examples of such techniques.[99]

The ensuing discussion will continue the constitutional approach to the problem and will deal with the balancing of personal privacy against the governmental interests.

The Balancing Approach

If a court were to find that possession of marijuana for personal use fell within one of the constitutional rights raised above, the marijuana possession statute would not be invalidated automatically. Under the prevailing view, where some sort of conduct is involved, the state's interest would be balanced against the constitutional right. Consequently, it is important to examine the general approach of the courts to constitutional questions in which personal liberties are limited by

---

[96] See text accompanying notes 61–62 *supra.*

[97] *E.g.,* Cal. Health & Safety Code § 11556 provides: "It is unlawful to visit or to be in any room or place where any narcotics are being unlawfully smoked or used with knowledge that such activity is occurring."

[98] State v. Abellano, 50 Haw. ——, 441 P.2d 333, 335 (1968) ruled unconstitutional on the basis of vagueness and privacy a statute making it criminal to be present at a cockfight.

[99] On the use of police dogs see "Purple Geese and Other Fighting Fauna," Time 41 (Oct. 14, 1968). On the use of police techniques see cases and materials cited note 5 *supra.*

state or federal law either criminally or as conditions to the receipt of any governmental benefit.

In general the current tests for deciding the constitutionality of criminal statutes conflicting with conduct falling within protected personal liberties, particularly those activities protected by the first amendment, can be condensed into three steps:

1. the restraints on personal liberties must rationally relate to a legitimate object of the police power (the minimum rationality test),
2. the state must demonstrate that such restraints outweigh the resulting impairment of constitutional rights (the balancing test),
3. no alternatives less subversive of constitutional rights are available (the least restrictive alternative test).

Such an analysis is essentially a combination of tests presently used by the United States Supreme Court in dealing with first amendment cases and is useful for that reason.[100] An enumerated approach has been expressly applied by the California Supreme Court in dealing with deprivations of governmental benefits where political rights, personal rights and rights of welfare clients were asserted.[101] The balancing test was also applied in a criminal case involving drugs in California. *People vs. Woody*[102] is an excellent example of the court's refusal to decide that a mere rational nexus between the statute and the state's avowed purpose is sufficient to uphold the statute. Instead the court applied the technique of balancing the infringement on the personal liberty against the interest of the state in regulating the individual's conduct with the state carrying the burden.

The defendant, an American Indian, was convicted for possession of peyote,[103] but contended that the law conflicted with his use of it

---

[100] *E.g.*, McLaughlin v. Fla., 379 U.S. 184, 196 (1964); Sherbert v. Verner, 374 U.S. 398, 406 (1963); Gibson v. Fla. Legislative Investigative Comm'n., 372 U.S. 539, 546 (1963); NAACP v. Button, 371 U.S. 415, 438–39 (1963); Bates v. City of Little Rock, 361 U.S. 516, 524 (1960).

[101] Bagley v. Washington Township, 65 Cal.2d 499, 501–02, 421 F.2d 409, 411, 55 Cal. Rptr. 401, 402 (1966) [political rights]; Rosenfield v. Malcolm, 65 Cal.2d 559, 561, 421 P.2d 697, 698, 55 Cal. Rptr. 505, 506 (1967) [political rights]; Finot v. Pasadena City Bd. of Educ., 250 Cal. App.2d 189, 58 Cal. Rptr. 520 (1967) [personal rights]; Parrish v. Civil Service Comm., 66 Cal.2d ——, 425 P.2d 223, 57 Cal. Rptr. 623 (1967); *noted* 18 Hastings L. J. 228 (1967) [privacy].

[102] 61 Cal.2d 716, 394 P.2d 813, 40 Cal. Rptr. 69 (1964).

[103] According to the court in Woody, peyote grows in small buds on the top of a small spineless cactus, *Lophorphora williams ii*, in Texas and northern Mexico. When taken internally, it causes vivid hallucinations and beyond this its users experience greater comprehension and even a sense of friendliness towards others. 61 Cal.2d at 720, 394 P.2d at 816, 40 Cal. Rptr. at 72. Cal. Health and Safety

as a form of religious expression as a member of the Native American
Church. The court, considering the record independently, examined
the conflicting interests of the state and the individual and reversed
the conviction.

> We have weighed the competing values represented in this case on
> the symbolic scale of constitutionality. On the one side we have placed
> the weight of freedom of religion as protected by the First Amend-
> ment; on the other, the weight of the state's "compelling interest."
> Since the use of peyote incorporates the essence of the religious expres-
> sion, the first weight is heavy. Yet the use of peyote presents only
> slight danger to the state and to the enforcement of its laws; the second
> weight is relatively light. The scale tips in favor of the constitutional
> protection.[104]

This is the prevailing test being used by the United States Supreme
Court as well. In *Griswold* the court rejected the minimum rationality
standard and reviewed the judgment of the state legislature.[105] Justice
Goldberg gave the reason for this in his concurrence:

> In a long series of cases this Court has held that where fundamental
> personal liberties are involved, they may not be abridged by the States
> simply on a showing that a regulatory statute has some rational re-
> lationship to the effectuation of a proper state purpose. "Where there
> is a significant encroachment upon personal liberty, the State may pre-
> vail only upon showing a subordinating interest which is compel-
> ling." [106]

In *Griswold* the alleged purpose of the Connecticut legislature was
to discourage extramarital relations; and the statute rationally pro-
moted this purpose. In spite of this the state did not carry the burden
of demonstrating that the purpose of the statute was compelling
enough to warrant the infringement of the right of privacy.

Even where a compelling interest might be shown by the state, a

---

Code § 11500 makes possession of any narcotic other than marijuana a felony.
For the planting provisions, see Cal. Health & Safety Code § 11540.

[104] 61 Cal.2d at 727, 394 P.2d at 821, 40 Cal. Rptr. at 77.

[105] 381 U.S. at 482. In cases where economic interests are involved, the Supreme
Court has invoked the minimum rationality standard holding that as long as
the state law in question is rationally related to some permissible purpose within
the police power of the state, the exercise of power is constitutional. *E.g.*, William-
son v. Lee Optical, 348 U.S. 483, 487–88 (1955); Ferguson v. Skrupa, 372 U.S.
726 (1963).

[106] 381 U.S. at 497, *quoting from* Bates v. Little Rock, 361 U.S. 516, 524
(1960).

further test must be satisfied: that there must be no alternative less restrictive of constitutional rights available. It would seem that the presence of alernatives less subversive of individual liberty is really part of the compelling interest argument. The state cannot have a "compelling interest" strong enough to outweigh the infringement of an individual's personal liberties if there are other alternatives less subversive of constitutional rights available. The broad sweep of the Connecticut statute was a major point in *Griswold* and Justice Douglas recognized it saying "a governmental purpose to control or prevent activities constitutionally subject to state regulation may not be achieved by means which sweep unnecessarily broadly and thereby invade the area of protected freedoms." [107]

The Connecticut legislature sought to attain its avowed purpose through means that had a "maximum destructive impact" on the rights of an individual. In such a situation narrower means are appropriate to achieve the same ends. [108]

As a matter of judicial review, when constitutional questions have been presented involving personal liberties, the courts have relied on their own evaluations of scientific facts and expert testimony by independently reviewing the whole record in order to weigh the interests. A constitutional question involving the "compelling interest" of a state is a mixed question of law and fact that necessitates such a review. The question before the court, therefore, is subject to a constitutional judgment in which the lower court's findings are not binding upon the appellate court. [109] One example of this with respect to drugs is *People vs. Woody* where the court examined the whole record and drew its own conclusions from the facts and testimony in holding that peyote could not work a permanent deleterious injury on the user. [110]

[107] 381 U.S. at 485, *quoting from* NAACP v. Ala., 377 U.S. 288, 307 (1964).

[108] 381 U.S. at 485. *See also* NAACP v. Button, 371 U.S. 415, 433 (1963); Shelton v. Tucker, 364 U.S. 479, 488 (1960); Talley v. California, 362 U.S. 60, 63 (1960).

[109] Oteri & Norris, "The Use of Expert and Documentary Evidence in a Constitutional Attack on a State Criminal Statute: The Marijuana Test Case," 56 Calif. L. Rev. 29 (1968). For discussion see Sherbert v. Verner, 374 U.S. 398, 406 (1963); Cox v. La., 379 U.S. 536 (1965). *cf.* Jackson v. Denno, 378 U.S. 368, 408 (1964) [voluntariness of confession re-examined]. See Karst, Legislative Facts in Constitutional Litigation, 1960 Sup. Ct. Rev. 75.

[110] 61 Cal.2d at 722, 394 P.2d at 818, 40 Cal. Rptr. at 74. The court, *id.* at 720, 394 P.2d at 816, 40 Cal. Rptr. at 72, also said: "An examination of the record as to the nature of peyote and its role in the religion practiced by defendants . . . compels the conclusion that the statutory prohibition most seriously infringes upon the observance of the religion." But see 39 Ops. Cal. Att'y Gen. 276 (1962).

In U.S. v. Kuch, 288 F. Supp. 439, 448-9 (D.D.C. 1968) the court reached the

Were the marijuana possession statute to be attacked as depriving
an individual of his right of privacy, it would appear that the reviewing court would take into consideration the entire record for independent judgment on the constitutional question. The court would
then apply the compelling interest, least restrictive alternative test.

The Governmental Interest

As this discussion has indicated, if a court found that possession of
marijuana came within the right of privacy or another constitutional
right, there would be no assurance that the statute would be declared
unconstitutional. If, under the balancing test, the state can successfully show a "compelling interest" why the personal right should be
abridged by methods which are not unnecessarily broad, the statute
will stand. For this reason it is important to examine the facts and
information available that might be introduced into the record as
evidence concerning marijuana and its effects on the user and society.
By the presence of such evidence in the record, an appellate court
could independently consider such facts in making its decision.

It is not within the scope of this article or the competence of the
author to delve into the scientifically complex factual bases of the
arguments for and against marijuana. This is the active concern of
those qualified in the relevant fields. In considering these governmental interests, methodical analysis is a prerequisite, since past
research has appeared to be selective at best, seemingly mixed with
many myths, misconceptions, and plain deception of rationale.[111] This

---

opposite result questioning the *Woody* decision. For a detailed view of the governmental interest see Finer, *supra* note 28, at 713–757.

[111] Dr. Joel Fort is one of the most outspoken critics of the deception which
has taken place. Dr. Fort has served on the medical staff of the U.S. Public
Health Service Hospital in Lexington, Ky., and with the U.N. Division of Narcotic
Drugs. He has been the director of both the Center for Treatment and Education
on Alcoholism in Oakland, Calif. and the Health Department Center for Special
Problems in San Francisco, California, and was a consultant on Drug Abuse for
the World Health Organization. See Fort, "Social Problems of Drug Use and
Drug Policies," 56 Calif. L. Rev. 17 (1968); Fort, *supra* note 61; and Fort,
"AMA lies about pot," 7 Ramparts Mag. 12 (Aug. 12, 1968). See also Finer,
supra note 28 at 755–56.
The most recent study is Weil, "Clinical and Physiological Effects of Marijuana
in Man," 162 Science 1234 (Dec. 13, 1968). Bibliographies can be found in
Israelsam, "Selected Bibliography on Marijuana and LSD-type Drugs," 56 Calif.
L. Rev. 160 (1968) and in U.S. v. Kuch, 288 F. Supp. 439, 452 (D.D.C. 1968)
[judicial notice taken]. See Mandel, "Problems with Official Drug Statistics," 21
Stan. L. Rev. 991 (1969).

scarcity of authoritative evidence is particularly evident when the information concerning marijuana is compared with what is known about other substances such as alcohol, tobacco, and the hard narcotics.

The legislator, judge, lawyer or interested observer should ask what considerations are within the scope of the police power—that is what are the *proper* governmental interests? What facts, studies or arguments support or detract from the claim? Finally, what weight does the conclusion carry alone and together with other governmental interests with respect to the constitutional rights asserted or, for that matter, the costs involved in the legislative determination?

From the most frequently advanced and widely publicized arguments marshalled against the use of marijuana and therefore its possession three categories can be constructed:

1. that use of marijuana leads to criminal acts (violent crimes, sex crimes, bizarre acts),
2. that use of marijuana is a steppingstone to addiction to other narcotics (marijuana is not physically addictive),
3. marijuana use is harmful to the user (suicides, psychosis, physical and psychological deterioration, alienation).

There also appears to be another group of reasons which does not get much articulation and constitutes a fourth category. That is, society just will not tolerate this sort of conduct and its societal effects ("hippieism," passive or contemplative life styles, social dependence). Such reasons are difficult to refute since they do not necessarily rest on factual grounds for their support.

The following discussion will consider these categories only generally, indicating which issues represent real governmental interests and why.

CRIMINAL ACTIVITY

The answer to the question whether use of marijuana gives rise to criminal acts may be divided into three parts. The first is that governmental interest is really aimed at crimes not caused by drug use. Drug oriented or "secondary crimes" such as possession with intent to sell,[112] failure to pay taxes on marijuana,[113] being present in a place where marijuana is used,[114] and being under the influence of mari-

---

[112] *E.g.*, Cal. Health & Safety Code § 11530.5.
[113] *E.g.*, 26 U.S.C. §§ 4741–4744 (1964).
[114] *E.g.*, Cal. Health & Safety Code § 11556.

juana[115] are criminal acts only because the drug itself is part of the crime. As one act is made criminal, an entire process becomes criminal; and it is in that sense only that criminal activity is increased.[116] It should be noted here that since marijuana is not physically addictive, the user will not be under a physical compulsion to steal and commit other crimes to support a habit.

Secondly, the statistics that the majority of marijuana users are first offenders, and that marijuana therefore introduces them to a life of crime that brings them into contact with other criminals, are self-contradictory.[117] Such statistics simply indicate that the use of marijuana may lead to being arrested for the offense of possession of marijuana or related offenses; but for those statutes there is no further criminal activity.

The third and real governmental interest is whether or not the use marijuana releases certain antisocial tendencies that result in crimes against the property or person of another. This is the classic image of the depraved "dopefiend," given wide coverage in the early literature on the subject. Although Dr. A. Lindesmith supposedly exposed this argument to be a myth in 1940,[118] it is a valid governmental interest which should be closely considered. Yet the same argument the United States Supreme Court made in *Stanley vs. Georgia* concerning the tenous link between obscenity and crime can be made about any deviant social behavior or crimes of violence which might be found to stem from exposure to marijuana. Such concerns are not matters of the state's interest until they are manifested in the actual crime. "Among free men, the deterrents ordinarily to be applied to prevent crime are education and punishment for violations of the law. . . ."[119]

ADDICTION

The government's prevention of marijuana use as a steppingstone to addictive narcotics would be a valid interest if we assume (1) that such use does *in fact* lead to addiction, and (2) that the state has an interest in keeping an individual from "socially" destroying himself in utilitarian terms. This sort of governmental interest is based upon a paternalistic "best interest" theory which claims that the addict like the person who would commit suicide is not competent to make this kind of decision. Indeed, Blackstone complained that juries in

[115] *E.g.*, Cal. Health & Safety Code § 11721.
[116] E. Schur, Crimes without Victims, 174 (1965); Becker, *supra* note 3, at 1–18.
[117] See statistics cited note 4 *supra*.
[118] Lindesmith, " 'Dope Fiend' Mythology," 31 J. Crim. L. & Crim. 199 (1940).
[119] 394 U.S. 557, 566–67 (1969).

England used to hold those who committed suicide not guilty of this heinous crime by reason of their insanity, since no sane man would take his life.[120] This avoided the severe penalties of cutting off the hand that committed the act, driving a stake through the body, forfeiture of the deceased's estate and damage to the family name. Although these penalties no longer exist, the question is a jurisprudential one whether the "best interest" theory should persist and to what degree.

Contrary to J. S. Mill's argument that this is a personal choice and no business of the state, H. L. A. Hart would argue with respect to drugs that there is a "general decline in the belief that individuals know their own interests best." [121] This view has been roundly criticized with the counterargument that the state becomes entirely involved at this point with a person's life and intimate personal choices without any justifying social interest other than saving a person from himself (whatever that means).[122] There would seem to be no stopping place other than total legislative discretion under this kind of "best interest" reasoning. This same kind of objection also becomes relevant when the question of marijuana's effect on the user arises.

A valid governmental interest could exist in the case of addiction where the addict and his dependents become economically dependent on the state. This, however, is a highly contingent governmental interest that depends on the wealth and family of the addict. It might be asked whether a rich bachelor should be held legally accountable for crimes relating to his addiction in the same way as a poor man with a large family.[123]

The statistics correlating the use of marijuana with addiction to other drugs raise a threshold problem. More basic reasons may exist for addiction, such as psychological or environmental factors.[124] Assuming addiction is a valid state interest, this question of *causation in fact* is a relevant consideration.

HARM TO THE USER AND THE PUBLIC DECENCY

The most significant area of controversy is raised by the questions how much and what kind of harm to the user justifies a governmental interest in preventing him from using the drug? As discussed above,

[120] 4 Blackstone, Commentaries 189 (Cooley 4th ed. 1899).
[121] H. L. A. Hart, Law, Liberty & Morality 32–33 (1963).
[122] Finer, *supra* note 28 at 722.
[123] *Cf.* American Motorcycle Ass'n v. Davids, 11 Mich. App. 351, 158 N.W.2d 72 (1968) *noted in* 82 Harv. L. Rev. 469 (1968) [statute requiring motorcyclists to wear helmets not within legitimate goal of police power].
[124] Clausen, "Social and Psychological Factors in Narcotics Addiction," 22 Law & Contemp. Probl. 34, 43 (1957).

with respect to addiction a basic consideration is whether personal harm is a valid governmental interest at all. The objection to the best interest theory becomes all the more acute when, unlike suicide which obviates future personal choice, the harm to the user is not a conclusive fact but speculative or a mere risk at best. Furthermore, to balance a right of personal privacy with a governmental interest in protecting a person from his own actions gives rise to a paradoxical situation. Does the Constitution create a personal right, only to have that right limited by a *conciding* governmental interest? It would seem that more should be required of the state in logic and fairness to override a primary constitutional right or even general values of privacy and personal autonomy.

Where only the drug user is directly affected, certain values are involved in deciding whether or not there is any "harm" to society. This is the point where morals and empirical evidence become confused and where the debate over regulation of marijuana will probably focus unless some inherently destructive agent or characteristic of the drug is discovered that significantly involves others, such as chromosome damage.[125] The basic question is what interest does society have in preventing marijuana use if new life styles are adopted because of use of the drug that "shock" the public's moral conscience (and perhaps lower the Gross National Product)? If a quietistic or contemplative state is encouraged or attained in which the person no longer reveres commonly held values of work and success, is this a basis for limiting the use of such a drug? What objections could be raised to the use of a substance which might provide the user with different and perhaps socially unacceptable insights or perspectives? Assuming that there is no permanent physical effect,[126] we are no longer concerned with the person's "best interest" but a purely societal interest in maintaining certain moral, economic and social values.

This question has been abstractly fought out in the controversy between Lord Patrick Devlin and H. L. A. Hart, leading English jurists.[127] Hart maintains that morality, as such, cannot be given force of law in a society that accepts individual liberty as a value. To limit personal choice to use marijuana privately on the grounds that the mere belief that its use is wrong, therefore harmful, is inconsistent with individual liberty and effectively reduces this liberty to do "those

[125] See Weil, *supra* note 110.

[126] Finer, *supra* note 28, at 728; J. S. Mill, On Liberty 125–26 (World's Classics ed. 1966); Laughlin, *supra* note 1, at 39–40.

[127] *See generally* P. Devlin, The Enforcement of Morals (1965); H.L.A. Hart, *supra* note 19; Dworkin, Lord Devlin and the Enforcement of Morals, 75 Yale L.J. 986 (1966); and B. Mitchell, *supra* note 40.

things to which no one else seriously objects."[128] Clearly a deadly veto power would be given majoritarian beliefs or revulsions over minority conduct and nonconformity which only indirectly affect the society. It would not then be surprising to find this supposed governmental interest dressed up in scientific claims that drugs cause "psychotic" reactions or other medically acceptable labels for nonconforming conduct and beliefs.[129] This shifts the burden back onto the individual raising the "harm to the user" issue once again. The few cases dealing with this aspect have too readily accepted such medical characterizations of the drug experience without qualification.[130]

Given that the courts and the legislatures are not particularly attuned to this jurisprudential issue of "harm" to the user and society, there is a pressing need for more research and thought in this area by legal philosophers, particularly Americans knowledgeable in our constitutional values, and by psychologists, psychiatrists, and sociologists in conjunction with the law.

Conclusion

The laws against possession of marijuana and its use do not significantly control the proscribed conduct. The difficulty of detecting offenders, widespread skepticism of any rational basis for the law,

---

[128] Hart, *supra* note 119, at 47. Apparently the police power can control conduct in public which "shocks" the public decency. Nudity, drinking in public and other activities are so controlled. This would raise again the veto by majority recoil based not on indirectly finding out about the conduct, but a direct "shock." It would appear to be a distinction in degree only and subject to the same objections.

[129] *See generally* T. Szasz, *supra* note 3; Finer, *supra* note 28 at 723–24.
Sociologist Howard Becker suggests in a timely article that psychotic reaction may very well spring from the lack of an available person or group who will define to the user what he perceives or experiences thus alleviating panic and anxiety. In this light with sufficient psychological preparation and confidence he feels that psychotic reactions with all hallucinogenic drugs may be minimized. Becker, "History, Culture, and Subjective Experience: An Exploration of the Social Bases of Drug-Induced Experiences," 8 J. of Health and Soc'l Behavior, 163 (1967).

[130] Leary v. U.S., 383 F.2d 851, 862 (5th Cir. 1967) *quoting from* State v. Bullard, 267 N.C. 599, 605, 148 S.E.2d 565, 569 (1966): "It is not a violation of his constitutional rights to forbid him, in the guise of his religion, to possess a drug which will produce *hallucinatory symptoms similar to those produced in cases of schizophrenia, dementia praecox or paranoia.* . . . [emphasis added]
U.S. v. Kuch, 288 F.Supp. at 446: "The drug marijuana may often . . . precipitate psychotic episodes. Among other reactions, hallucinations and delusions, impairment of judgment and memory, and confusion and delirium are common." *See also* Kuch, *id.* at 449.

combined with the absence of a complainant because of the personal nature of the crime, make the laws quite difficult to enforce. In this light the concept of personal privacy deserves closer judicial and legislative scrutiny as a substantive constitutional guarantee and as a societal value. Personal privacy may be considered as standing alone in the Constitution of the United States or, more likely tucked into the first amendment. Whether or not privacy as a constitutional value is accepted, it remains a value to be weighed in any thorough consideration of the wisdom of the laws making use and possession of marijuana criminal. While lawyers, judges and legislators may speculate on the medical and sociological effects of marijuana and base such speculations on inconclusive information at best, severe penalties for its use and possession remain. It would seem that such speculations, combined with ignorance and fear of marijuana and its effects, is a rather tenuous base for making possession a crime at all, much less a felony. Hopefully with more authoritative information and a proper analysis of all the costs involved in maintaining such a law on the books, the decision whether to maintain the legal proscription of marijuana use and possession will become more precise and rational.

An Approach to Marijuana Legislation

William H. McGlothlin, Ph.D.

I propose to devote the bulk of this discussion to practical considerations in the control of drugs. However, it is probably useful to begin by taking a position with regard to the more abstract issue: whether or not the prohibition of behavior whose direct effects are limited to the individual should be a function of the state. Those who feel it should not be argue with respect to drug use: the individual has the absolute right to ingest whatever substances he wishes; the state has no more right to intervene with respect to the use of harmful drugs than it does with regard to harmful overeating. Those who take the contrary position argue: the harmful effects of drug use are not limited to the individual; it burdens society in a variety of ways such as drug-related crime, driving hazards, increased welfare costs to support the user and his children, and so on. Since society is thus adversely affected by drug use, opponents argue that the state is entitled to prohibit such drug use in the public interest.

The Role of the State

It is certainly clear that the very existence of government entails individual restraints. Certain individual freedoms are sacrificed in the interest of the over-all welfare of society, and in order to allow the practice of other freedoms. It is the function of the state to initiate whatever policies and laws are necessary to insure the survival and health of the society. It is conceivable to me in principle that the use of a drug could pose a sufficient threat to society such that the state would be justified in prohibiting its use. In other words, I would not arbitrarily exclude coercion against the individual user on the grounds that freedom of control over what one takes into one's body is sacrosanct or inviolable, even in a democracy such as ours, where individual freedom is prized by custom and protected by law.

I would therefore begin with the premise that the state has a broad

"An Approach to Marijuana Legislation" was presented at the Marijuana Symposium, at the University of California Medical Center, in San Francisco, on March 23–24, 1968, and was published in the Journal of Psychedelic Drugs 2, no. 1 (Fall 1968): 149–56. Copyright © 1968 by David E. Smith, M.D. Reprinted with minor changes by permission of the publisher and the author.

prerogative to evolve social policy in the over-all public interest; and that limitation of the state's authority is better based on rational assessment of consequences than on resort to some "higher authority." It follows then, that just as individual freedom is said to carry with it the notion of individual responsibility, the authority to restrain individual freedom should carry the responsibility that policy be based on objective consideration of society's over-all welfare.

Assessing the Threat Posed by Drug Use

A logical place to start this discussion is with an objective assessment of the threat or benefit to society resulting from the non-medical use of various drugs. The present controversy over marijuana illustrates the gross discrepancies between facts and beliefs that can develop regarding the basic effects of a drug. This is especially true when society refuses to recognize the actual basis of the threat, and rationalizes its fears by unwarranted association of drug use with antisocial behavior in other areas.

Some of the factors that should be considered in determining the social impact of the use of a particular drug are physiological effects resulting from acute or chronic use; the tendency to produce physiological or psychological dependence—and over what period of use; the release of antisocial behavior; the effects on motor activity, especially automobile driving; and the tendency to produce long-lasting undesirable personality changes. Other factors are drug cost; ability to measure and control the drug's potency; convenience of mode of intake (oral or intravenous); ability for self-titration to control effect; protection against overdose; availability of antidote; specific effects attainable without unpredictable side effects; predictable duration of drug action; hangover or other short-term properties that may affect work or other activities; ability to return to normalcy on demand; and ability to detect the presence of drug (for monitoring drivers or for other purposes).

Especially for recreational drugs such as marijuana and alcohol one of the most neglected questions is the individual benefits that motivate the user to take the drug. Some of the possible positive features that should be considered are aid to pleasure, relaxation, and aesthetic appreciation; enhancement of appetite and other senses; enhancement of interpersonal rapport, warmth, love, emotionality; variety of experience, newness of perception and thinking; and enhancing the enjoyment of vacations, weekends, or other periods devoted to recreation, rest, and pleasure.

Other effects of non-medical drug use may have more far-reaching ramifications for society in general. Does the drug use provide an emotional escape-valve similar to institutionalized festivities employed by other cultures? What is its effect on personality, life style, aggressiveness, competitiveness? Does it affect military effectiveness through increased passivity? Would its adoption by large numbers affect the direction of society, e.g., would the use of peyote change the direction of the Indians by creating a pan-Indian movement (the hippies would advocate a similar cure for the ills of our present society).

Are Drug Laws an Effective Deterrent?

In considering the legal sanctions against the use of a drug, three related questions need to be considered at the outset.

1. How many persons would abuse the drug if legal controls were removed or not adopted?
2. Do the laws deter use, or perhaps encourage it, as has been suggested with relation to rebellious youth?
3. Is the drug abuser a sick person who, if one drug is prohibited, will find another drug, or some equally destructive behavior as a substitute?

More specifically, each of these questions needs to be examined in the context of criminal sanctions against both the user and the distributor, as opposed to sanctions against sale only.

Clearly, if the law is protecting against a nonexisting harm, society is better off without the law. The number of persons who would use currently illegal drugs if the legal penalties were removed cannot be estimated with any reasonable degree of accuracy. The recent elimination of all laws pertaining to written pornography in Denmark, for example, apparently resulted in no ill effects. On the other hand, the strikingly higher incidence of opiate addiction among physicians over that for the general population would seem to argue that removal of the controls on opiates would result in increased use; although the higher addiction rate among physicians actually may be due to their familiarity with, and acceptance of, drugs as well as the drugs' availability.

The incidence of marijuana use as opposed to LSD use supports the position that legal penalities are by no means the overriding determiner of drug use. Most marijuana offenses are felonies; LSD use is typically a misdemeanor (depending on the state). Yet the number of persons using marijuana is several times that for LSD. While marijuana use is rapidly increasing in spite of the laws, LSD use is declining, apparently because of concern over the dangers rather than because of legal penalties.

It is interesting to speculate whether marijuana use would have spread to the middle class during 1937–1960 if the laws against marijuana had not been enacted. Since the current upsurge in marijuana use is obviously due to factors other than a change in the laws, the earlier lack of use may have been due to the absence of these factors rather than any deterrent effect of the law.

The argument that the drug abuser would simply find another means of escape or self-destructive behavior if the drug were not available is, I think, only partly correct. It does not appear, for instance, that all excessive marijuana users would have become alcoholics had their drug of preference been unavailable. It is also clear that persons are more vulnerable to the abuse of drugs at certain times in their lives, such as adolescence or highly stressful periods; and if a potential drug of abuse is unavailable at these times, an undesirable chain of events may well be avoided. Finally, since alcoholism ran result from sociogenic as well as psychogenic causes, marijuana abuse can undoubtedly follow a similar pattern.

The many factors involved, and the increasingly rapid change in cultural values, make it impossible to estimate confidently the social impact of legalizing marijuana. Probably a large number of persons who had not previously used marijuana would try it if it were legalized —if only because of curiosity generated by the recent widespread publicity. Rosenthal has suggested that persons who use marijuana to excess do so in spite of the law, and those who would use it only under legal conditions would most likely practice moderation. My own guess is that if sale as well as use were made legal, both the use and abuse would show a marked increase. It is perhaps true that some of the present day faddish use among youth would diminish, but this would probably occur anyway, since the popularity of fads and rebellions are typically short-lived.

Sanctions Against Distribution Only

There is a general consensus that the government has not only the right, but the obligation, to enforce certain practices with respect to drugs in general. These include testing, quality control, prescription system, advertising, and labeling. There is also general agreement that the government should control, or prohibit if necessary, the manufacture, importation and distribution of non-medical drugs when the net consequences of such drugs are considered harmful to society. Disagreement exists at the point where the advantages of restricting availability are outweighed by the harm resulting from the illicit supplying of the demand for the drug, such as occurred during the prohibition of alcohol. Regulation, as opposed to prohibition, permits the orderly control of potency, and the conditions under which the drug may be sold. It also permits taxation and eliminates the support of organized crime, as well as the criminogenic aspects of forcing the user to deal with illegal sources. On the other hand, prohibition of sale clearly indicates social disapproval, whereas open sale does not.

Sanctions Against Both the User and the Seller

One line of argument, repeatedly advanced by enforcement agencies, is that laws against possession are needed to obtain convictions against sale. They argue it is difficult to draw the line between possession for personal use and possession with intent to sell; the apprehension of the seller is made easier by using simple possession charges to secure the cooperation of the user against the seller; and, in the case of heroin, the user and the seller are frequently one and the same at the retail level. The Federal Bureau of Drug Abuse Control has operated for the past three years under the Dangerous Drug Law, which prohibits sale but not possession for personal use. This could provide an excellent opportunity to examine the validity of the argument that laws against the user are needed to prosecute the seller. However, if recent Administration proposals are enacted, federal penalties will also be imposed on the user of LSD and other dangerous drugs.

Although I assume that the imposition of criminal sanctions at the user level did not fall outside the state's over-all jurisdiction on absolute grounds, there are nevertheless some very compelling arguments against such a policy. The enforcement of such laws inevitably encourages the violation of constitutional guarantees of privacy, as well as various other practices, such as informers' posing as students, hippies, or other potential drug users. The higher courts generally rule in favor of the defendant in cases where constitutional rights are violated, even when the action of the individual concerned constitutes a very real threat to society (for instance, leaders of organized crime). Yet enforcement officers run roughshod over the rights of individuals suspected of using drugs, by means of rousting on the street and illegal search and seizure of automobiles or private homes. Although the informed defendant is often able to have evidence obtained in such a manner ruled inadmissible, he has no resource against the arresting officer except in the most blatant of violations. The net result is that enforcement officers are compelled to observe constitutional rights of many persons committing very grave offenses, but may ignore them with impunity in regard to the relatively petty offense of drug use.

Drugs That Permit Both Use and Abuse

For drugs like alcohol, marijuana, and perhaps the strong hallucinogens, the practical problem from society's point of view is that the majority may use them without harm to either the individual or society, yet these drugs do have an abuse potential for the minority. Other drugs like heroin, cocaine, amphetamines, and barbiturates (when used to produce intoxication) have few redeeming qualities to weigh against their abuse potential. For drugs that lend themselves to use as well as abuse, the problem of penalizing the majority because of the abuse by the minority is a prime issue. The Supreme Court specifically dealt with this question in a ruling made at the time of the Volstead Act:

> The ultimate legislative object of prohibition is to prevent the drinking of intoxicating liquors by anyone because of the demoralizing effect of drunkenness upon society. The state has the power to subject those members of society who might indulge in the use of such liquors without injury to themselves to a deprivation of access to liquor in order to remove temptation from those to whom its use would demoralize.

On a few occasions exceptions have actually been carved out of the law to permit use of a drug otherwise prohibited. Sacramental use of wine was permitted during prohibition, and the ritualized controls of the Native American Church are considered sufficient to safeguard Indians against the abuse of peyote. More frequently, society has informally disregarded the enforcement of the law for certain groups or for certain locations. At the time when jazz musicians were virtually the only persons outside the lower socioeconomic minority groups to use marijuana, police frequently overlooked their use of drugs because they were otherwise productive and did not cause trouble. There is sometimes differential treatment on a geographic basis, with bohemian settlements largely left alone except when drug use is particularly blatant, or local political factors are evident. Other illegal activities such as prostitution, homosexuality, and gambling are also sometimes tacitly allowed in certain districts of a city. Sometimes the affluent or privileged are similarly allowed to violate the law, as in the case of gambling in private clubs or homes.

Another means of dealing with the problem of allowing use but controlling abuse is through compulsory treatment. This is currently employed to a limited extent with alcoholics. Finally, the reduction of possession offenses from felony to misdemeanor would permit much more realistic flexibility in prosecuting through legal channels.

A Congruent Drug Policy

What is especially needed is a concerted effort to produce congruency among the various drug policies and laws. What we have at present is an ill assortment of approaches that is not only lacking in consistency but often operates in clearly contradictory ways. The difficulty does not lie in defining the direction that the over-all policy should take. This may be described as protecting the health and welfare of society within the degree of limitation on individual freedom that is consistent with our political beliefs. The problem lies in the fact that much of the present incongruence is based on unrecognized attitudes and fears that must be explicitly defined before a congruent policy can emerge. This is a mammoth educational task; however, certain steps could speed up the process. One very useful move, which Joel Fort has long advocated, is to treat alcohol abuse and other drug abuse as a single problem. Once this is accomplished some of the most glaring inconsistencies must come into perspective.

For instance, if we are serious about reducing the harm caused by excessive drug use, we must examine the contributions of the massive advertising programs promoting the use of alcohol and tobbaco, and weigh this against the economic and other costs of intervening in our free enterprise system. The length to which we are capable of blindly following an economic policy at the expense of our over-all welfare is illustrated by our supplying Japan with vast amounts of scrap iron for its arms industry virtually to the day of the Pearl Harbor attack. We must ask: if public drunkenness is the manifestation of an illness to be treated rather than prosecuted, is dependency on other drugs not also an illness? We should critically examine the legal reasoning that concludes that being an addict is not a crime, but possessing the substance necessary to be an addict is a felony deserving of a five- or ten-year prison sentence. When the Narcotics Bureau argues that it has reduced heroin addiction by making it a highly expensive habit, we should weigh this result against the expense to the victims burglarized, the increased number of prostitutes, and the large profits to organized crime. We should evaluate the deterrence of the marijuana laws against the resulting alienation, disrespect for the law, and secondary deviance involving a sizeable portion of a whole generation of youth.

Our present attempts to deal with the drug problem consist of a well-established criminal law approach and the beginnings of a treatment-oriented rehabilitation program. It is not at all clear that these two approaches operate together in a congruent fashion. As Richard Blum has noted, the definition of the legal offender is precisely stated in terms of certain behavior, e.g., possession of marijuana; yet the health approach defines the drug user's condition along much broader medical, psychological, and sociological lines. The distinction is strikingly evident in the case of marijuana use, where no one as yet has suggested a treatment-rehabilitation program to parallel the legal approach. The immediate goals are also different—the task of the police is to apprehend and bring to trial a maximum number of law violators, whereas the health approach seeks to modify behavior that is harmful to the individual and society. Finally, the results may be opposed. The criminal law approach creates a deviant subculture that is alienated from and hostile to society; by contrast, the health approach encourages adjustment within society.

Lest I leave the impression that I am unalterably opposed to a punitive legal approach, I shall give an example of a situation where such a policy might be considered congruent with the goal of promoting the over-all welfare of society. For many years the number of persons addicted to heroin in England was on the order of three or four hundred. They were primarily older medical personnel or persons who became addicted through medical treatment. A social policy of maintaining the addiction through medical sources when withdrawal was considered unworkable proved quite effective. In recent years there has been a rapid rise in heroin addiction, primarily among young persons similar to the American addict, and the number of addicts is now estimated to be around 1,500. The demand for heroin is producing a black market, and there is concern that its use will spread to the dimensions observed in the United States. One possible solution might be compulsory commitment of the 1,500 persons presently addicted, and prohibition of further prescriptions for heroin through medical sources. This would effectively eliminate most demand for heroin, and hence the black market should cease to exist. With no available heroin, there would be no, or virtually no, subsequent addicts. While this is a drastic policy (from the standpoint of the present addicts) it might still qualify as being in the best interest of society if it prevented addiction of much larger numbers in subsequent generations.

Finally, in a somewhat speculative vein, I should like to suggest that part of the lack of congruence among drug policies in the United States is due to the fact that economic and technological factors are changing at a faster rate than are cultural attitudes and values. The drug laws in this country have always been an attempt to legislate morality, although they have been justified in terms of preventing anti-social acts. These laws and attitudes evolved at a time when the Protestant ethic, and the competitive achievement-oriented value system were very much in dominance. The passive withdrawal to a life of drug-induced fantasy has been an extremely threatening concept.

Now we are told we are verging on an economy of abundance rather than scarcity; an age of automation will eliminate half or more of the labor force necessary for the production of goods; the concept of work will have to be redefined to include nonproductive pursuits that are now considered hobbies; a guaranteed annual income program will likely be in effect within five to ten years. The children of today's middle class have never experienced a depression or any appreciable difficulty in satisfying their material needs. They do not share the materialistic value system to the same extent as their parents because they have little fear of material deprivation.

There also appears to be an increasing acceptance of pleasure in its own right, rather than something that needs to be earned as a reward for hard work. The traditional American attitude towards pleasure was quite evident in the opinion recently given by Judge G. Joseph Tauro in upholding the constitutionality of the Massachusetts marijuana laws.[1] In denying that the fundamental right to the pursuit of happiness is violated by the marijuana laws, he argued that such a right must be "essential" to continued liberty, as are those rights "closely related to some commonly acknowledged moral or legal duty and not merely to a hedonistic seeking of pleasure." In affirming that the state was justified in permitting alcohol and prohibiting marijuana, Judge Tauro argued that alcohol was used most frequently as a relaxant and "as an incident of other social activities," whereas marijuana was "used solely as a means of intoxication," i.e., pleasure.

If the age of economic abundance, automation, and greatly increased leisure becomes a reality, it is doubtful that these viewpoints toward pleasure (hedonistic or otherwise) will survive. Such an age would not necessarily be accompanied by increased drug usage; however, it does appear that the popularity of marijuana and the stronger hallucinogens might increase at the expense of alcohol use. The former psychedelic drugs are more compatible with an inward-turning orientation and an enhancement of sensual and aesthetic pleasures. Alcohol is more compatible with an aggressive, outward-turning and achievement-oriented society. Excessive drug use would be seen as a threat

---

[1] See above, pp. 6–7.

to the individual alone—not as "a threat to the very moral fabric of society." The over-all welfare of society would be much less dependent on the productivity of the individual, and the value system that demands that pleasure be earned through work would be obsolete.

In conclusion, I predict that whether or not the age of abundance arrives, social policy, with some minor reversals, will generally move in the direction of permitting greater individual freedom with respect to drug use. Society will promote the concept of allowing adults the privilege of informed decision. The crucial problem that will remain is that of protecting those who are too young to make an informed decision.

Running Out of Era: Some Nonpharmacological Notes on the Psychedelic Revolution

Mark Messer, Ph.D.

Some time ago an enthusiastic student explained to me that "if we could somehow drop some LSD into LBJ [President Lyndon Baines Johnson]" many of the problems that confront our society today could be solved. This solution seems to me to be sociologically naive. It is my belief that if we could somehow get 100 nineteenth-century English bankers together and give them some LSD, at least 95 of them would have "bummers" [adverse drug reactions]. But give the same drug to 100 mid-twentieth-century American young people, and 95 or more of them will have a good experience.

This is because the English bankers and LBJ are not where the kids "are at." And where one is at is not a question of pharmacology; it is a question of culture and historical location. Expressed differently, the reason so many of today's youth can say "yes" to a drug experience of the marijuana or LSD type has little to do with the consciousness-altering chemicals in themselves. Rather, they can say "yes" to the experience because of their historical location in the center of a storm of cultural forces, which has already altered their consciousness and which the drugs augment and make lucid. In short, a mind-altering drug *shows* them where they are at; it does not *put* them there.

Rather than discussing the drugs as such, then, I want to discuss something of the historical location and cultural forces that I think are centrally relevant to the psychedelic (cultural) revolution.

"Running Out of Era: Some Nonpharmacological Notes on the Psychedelic Revolution" was published in the Journal of Psychedelic Drugs 2, no. 1 (*Fall 1968*): 157–66. Copyright © 1968 by David E. Smith, M.D. Reprinted with minor changes by permission of the publisher and the author.

At the outset, I want to make an assumption: that every historical epoch has as its driving force or impetus a *myth*. This notion is not an uncommon one amongst philosophers of history, historians, and social scientists. It is most clearly stated, I think, by Susanne Langer in her important book, *Philosophy in a New Key*.[1] Langer suggests that myth is the first form of a new symbolic system, a new dream, a new way of seeing the world. Myths are not discursive: they are essentially ineffable or inarticulable forms of "thought" that find their expression in ritual and art. A myth, then, is the first embodiment of a new world view, but it can do no more than initiate and present this world view. The highest development of which myth is capable, according to Langer, is epic poetry. We cannot abstract and manipulate its concepts any further within the mythical mode. From this point onward, there must be a rationalistic period in which the spirit of the myth is made substance in the form of discursive writing and purposive action. Some day when the vision is totally rationalized, the ideas exploited, exhausted, and acted out, then a *new myth* must be invented, there must be a new vision. This is what is referred to as a "symbolic transformation," that is, a radical redefinition of the whole cultural situation.

It seems to me that the American dream (or myth) of success—that anyone can "make it"—is really just a sub-myth: the larger myth (and the larger historical epoch) involves the last several centuries of the Western world. The spirit of this larger myth (the world view or symbolic system) is something like Prometheus unbound, autonomous man as the measure of all things, dominant over nature, goal directed, with the Faustian-like tendencies to move onward and upward, over and against; in short, *man making it!*

I do not feel qualified to discuss the mythic phase of this historical epoch, expressed in ritual and art, but I think Milton's *Paradise Lost* might well have been the slightly belated epic poem that marked the turning point to rationalization and enactment of the myth. John Calvin provided an example of making the myth of autonomous man discursive, articulate, and a formula for action. The following passage, written in about 1550, is typical.

Let us every one *proceed* according to our small ability, and prosecute the *journey* we have begun. No man will be so unhappy but that he may everyday make some progress, however small. Therefore, let us not cease to strive, that we may be incessantly advancing in the way of the Lord, nor let us despair on account of the smallness of our success; for however our success may not correspond to our wishes, yet

[1] Susanne K. Langer, *Philosophy in a New Key* (Cambridge: Harvard University Press, 1942).

our labor is not lost, when this day surpasses the preceding one; provided that with sincere simplicity we keep our end in view, and press forward to the goal, not practicing self adulation, nor indulging our own evil propensities, but perpetually exerting our endeavors after increasing degrees of amelioration, till we shall have arrived at a perfection of goodness, which indeed, we seek and pursue as long as we live . . .

What Calvin is saying in this remarkably "lineal" passage is, "Don't just stand there, *do* something!" And as Weber points out, the striving to do one's best religiously was readily interpreted to mean doing one's best in the "post assigned to him by his Lord," namely, his *occupation*. "What are you going to *do* when you grow up?"

About 410 years later, Tim Buckley wrote:

> The velocity addicts explode on the highways
> Ignoring the journey and moving so fast
> their nerves fall apart and they gasp but can't breathe
> They run from the cops of the skeleton past
> Petrified by tradition in a nightmare they stagger
> Into nowhere at all, and then look up aghast
> And I wave goodbye to speed
> And smile hello to a rose.

It is as if Buckley were saying, "Don't just *do* something, *stand* there!" And we've come full circle. He continues:

O the new children play	I am young
Under Juniper trees	I will live
Sky blue or gray	I am strong
They continue at ease	I can give
Moving so slow	You the strange
That serenely they can	Seed of day
Gracefully grow	Feel the change
And yes still understand	Know the way*

But let us go back to the sixteenth century and the rationalization of the myth. Enter rationalization itself with the "age of reason" and "enlightenment" in the succeeding two centuries. Enter the rationalization of power with democracy and the rationalization of economics with capitalism. Find the peak of the historical epoch—its flowering —in the first half of the nineteenth century for Europe, and in the second half of that century for America. Then witness the overripen-

---

ing of the myth and the simultaneous appearance of irrational art, literature, and philosophy: Nietzsche, Marx, Heidegger, Husserl, Freud, Sartre, Berdaev, Camus, Chardin, Dadaism, Cubism, Abstract Expressionism, Joyce, Beckett, Malraux, Faulkner, Hemingway.

The artist and the sensitive literary soul, however, are always historically precocious. In the words of the *Buffalo Springfield,* he has a way of "hanging up his eyelids and running down the hall," screaming while the rest of us sleep soundly in the adjoining bedrooms. What about the rest of us? We persist as true believers and continue to overdevelop and overripen. Science flourishes (this is the epitome of acting out the rationalization of the myth), and the inquiring, manipulating, controlling, achieving spirit has really become man over and against. We have fragmented and specialized the goals toward which we have been oriented to the extent that we now have tens of thousands of professional journals, some of them with information on how to handle this information overload with computers.

And the economy? It has become overdeveloped to the extent that it has to produce the consumption for its own products!

And the political system? Too horrendous to discuss. Suffice to say that the political system together with the psychedelic experience is largely responsible for the popularity of the slogan that "reality is an illusion."

By its own internal logic, of course, the myth of Faustian man ever ascending to more and more knowledge and control is a never-completed project. Any biochemist or solid-state physicist will tell us that we are just getting started. But I think it is instructive to recall that Dr. Faustus himself threw up his hands late in his career and proceeded to sell his soul for the opportunity to engage in a different myth. It seems to me conceivable that a large segment of people might enter the stream of an overripe history at such a point that they collectively sense that the "Faustian Frontier" is closed, though by its own logic it never can be. Experientially, it might be perceived that the phallic rocketship's probing of the cosmos itself is going "just about far enough." This degree of goal-stretching might well be the point at which enterprising knowledge explosion reverses itself and becomes the simultaneous presentation of information overload—the whirring of computers—that can only be characterized as implosion, a coming back on to itself. This would be symbolic transformation, and it would mark the invention of a new myth.

A book recently was published about the so-called beatniks of the 1950s. The title of this book is rather un-Faustian; it is called *Nothing More to Declare.* Bob Dylan, perhaps the poet laureate of the so-called hippies of the 1960s, simply asks, "What else can you show me?"

Nothing More to Declare suggests the end of a myth, "What else can you show me" suggests the beginning of another. This, I think, describes where the members of the psychedelic revolution "are at." Because of their historical location at the end of a myth, that is, at the end of a cultural era, they perceive the rewards of the going social order as unrewarding—as overripe. In Paul Goodman's terms, these people have "grown up absurd." The generation gap seems to have widened to the extent that it is now a *cultural* gap as well.

Karl Mannheim,[2] who first articulated such an historical location approach to generations, suggested that certain times in history are critical. There are certain nodal points in history; generations entering history at these points are critically situated. Though there is always the risk of elevating the importance of our own time, it is my conviction that the current generation is unique enough that to treat it in terms of a phase in the life cycle that will be outgrown rather than in terms of its peculiar historical situation is to be misled and deluded. If this generation is on a moral holiday, it may not return to work. It may, in fact, well be the vanguard of a new cultural era, that is, a new mythology.

What is implied here is that the introduction of a new wave of people into the historical stream provides a situation of fresh contact with the culture, which does not so much cause cultural change but *permits* cultural change. The causes of change are inherent in the social and historical process itself. The psychedelic generation is simply located in a strategic position, so that it can perceive the overripeness of the old order. Likewise, the psychedelic drugs do not so much cause altered consciousness but permit the perception of a consciousness *already* altered in the direction of a more appropriate world view. If this is the case, then one can argue that, at least in some historical periods, the young become seers for the old.

In the remaining portion of this paper I am going to discuss what I think to be several important components of the shared history of the generation that is most readily associated with the psychedelic revolution. More specifically, I want to present this discussion in terms of three historical "inputs" that seem to give this age group a temporal "location" that may permit significant cultural change—the historical location of the new youth relative to other age groups, to the affluent state of the society, and to certain technological factors.

[2] Karl Mannheim, *Essays on the Sociology of Knowledge,* chap. 7, "The Problem of Generations" (London: Routledge & Kegan Paul Ltd., 1952).

Historical Location Relative to Other Age Groups

In a complex society, many more influences than that of the family
are at work making us what we are. It becomes clear that men resem-
ble their times more than their fathers. A very important element in
the shared history of any age group, nevertheless, is the experience
it has of that age group that immediately precedes it in the historical
stream. For the current generation, this older group consists of people,
now in their thirties and forties, who were teenagers in the decade
following World War II. The seriousness that characterized this
postdepression and postwar period, added to the go-carefulness of
McCarthyism, helped produce what has been described as "the oldest
younger generation." [3] This is a generation that willed itself directly
from childhood into adulthood. The suburbanized organization man
that resulted presents many of the current generation with an example
that is conducive to "growing up absurd."

It appears, furthermore, that the organization man has lost his commitment to his own life style. The current generation is, for the most
part, not even asked to take up a way of life against which it can
rebel. Perceiving a certain "end of ideology" in his elders, the new
youth is left with a void. He can either choose that void as a way of
life itself (as Keniston's "uncommitted" [4] seem to have done), or he can
invent an entirely different kind of game. The participants of the
psychedelic revolution seem to have chosen the latter course.

One of the nonpharmacological factors that seems to characterize
this new game is its apolitical nature. In the words of Bob Dylan,
"there's no left wing and right wing; only up wing and down wing."
As Simmons and Winograd [5] have observed, this is a kind of ir-
reverence that goes beyond openly aggressive challenging. For political and economic belief systems to be defied is one thing; but for
them to be simply ignored and dismissed out of hand is something
else. "This withdrawal has aroused some of the greatest resentment
and opposition since it is perhaps the gravest affront to an established
ethic not to be taken seriously." [6]

Alabama is prepared to have its capital city marched upon but

---

[3] Ludwig Marcuse, "The Oldest Younger Generation," *The New Partisan Reader*
(New York: Harcourt, Brace & World, Inc., 1953).

[4] Kenneth Keniston, *The Uncommitted* (New York: Harcourt, Brace and
World, 1965).

[5] J. I. Simmons, and Barry Winograd, *It's Happening* (Santa Barbara: Laird
Publications, 1966).

[6] Ibid., p. 13.

California seems to be unprepared to have free food and clothing distributed in its parks every afternoon at four o'clock. A policeman is prepared to confront switchblades and even antiwar pickets, but apparently he is not prepared to confront a young man with flowers in his long hair and a bell around his neck handing him some incense. Universities are prepared to have goldfish swallowed (that's a fad), but they appear less prepared to have students turn themselves into a work of art (that's a threat). The established ethic, in short, is prepared to be defied, but it is not prepared to have its "mind blown." It may well be this unpreparedness of the present establishment that will mark its demise. Yet how can any system defend itself if the threat is a symbolic transformation? If the old myth is irrelevant, so are its guardians.

This important apolitical theme in the psychedelic ethos is interpreted, at least partially, as a response to the preceding age group. The historical location of what Donovan refers to as the "dawning generation" places them adjacent to the ideological void that characterizes their immediate predecessors. Forced to confront a meaningless (or finished) contest, they may decide to invent a new game rather than join the old as opponents to a team that has lost its spirit. Even to picket the old game for having unfair rules is still political action, because one must go to the old stadium. The managers may not like the demonstration, but at least they understand it. To invent a new game, however, and to play it in an entirely different arena, is apolitical action. Politics is part of the old game. Again, to be defied is one thing; to be simply ignored and dismissed out of hand is something else. The one may bring about social change, but the other portends to cultural change. The one is a *redistribution* of things already valued (like contesting political systems); the other is a *redefinition* or transformation of values.

It may be charged that to opt out (or drop out) is to act in support of the established ethic by default. The political radicals level this charge against the members of psychedelica. But the possibility also exists that it is precisely direct political action that is most easily co-opted into the prevailing mentality. Those whom the system cannot buy off may well be those who have "nothing more to declare" in the old arena. In the words of Herbert Marcuse:

> Their opposition hits the system from without and is therefore not deflected by the system; it is an elementary force which violates the rules of the game, and in so doing, reveals it as a rigged game. . . .
> The fact that they start refusing to play the game may be the fact which marks the beginning of the end of a period.[7]

[7] Herbert Marcuse, *One-Dimensional Man* (Boston: Beacon Press, 1966), p. 256.

Historical Location Relative to the Economy

Unlike most of the previous bohemian movement, the hippy ethos does not appear to be fiercely antimaterialistic. Affluence is an important part of the shared historical experience of this age group, and, for the most part, it is neither denied nor decried.

What is denied is the mythical mandate of material success. Again, historical location of the hippies seems to be a terminal—they have arrived. This is the first time in history when a really significant portion of the youth generation in America has come out of homes where the dream of success has become a reality. Their subjective experience of the economic project is that the project is completed, and they find themselves in a position to say, "OK, I've had enough; what else can you show me?"

But it is important to understand that this attitude itself rests on a firm economic base. We must take as a given that a certain level of affluence and technological development is necessary for the emergence and maintainance of a psychedelic life style. Critics of the psychedelic or hippy scene get very disconcerted at this point. Obvious but crucial questions are raised. Who will mind the shop? If many members of one generation opt out of the very economic system that both produces and sustains them, what is to become of the system? But these questions reveal preoccupation with the Faustian myth— the struggle *for* existence. If a large number of people are located at the end of a project, and they perceive that the project has been fulfilled, then they start asking qualitatively different questions. What about the pacification *of* existence? The participation or indulgence *in* existence? "Don't just *do* something; *stand* there!"

Yes, for the most part the members of the psychedelic revolution *are* parasites. This, perhaps, is what makes the phenomenon most instructive. If we are to believe the literature on automation and cybernation, *all of us* are going to be parasites. In fact, most of us already are. Rather than lamenting the economic worthlessness of the hippies, perhaps it behooves us to take them as exemplary of an unabashed perception of the economic reality of our time. To live *off* machines rather than live *like* machines is to accept honestly one's historical location. The machine is not decried. It is put in its proper place and then celebrated. As one participant in the psychedelic revolution put it, "What we want is an electronic Tibet." When the concept of "work" becomes culturally irrelevant, then so will the concept of "parasite." This is a crucial symbolic transformation, and this, I think, is where the psychedelic revolution "is at" in terms of the economy.

Historical Location Relative to Technology

The current generation is the first whose shared history included television, computers, and transistors as a *given*. This may be of signal importance in any attempt to understand the world view—the socially constructed reality—of the psychedelic revolution and, more generally, the emerging youth culture. In an effort to interpret Marshall McLuhan's thinking on these matters, Richard Kostelanetz has written:

> . . . the electronic media initiate sweeping changes in the distribution of sensory awareness—in what McLuhan calls the "sensory ratios." . . . The new media envelop us, asking us to participate. McLuhan believes that such a multisensory existence is bringing a return to the primitive man's emphasis upon the sense of touch, which he considers the primary sense, "because it consists in a meeting of the senses." . . . He sees the new media as transforming the world into a "global village," where all ends of the earth are in immediate touch with one another, as well as fostering a "retribalization" of human life.[8]

The number of mixed-media shows that involve the simultaneous presentation of total hearing, seeing, smelling, and touching stimulation has increased steadily over the last two or three years. A statement from one of these shows indicates that "we are all at work beating the tribal drum of our new electronic environment. . . . We flood the sense-receptors of the audience to the point where time sense is warped, emotions run free, and love of the world suffuses each spectator's body."

A curious pattern seems to be emerging. There is at least some indication that a postindustrial level of technology is creating the rudiments of preindustrial (in fact, preliterate) thinking and social organization. This must be what McLuhan means when he says "we have evoked a super-civilized sub-primitive man."[9] This retribalization is seen as a consequence of an altered consciousness or symbolic transformation that is more consistent with nonlineal electronic circuitry than with the lineal typographical and industrial culture that has characterized the Faustian epoch.

[8] Richard Kostelanetz, "Understanding McLuhan (In Part)," *The New York Times Magazine*, January 29, 1967. Reprinted by permission.
[9] Marshall McLuhan, "Five Sovereign Fingers Taxed the Breath," Edmund Carpenter and Marshall McLuhan, eds., *Explorations in Communications* (Boston: Beacon Press, 1960), p. 208.

We need not look only to the participants in the psychedelic revolution to sense a new mode of thinking. Those of us who are teaching will recognize in many of our students what McLuhan recognized in the young man who commented: "You see, my generation does not have goals. We are not goal-directed. We just want to know what is going on." McLuhan suggested that "the point that this person was making was that it is absurd to ask us to pursue *fragmentary goals* in an electric world that is organized integrally and totally." [10]

It is as if the very system of highly distinct and segmented goals that characterized a culture that could produce an electronic technology has now created its own obsolescence. The new technology is the medium that calls for a new (integral) cultural content. This is what I mean by suggesting that technological factors figure heavily in the shared historical experience of a generation that has within itself the potential for radical cultural change—for symbolic transformation.

A characteristic of the new ethos, which seems very much related to this postindustrial quest for total involvement, is the development of a tremendous interest in religion and cosmology. It is this phenomenon, perhaps more than any other, that is said to be the essence of the drug experience.[11] If drugs are the sacrament of a new religion, they are so in the same sense that the media mix is the mass of a new religion. The media mix is said to simulate a psychedelic drug experience. It is my suggestion here that both the drugs and the media mix simulate the electronic world in which we live, and such simulation *is* the religious experience.[12] Men need religion to make meaningful sense of the world in which they find themselves. Traditional Western religious forms made sense of Calvin's fragmented and goal-oriented world, but that project is completed—that myth has run its course. Now the quest is for a religious form appropriate to the simultaneity of an electronic-organic postindustrial world.[13] This, I think, is why so many participants in the psychedelic revolution are rediscovering cosmological Christianity, as well as reading the *I Ching*, consulting oracles, engaging in yoga, reciting Buddhist, Taoist, and Hindu chants, meditating on nature and mystical unity, and speaking of cosmic forces, strange vibrations, and spherical archetypes.

[10] Marshall McLuhan, "Address at Vision 65," mimeographed.

[11] There has been a considerable amount of literature on the religious nature of the psychedelic drug experience. See, for example, "Psychedelic Drugs and Religion," *Journal of Psychedelic Drugs* 1, no. 2 (Spring 1968).

[12] This notion of religion as a cultural symbol system that articulates world views and meaning is expressed clearly in the extensive writings of Clifford Geertz.

[13] See Thomas Luckmann, *The Invisible Religion: The Transformation of Symbols in Industrial Society* (New York: The Macmillan Company, 1967).

We have always had with us in our society occultists, astrologists, and people of exotic faith systems. But there seems to be something qualitatively more telling about our culture when even so small a portion of (largely middle-class) young people come up with such a radically different world view. These people are living in the kind of truth system that Sorokin has called "ideational," one that for years he has predicted will replace the overripe "sensate" truth system that has dominated Western culture for the past several centuries.[14]

I do not want to say that "this is it!"—that a symbolic transformation toward a new world view has fully taken place, but I do suggest that there seems to be something more than a fad or a phase in the life cycle going on, and that this something runs deeper than the ingestion of hallucinatory drugs. I think that, because of their historical location, a considerable portion of today's youth can perceive that we are "running out of era." These people are busy inventing a new myth, that is, a new reality.

[14] Pitirim A. Sorokin, *Social and Cultural Dynamics* (New York: American Book Company, 1937–41, 4 vols.).

Marijuana and the Politics of Reality

Erich Goode, Ph.D.

It is asserted that the marijuana controversy is primarily a political, rather than a scientific, debate. It is a struggle to establish moral hegemony. Stances toward marijuana use and legalization are largely a manifestation of prior basic underlying ideological commitments. Scientific truth or falsity seem to have little or no impact on the positions taken—although both sides will invoke scientific findings and in fact will actually believe them—and have been preselected to verify a position already taken. Widely used concepts such as "drug abuse" reflect the ideological character of the controversy.

Introduction

One of the more mystifying chapters in recent social research is the seemingly totally contradictory conclusions arrived at in regard to marijuana use. It is possible that no sector of social behavior is more disputed. To raise empirical questions concerning aspects of marijuana use is to arouse a hornet's nest of controversy. Even the fundamental question of the effects of the drug on the human mind and body is hotly disputed; two descriptions, both purporting to be equally "objective," often bear no relation to one another whatsoever.[1] Is marijuana a drug of "psychic dependence"? Or is it meaningless to speak of dependency in regard to marijuana? Does marijuana cause organic damage to the brain? Are its effects criminogenic? How does it influence the over-all output of activity—in popular terms, does it

"Marijuana and the Politics of Reality" was published in the Journal of Health and Social Behavior 10, no. 2 (June 1969): 83–94. Reprinted by permission of the American Sociological Association and the author.

The writing of this paper was facilitated by a grant (MH 15659) from the National Institute of Mental Health. The term "the politics of reality" seems to have been independently invented by politicians and symbolic interactionists, although to refer to two totally disparate concepts. Robert F. Kennedy used the term to mean something akin to Max Weber's Realpolitik, whereas Gregory P. Stone and Harvey A. Farberman, in their anthology (Stone and Farberman, 1969), parallel our meaning in this paper. I would like to thank Professor Farberman for suggesting the term to me, and for helpful criticism of an earlier draft of this paper.

[1] A recent anthology (Goode, 1969) includes sections which assert and supposedly demonstrate wholly contradictory answers to these questions.

produce "lethargy" and "sloth"? Does it precipitate "psychotic episodes"? What, specifically, is its impact on artistic creativity? What is the drug's influence on mechanical skills, such as the ability to drive an automobile? Does the use of marijuana "lead to" heroin addiction? These are questions which can be answered within the scope of empirical sociological, psychological and pharmacological scientific technique. Each query can be operationalized. Indices can be constructed; tests can be devised. Occasionally they are. Yet the zones of widespread agreement are narrow indeed. Surely this should puzzle the sociologist. We propose, therefore, to explore some of the likely sources of this controversy, and to attempt a partial explanation for this almost complete discord.

The Social Construction of Reality[2]

All civilizations set rules concerning what is "real" and what is not, what is "true" and what "false." All societies select out of the data before them a world, one world, the "world taken for granted," and declare that the "real world." Each one of these artificially constructed worlds is to some degree idiosyncratic, unique. No individual views reality directly, "in the raw," so to speak. Our perceptions are narrowly channeled through concepts and interpretations. What is commonly thought of as "reality," that which "exists," or simply "is," is a set of concepts, conceptual frames, assumptions, suppositions, rationalizations, justifications, defenses, all generally collectively agreed upon, which guide and channel each individual's perceptions in a specific and distinct direction. The specific rules governing the perception of the universe which man inhabits are more or less arbitrary, a matter of convention. Every society establishes a kind of *epistemological methodology*.

Meaning, then, does not automatically announce itself. Rather, it is *read into* every situation, event, entity, object, phenomenon. What one individual understands by a given phenomenon may be absolutely heterogenous to what another individual understands by it. In a sense, then, the reality itself is different. The only reality available to each individual consciousness is a subjective reality. Yet this insight poses a dilemma: we must see in a skewed manner or not at all. For, as Berger and Luckmann point out, "To include epistemological questions concerning the validity of sociological knowledge is like trying to push a bus in which one is riding" (Berger and Luckmann, 1966:13).

[2] The title of this section is taken from a book of the same name (Berger and Luckmann, 1966).

Sociologists, too, are implicated in this same process. But unless we wish to remain huddled in the blind cave of solipsism, the problem should not paralyze us. We leave the problem of the ultimate validity of sociological knowledge to the metaphysical philosophers.

If we wish to grasp the articulation between ideology and what Westerners call science, we must look to fundamental cultural beliefs which stimulate or inhibit the growth of scientific-empirical ideas. One form of this selection process, the course of defining the nature of the universe, involves *the rules of validating reality.* A procedure is established for accepting inferential evidence; some forms of evidence will be ruled out as irrelevant, while others will serve to negotiate and determine what is real. For instance, some religious systems have great faith in the validity of the message of the senses (Merton; Kennedy). Other civilizations give greater weight to mystical insight, to the reality beyond empirical reality (Needham: 417–422, 430–431).

The sociologist's task only begins on this vast cultural canvas. While the "major mode" of the epistemological selection and validation process involves the decision to accept or rule out the data of our senses, within this tradition, minor modes of variation will be noticed. Clearly, even societies with powerful scientific and empirical traditions will contain subcultures which have less faith in the logic of the senses than others. Moreover, all cultures have absorbed one or another mode of reasoning *differentially,* so that some institutions will typify the dominant mode more characteristically than others. Certainly few in even the most empirical of civilizations will apply the same rules of evidence in the theater of their family as in their workaday world.

The more complex the society, the greater the number of competing versions concerning reality. The Positivists were in error in assuming that greater knowledge would bring epistemological convergence. The arenas of controversy are more far-flung than ever before. Now, instead of societies differing as to how they view the real world, subsegments of society differ. This poses a serious problem for those members of society who have an emotional investment in stability and in the legitimacy of their own special version of reality. The problem becomes, then, a matter of *moral hegemony,* of legitimating one distinctive view of the world, and of discrediting competing views. These rules of validating reality, and society's faith in them, may serve as *strategies* in ideological struggles. Contending parties will wish to establish veracity by means of the dominant cultural mode.

All societies invest this selection process with an air of *mystification,* to use Peter Berger's phrase (1967:90–91, 203): "Let the institutional order be so interpreted as to hide, as much as possible, its *constructed* character. . . . [The] humanly constructed nomoi are given a cosmic status. . . ." (1967:33, 36). This process must not, above all, be seen as whimsical and arbitrary; it must be grounded in the nature of reality itself. The one selected view of the world must be seen as the *only possible* view of the world; it must be identified with the real world. All other versions of reality must be seen as whimsical and arbitrary and, above all, *in error*. At one time, this twin mystification process was religious in character: views in competition with the dominant one were heretical and displeasing to the gods— hence, Galileo's "crime." Now, of course, the style is to cloak what Berger terms "fictitious necessities" with an aura of scientific validity. Nothing has greater discrediting power today than the demonstration that a given assertion has been "scientifically disproven." Our contemporary pawnbrokers of reality are scientists.

Value and Fact in Negotiating the Marijuana Reality

Probably no area of social life reflects this selective process more than drug use. Note the pharmacological definition of a "drug": ". . . a drug is broadly defined as any chemical agent that effects living protoplasm. . . ." (Fingl and Woodbury, 1965:1). Yet very few in our society will admit to the use of drugs, including the man who smokes two packs of cigarettes a day, the barbiturate-dependent housewife, and the near-alcoholic. Society has constructed the social concept (if not the pharmacological definition) in such a way that it excludes elements which are substantially identical to those it includes. What is seen as the essential reality of a given drug and its use, then, is a highly *contingent* event. What society selects as crucial to perceive about drugs, and what it ignores, tells us a great deal about its cultural fabric.

The scientist makes a clear distinction between those questions which can be tested empirically and those which are wholly in the realm of sentiment. A man may have an opinion about whether marijuana causes crime, but the question is, ideally at least, answerable. As long as the combatants agree on the rules of the road, there is supposedly a more or less clear right and wrong here. But the question of whether marijuana is *evil* or not is intrinsically unanswerable, within an empirical and scientific framework; it depends completely on one's perspective. However clear-cut this distinction is in the scientist's mind, as a tool for understanding the combatants' positions in this controversy it is specious and misleading, for a variety of reasons.

To begin with, the strands of value and fact intersect with one another so luxuriantly that in numerous reasoning sequences they are inseparable. What one society or group or individual takes for granted as self-evidently harmful, others view as obviously beneficial or even necessary. In crucial ways, the issue of harm or danger to society as a result of the drug pivots on moot points, totally unanswerable questions, issues that science is unable to resolve. Science requires that certain basic issues be resolved before any reasonable solution can be reached. And for many crucial debated marijuana questions, this modest requirement cannot be met. In other words, before we raise the question of whether marijuana has a "desirable" or a "noxious" effect, we would first have to establish the fact of the desirability or the noxiousness to whom. We must concern ourselves with the differential *evaluations* of the same "objective" consequences. Many of the drug's effects—agreed upon by friend and foe alike—will be regarded as reprehensible by some individuals and desirable or neutral by others. Often anti-marijuana forces will argue against the use of the drug, employing reasons which its supporters will also employ— in *favor* of its use. In other words, we have here not a disagreement in what the effects are, but in whether they are a "good" or a "bad" thing. This is probably the most transparently ideological of all of the platforms of debate over marijuana. Three illustrations of this orbit of disputation should suffice.

With marijuana use more prevalent than today would come the billowing of a distinct esthetic. The state of marijuana intoxication seems to be associated with, and even to touch off, a unique and peculiar vision of the world. That the marijuana-induced vision is distinctive seems to be beyond dispute (Anonymous, in Goode, 1969; Adler, 1968; Ginsberg, 1966; Ludlow, 1965); that it is rewarding or fatuous is a matter for endless disputation. Inexplicably, the drug seems to engender a mental state which is coming into vogue in today's art forms. An extraordinarily high proportion of today's young and avant-garde artists—film-makers, poets, painters, musicians, novelists, photographers, mixed media specialists—use the drug and are influenced by the marijuana "high" (Anonymous, in Goode). Some of the results seem to be an increasing irrelevance of realism; the loss of interest in plot in films and novels; a glorification of the irrational and the seemingly nonsensical; an increased faith in the logic of the viscera, rather than in the intellect; a heightened sense for the absurd; an abandonment of traditional and "linear" reasoning sequences, and the substitution of "mosaic" and fragmentary lines of attack; *bursts* of insight rather than *chains* of thought; connectives relying on internal relevance, rather than a commonly understood and widely accepted succession of events and thoughts; love of the paradoxical, the perverse, the contradictory, the incongruous; an "implosive" inward thrust, rather than an "explosive" outward thrust; instantaneous totality rather than specialization; the dynamic rather than the static; the unique rather than the general and the universal.[3]

Those with conventional, traditional and "classic" tastes in art will view these results in a dim light. A recent anti-marijuana tract, for instance, comments on the highly unconventional and antitraditionalist novelist William Burroughs' approval of marijuana's influence on his creative powers: "The irony is that Burroughs meant his remark as an endorsement" (Bloomquist, 1968:189). The sociologist of knowledge seeks to understand and explain the bases from which man's intellectual efforts spring. He will notice the prominent place in this debate of the manner in which matters of taste, such as artistic esthetics, are intimately and inseparably bound with views of the empirical reality of the drug. He who is opposed to the use of marijuana, and who believes that it is (empirically) harmful, is very likely to dislike contemporary art forms, and vice versa. The two are not, of course, necessarily causally related, but rather emerge out of the same matrix.

Marijuana's reputed impact on sexual behavior is all to the good to some who are comfortable with an unconventional view of sex. To the sexually traditional, the fact that marijuana could disrupt man's (and woman's) traditional patterns of sexuality is an out-of-hand condemnation of the drug. While marijuana's opponents would label any imputed increase in sexual activity as a result of the drug [4] "promiscuity" [5] and would roundly condemn it, the drug's apostles would cheer society's resurgent interest in the organic, the earthy, the sensual.

The argument that marijuana is a "mind altering" drug has discrediting power to him who thinks of the everyday workings of the mind as "normal" and desirable. But to the explorer of unusual and exotic mental realms, its mind-altering functions are an argument in its favor. The ideologues of the psychedelic movement—and mari-

---

[3] The parallel between the mental processes associated with the marijuana "high" and the "tribal" mind typified by McLuhan (1964) is too close to escape mention.

[4] There is some question about marijuana's sexual impact. Although pharmacologists today generally feel that marijuana is either non-sexual or even anti-sexual (anaphrodisiac) in its effects in the strict physiological sense, marijuana users often feel that the drug acts as a pleasure-stimulator. In a study by the author still in progress at the time of this writing, of 200 marijuana users, 44 percent said that marijuana increased their sexual *desire*, and 68 percent said that it increased their sexual *enjoyment*.

[5] A recent court ruling by Joseph Tauro (1967), Chief Justice of the Superior Court of Massachusetts, held that "sexual promiscuity" was one of the undesirable consequences of marijuana use; Justice Tauro rejected the defendants' appeal. Strangely, *Time* magazine claimed that Tauro's ruling would be judged fair by even the staunchest of marijuana supporters.

juana is considered by most commentators as the weakest of the psychedelic or "hallucinogenic" drugs—claim that every member of society is lied to, frustrated, cheated, duped and cajoled, and thus grows up totally deceived. Barnacles of attitudes, values, beliefs, layer themselves upon the mind, making it impossible to see things as they truly are. This ideology maintains that far from offering an "escape from reality," the psychedelic drugs thrust man more intensely *into* reality. By suspending society's illusions, the "voyager" is able to see reality "in the raw," with greater verisimilitude. Aldous Huxley (1963:34) exclaimed, under the influence of mescaline, "This is how one ought to see, how things really are."

The anti-psychedelic stance will, of course, deny the validity of this process. What is "real" is the world as the undrugged person perceives it. Any alteration of the "normal" state of consciousness is destructive and inherently distorting. Drug use, it is claimed, is "a way to shut out the real world or enter a world of unreality"; the psychedelic drug user attempts to "take a trip away from the real world and to a society of his own making." (AMA, 1968, 6:1, 4). But what is astonishing about the controversy is that both sides presume to know precisely what *reality* is. Whichever version we choose to guide our senses, we should not fail to notice the ideological character of the controversy. Both orientations are to a large degree arbitrary, conventional. Epistemological questions cannot be resolved by fiat or empirical test. Even the natural sciences rest on faith, an unprovable assumption that the senses convey valid information. Yet each side insists that it alone has a monopoly on knowing what is true and what false, what is real and what illusory. Both sides attempt to mask the capricious nature of their decision with an air of legitimacy and absolute validity. Taking a relativistic stance toward both perspectives, we are forced to regard both to be statements of political persuasion.

An essential component of dominant medical and psychological thinking about illicit drug use is that it is undesirable, that the user should be "treated" in such a manner that he discontinues use. The user is felt, rightly or wrongly, to threaten some of the more strongly held cultural values of American society:

> In my opinion, psychopharmacologic agents may be divided into two major categories depending on the manner in which they either help or hinder the individual in his adaptation to society.
>
> Drugs may be used in one of two ways to help relieve . . . tensions: by sufficiently diminishing emotional tension to permit the individual to function or by allowing the individual to totally escape from reality. Sedatives, tranquilizers, and antidepressants . . . often permit

an individual to function more effectively. Psychedelic drugs . . . allow the individual to escape from reality so that he need not function at all. The first group of drugs is often useful to society; the second group would only destroy it (Kissin, 1967:2).

Given the basic premises on which statements such as these are based, it is difficult to understand just what the notion of detachment and objectivity toward drug use might mean.

Another locus of unresolvable controversy, where value and fact interlock inseparably, is the question of a *hierarchy of values.* An impartial stance is claimed by combatants in a multitude of pseudoscientific questions. Here, even the value issues may be resolved. Everyone agrees that marijuana may precipitate psychotic episodes, and that, further, psychotic episodes are a "bad thing." The issue then becomes not, does it occur, or, is it good or bad, but: Do marijuana's claimed dangers outweigh its possible benefits? Should we restrict society's right to access to drugs so that we may minimize the potential harm to society? How does one set of values stack up against another? One might, by donning a white coat, pretend to scientific objectivity in answering this question, but it might be wise to remember that even the emperor didn't succeed in the ruse.

The Logistics of Empirical Support

A second powerful reason why strictly empirical arguments seem to have exerted relatively little hold in the marijuana controversy, aside from the intricate intertwining of value and fact, seems to be a basic panhuman psychic process which leads to the need for the confirmation of our strongly held biases; moreover, empirical reality, being staggeringly complex, permits and even *demands* factual selection. We characteristically seek support for our views: contrary opinions and facts are generally avoided. This opens the way for the maintenance of points of view which are contradicted by empirical evidence. And there is invariably a variety of facts to choose from. It is a comparatively simple matter to find what one is looking for in any moderately complex issue. Each individual facing an emotionally charged issue selects the facts which agree with his own opinions, supermarket-like. Individuals do not judge marijuana to be "harmful" or "beneficial" as a result of objective evidence, rationally weighed and judiciously considered. The process, rather, works in the opposite direction: the drug is considered harmful—as a result of customs which articulate or clash with the use and the effect of the drug, as a result of the kinds of people who use it, and the nature of the "reading" process society applies to these individuals, and as a result of campaigns conducted by "moral entrepreneurs" (Becker, 1963), as well as innumerable other processes—and *then* positive and negative traits are attributed to the drug. The explanation for perceiving the drug in a specific manner *follows* attitudes about it. A man is not opposed to the use or the legalization of marijuana *because* (he thinks) it "leads to" the use of more dangerous drugs, because it "causes" crime, because it "produces" insanity and brain damage, because it "makes" a person unsafe behind the wheel, because it "creates" an unwillingness to work. *He believes these things because he thinks the drug is evil.* The negative consequences of the use of marijuana *are superadded to support a basically value position.* But everyone, Pareto says, seeks to cloak his prejudices in the garb of reason, especially in an empirical age, so that evidence to support them is dragged in *post hoc* to provide rational and concrete proof.[6]

Conceptions of true and false are extravagantly refracted through social and cultural lenses to such an extent that the entire notion of empirical truth becomes irrelevant. "True" and "false" become, in fact, what dominant groups define as true and false; its very collectivity establishes legitimacy. A pro- or anti-marijuana stance reflects a basic underlying attitudinal syndrome, ideological in character, which is consonant with its drug component. Prior to being exposed to attitudes or "facts" about marijuana, the individual has come to accept or reject fundamental points of view which already lead him to apprehend the reality of marijuana in a definite manner. These ideological slants are not merely *correlates* of related and parallel attitudes. They are also *perceptual screens* through which a person views empirically grounded facts. In other words, marijuana provides an *occasion* for ideological expression.

Perceptions of the very empirical reality of the drug are largely determined by prior ideological considerations. Almost everyone facing the issue already has an answer concerning its various aspects, because of his attitudes about related and prior issues. He finds facts to suit his predilections—whether supportive or critical—and commandeers them to suit his biases. The essential meaning of the marijuana issue is the meaning which each individual brings to it. The marijuana "reality"

---

[6] Clearly, not many interested participants in a given controversy are aware of the rules of the scientific method. They may feel that they are empirically proving a point by submitting concrete evidence, yet the mode of reasoning merely confirms their ideological biases. "Proof" by enumeration exemplifies this principle. The criminogenic effect of marijuana is "demonstrated" by a listing of individuals who smoke marijuana who also, either under the influence or not, committed a crime. Munch (1966) and Anslinger and Tompkins (1953: 23–25) exemplify this line of reasoning.

going on before us is a vast turmoil of events which, like all realities, demands factual selection. Yet the selection of facts is never random. It is always systematic, it always obeys a specific logic. Any message can be *read into* the impact of the drug; anything you wish to see is there. We support our predilections by seeing in the drug only that which supports them. If the critic wants to see in the drug and its use violence, sadism, rape and murder, they are there, buried in the reality of marijuana.[7] If the drug supporter wishes to see peace and serenity, it is no difficult job to find them.

This is not to say, of course, that no research has ever been conducted which approaches scientific objectivity. (Scientific objectivity is, as we pointed out above, one form of bias, but since on most issues all participants in the dispute pay their respects to it, this axiom is apolitical in its import). It is to say, however, that not all participants in the marijuana controversy have been trained as scientists, nor do they reason as scientists. *Interpretations* of the marijuana studies are more important to us here than the studies' findings themselves. Out of a multitude of findings a diversity of mutually exclusive conclusions can be reached. The multitude of results from the many marijuana reports forms a sea of ambiguity into which nearly any message may be read. The researcher's findings do not announce themselves to the reader. Any opinion may be verified by the scientific literature on marijuana. Mayor La Guardia's Report (The Mayor's Committee on Marihuana, 1944) rivals the Bible in the diversity of the many conclusions which have been drawn from it.

Marijuana's proponents take heart in its conclusions (Rosevear, 1967:111–112), and nearly all of the report has been reprinted in a recent pro-marijuana anthology (Solomon, 1966). Yet anti-marijuana forces find in the study solid evidence for the damaging effects of the drug (Bloomquist, 1968:122–126; Brill, 1968:20–21; Louria, 1968:105). Our point, then, is that drawing conclusions from even the most careful and parsimonious scientific study is itself a highly *selective* process. The welter of findings are subject to a systematic sifting process. Often the researcher finds it necessary to disassociate himself from the conclusions which others have reached on his work. For instance, a sensationalistic popular article on LSD (Davidson, 1967) was denounced as a "distortion" and "an atrocity" by the very scientists

---

[7] In its Field Manual, the Federal Bureau of Narcotics requests district supervisors to obtain from state and local officials "reports in all cases . . . wherein crimes were committed under the influence of marijuana." To illustrate the selective process involved in this request, imagine the impressive dossier which might result from a request that reports be conveyed on anyone *wearing a hat* while committing a crime; a case could thus be made on the criminogenic effects of hat-wearing.

whose research it cited. More attention ought to be paid, therefore, to the "reading" process of drawing conclusions from scientific work, rather than the findings themselves. In fact, specifically what is meant by the "the findings themselves" is unclear, since they can be made to say so many different and contradictory things.

Strategies of Discreditation

Naming has political implications. By devising a linguistic category with specific connotations, one is designing armaments for a battle; by having it accepted and used, one has scored a major victory. For instance, the term "psychedelic" has a clear pro-drug bias: it announces that the mind works best when under the influence of a drug of this type. (Moreover, one of the psychedelic drug proselytizers, in search of a term which would describe the impact of these drugs, rejected "psychedelic" as having negative overtones of psychosis.) Equally biased is the term "hallucinogen," since an hallucination is, in our civilization at least, unreal, illusory and therefore undesirable; the same holds for the term "psychotomimetic": capable of producing a madness-like state. The semantics and linguistics of the drug issue form an essential component of the ideological skirmishes[8] (Fort, 1967:87–88; Goode, 1969).

Drug "abuse" is such a linguistic device. It is often used by physicians and by the medically related. Encountering the use of the term, one has the impression that something quite measurable is being referred to, something very much like a disease, an undesirable condition which is in need of remedy. The term, thus, simultaneously serves two functions: (1) it claims clinical objectivity; (2) it discredits the action which it categorizes. In fact, no such objectivity obtains in the term, and its use is baldly political. Drug abuse is the use of a drug in a way that influentials with legitimacy disapprove of. Their objections are on moral, not medical, grounds, although their argument will be cast in medical language. The American Medical Association, for instance, defines the term: "drug abuse [is] taking drugs without professional advice or direction" (AMA, 1967:2). Nonmedical drug

---

[8] As an example of how naming influences one's posture toward a phenomenon, note that the Bureau of Narcotics and Dangerous Drugs has jurisdiction over "addicting" drugs, which supposedly includes marijuana, while the Food and Drug Administration preside over "habit-forming" drugs. Because of this jurisdictional division, the bureau is forced into the absurd position of having to claim that marijuana is an "addicting" drug, and to shore up this contention, it supplies drug classifications which follow jurisdictional lines (School Management, 1966a), as if they had some sort of correspondence in the real world.

use is, in the medical view, *by definition* abuse. *Any* use *of any* drug outside a medical context, regardless of its consequences, is *always* undesirable, i.e., is by definition, abuse.

A linguistic category both crystalizes and influences responses to, and postures toward, a phenomenon. The term "abuse" illustrates this axiom. It announces that nonmedical drug-taking is undesirable, that the benefits which the drug-using subculture proclaims for drug use are outweighed by the hard rock of medical damage. Yet, since the weighing of values is a moral, not a medical process, we are full-face against an ideological resolution of the issue, yet one cast in a scientific and empirical exoskeleton. Further: *the linguistic category demands verification.* By labeling a phenomenon "abuse," one is willy-nilly under pressure to *prove* that the label is valid. The term so structures our perceptions of the phenomenon that it is possible to see only "abusive" aspects in drug use. Therefore, data must be collected to discredit the beneficial claims of drug use.

Another strategy of disconfirming the marijuanists' claims to legitimacy is the notion, closely interconnected with drug use as "abuse," of marijuana use as being the manifestation of medical *pathology.* This thrust bears two prongs: (1) the *etiology* of marijuana use as an expression of, or an "acting out" of, a personality disturbance (Ausubel, 1958:98–100, 102–103, 106; AMA, 1967:369–370; AMA, 1968b:2, Halleck, 1967:4–5);[9] (2) the effects of the drug as a precipitator of temporary but potent *psychotic episodes* (Farnsworth, 1967:434–435; Farnsworth and Weiss, 1968; Isbell et al., 1967; Keeler, 1967 and 1968; Ungerleider et al., 1968:355).[10] By assigning marijuana use to the twilight world of psychic pathology, its moral and willful character has been neutralized. The labeled behavior has been removed from the arena of free will; its compulsive character effectively denies that it can be a viable alternative, freely chosen.[11] An act reduced to both symptom and cause of pathology has had its claims to moral rectitude neutralized and discredited. As a manifestation of illness, it calls for "treatment," not serious debate. In a sense, then, physicians and psychiatrists have partially replaced policemen as preservers of the social

[9] Most formulations, however, include the important qualification that the more the user smokes, the greater is the likelihood of a personality disturbance; the less he smokes—the "experimenter" and the "occasional," as opposed to the "regular," smoker—the greater is the likelihood that accidental, cultural, social, contextual, factors play a role.

[10] Likewise, as above, the greater the dosage, the greater is the chance for such episodes to occur; at lower dosages, it is less likely.

[11] A recent discussion (Stone and Farberman, 1969) argues that assigning the status of medical pathology is an effective device for neutralizing the legitimacy of a political opponent's ideology.

order, since attempts at internal controls have replaced external sanctions. Both presume to know for the subject how he "ought" to act. Yet the new sanctions, based on an ideology which the deviant partially believes in—scientific treatment of a medical illness—becomes a new and more powerful form of authoritarianism.

Generally, some sort of explanation, particularly one involving compulsion and pathology, is called for wherever it is not rationally understandable to the observer—that is, it "doesn't make sense." An anomalous and bizarre form of behavior demands an explanation. We can understand repeated dosages of poetry because we all approve of poetry, so that no special examination is necessitated. It is only where the behavior violates our value biases that we feel it necessary to construct an interpretation. There is the built-in assumption that the individual *should* be able to do without recreational drugs, that their use is *unnecessary*, and a life without them is the *normal* state of affairs. Violation of our expectations requires an explanation. No explanation for *abstinence from* drugs is necessary, since our biases tell us that that is the way one "ought" to live.

Looking at all of the actions of which society disapproves—"deviant" behavior—we notice that they share fundamental similarities. However, these similarities inhere not so much in the acts themselves as in the way society responds to them. One of the more interesting responses is the tendency to impute psychological abnormality to their authors. The issue of whether such judgments are "correct" or not is less relevant to us as in the nexus between the kinds of acts which attract such judgments, and the nature of the society in which they are made. It is said that Freud once had a patient who believed that the center of the earth was filled with jam. Freud was not concerned with the truth or falsity of that statement, but with the *kind of man* who made it. Similarly, the sociologist of knowledge concerns himself with the kinds of explanations a society fabricates about behavior in its midst, and what those explanations reveal about that society. It should be regarded as extremely significant that deviant behavior seems to have attracted explanations which activate a principle of psychological abnormality. The sociologist legitimately raises the question as to what it is about American society which begets a personality abnormality explanation for marijuana smokers, as well as heroin addicts (Chein et al., 1964), homosexuals (Bieber, 1962; New York Academy of Medicine, 1964), unwed mothers (Young, 1945 and 1954), criminals (Abrahamsen, 1960), juvenile delinquents (Grossbard, 1962), prostitutes, as well as a host of other deviant groups and activities. The fact that each of these social categories—and the activities associated with them—are severely condemned by American society makes the nature of the process of constructing pathology interpretations of deviance at least as interesting as the etiology of the deviant behavior itself. In all of these cases, adopting a medical approach to the deviant and his behavior effectively neutralizes his moral legitimacy, as well as the viability of his behavior. In this sense, the constructors of such theories serve to mirror the basic values of American society.

Overview

It is the sociologist's job to discover and explicate patterns in social life. When one side of a protracted and apparently insoluble controversy activates arguments that involve such putatively repugnant components as: "socially irresponsible," "vagabond existence," "outlandish fashions," "long hair," "lack of cleanliness," and "disdain for conventional values" (Farnsworth, 1967), while the other side emphasizes factors which it deems beneficial, and which sound very different: "discovery," "optical and aural aesthetic perceptions," "self-awareness," "insight," and "minute engagement" (Ginsberg, 1966), we are ineluctably lead to the conclusion that the controversy is a matter of taste and style of life, that it revolves about basically unanswerable issues, and its adjudication will take place on the basis of power and legitimacy, and not on the basis of scientific truth. In fact, given the nature of the disputation, it is difficult to know exactly what is meant by scientific truth. The problem becomes one of gathering support for one or another bias, rather than the empirical testing of specific propositions, whatever that might entail.

The American Medical Association urges educational programs as an "effective deterrent" to marijuana use (AMA, 1968a:92). It is not, however, the sheer accumulation of information about marijuana which the AMA is referring to, since any marijuana user knows more than the average nonuser about the effects of the drug. What is being referred to is *attitudes toward* the drug, not factual information:

> . . . district officials are so fired up, they'd interrupt the routine of the whole district just to make sure our kids hear a good speaker or see a movie that will teach them the basic fact: *stay away from drugs.*

> In order to know exactly what it is that they should stay away from, students must know the *nature* of drugs . . . they're provided with basic facts. These facts aren't given "objectively"—they're slanted, so there's not the slightest doubt that students understand just how dangerous drugs can be.

You can call it brainwashing if you want to. We don't care what you call it—as long as these youngsters get the point. (School Management, 1966b:103).[12]

Not only is the "meaning in the response," but both meaning and response are structured by power and legitimacy hierarchies. Society calls upon certain status occupants to verify what we wish to hear. These statuses are protective in nature, and are especially designated to respond to certain issues in a predetermined manner. Threats to society's security must be discredited. An elaborate charade is played out, debating points are scored—with no acknowledgment from the other side—and no one is converted. Inexorably, American society undergoes massive social change, and the surface froth of marijuana changes with it.

Summary

1. Civilizations differ in their rules for validating reality.

2. The particular manner in which a given culture chooses to view the material world is an arbitrary and conventional decision.

3. Yet this decision must be, and generally is, accorded a semi-sacred status.

4. Empirical and scientific rules and statuses have become basic arbiters of reality for the recent West.

5. Yet, different subcultures within the same society vary in their conceptions of what is real.

6. Yet these subcultures also vary significantly in their access to power and legitimacy.

7. He who is dominant in a given society attempts to enforce his version of reality on the rest of society, both in terms of legitimacy (i.e., moral hegemony), and in terms of making sure that others who disagree with him do not do anything which he disapproves of. He generally believes that he does this for the good of society, for the good of the individual whose behavior is restricted, because it is both moral and scientifically sound. In other words, society is not merely an agglomeration of different individuals and social groups, each neutral to one another, getting "equal time," but is made up of elements which are differentially able to enforce and impose their own unique version of reality on others.

8. Imposing a dominant mode of thinking about reality—as well as behavioral compliance in correspondence with that definition—involves questions of strategy.

[12] The interview is with Dr. Sidney Birnbach, director of school health, physical education and safety in the Yonkers, New York, school system.

9. Thus, the scientific status of one or another version of reality becomes a political and a tactical issue.

10. Yet the complexity of empirical phenomena, along with widespread unfamiliarity with scientific reasoning processes, and the degree of emotion engaged by the issue, combine to make a "genuine" scientific adjudication of the debate spurious and nonexistent.

11. Moreover, many of the issues surrounding the controversy are ideological, matters of taste, beyond the test of scientific instruments (*de gustibus non est disputandum*); they sum up styles of life, ways of viewing the universe. They represent inviolable cultural perspectives, attitudinal gestalts, outlooks on the world, which shape the individual's behavior patterns, which represent taken-for-granted realities, irrefutable and unquestionable.

12. These basically nonrational beliefs shape perceptions of empirically testable assumptions. He who thinks of marijuana use as morally wrong is likely to exaggerate its criminogenic effects; he who thinks of it as beneficial will minimize its impact on crime.

13. It is not uncommon to assume that from the acceptance of a particular empirically relevant belief that he who has a belief which is in disagreement with my own is *wrong*, ignorant, and possibly stupid as well.

14. The line between what can and cannot be tested empirically is fuzzy, nonexistent and irrelevant to most people. Therefore, not only is he who disagrees with me on scientific matters wrong and ignorant, but he who disagrees with me on matters of taste and style of life is also wrong and ignorant.

15. Marijuana can be thought of as a kind of *symbol* for a complex of other positions, beliefs and activities which are correlated with and compatible with its use. In other words, those who disapprove of marijuana use often feel that he who smokes must, of necessity, also be a political radical, engage in "loose" (from his point of view) sexual practices, and have a somewhat dim view of patriotism. Marijuana use is seen (whether rightly or wrongly) to sum up innumerable facts about the individual, facts which can clearly place him along the conservative-liberal-radical dimension in a number of areas of social and political life.

16. In view of these and other intricacies, the debate over marijuana use is unlikely to be solved in the foreseeable future.

References

ABRAHAMSEN, DAVID. 1960. The Psychology of Crime. New York: Columbia University Press.

ADLER, RENATA. 1968. "The screen: Head, monkees movie for a turned-on audience." The New York Times (November 7).

AMERICAN MEDICAL ASSOCIATION. 1967. "Dependence on cannabis (marijuana)." Journal of the American Medical Association 201 (August 7):368–371. 1968a. "Marihuana and society." JAMA 204 (June 24:1181–1182. 1968b. "The Crutch That Cripples: Drug Dependence." (a pamphlet)

ANSLINGER, HARRY J. and W. G. TOMPKINS. 1953. The Traffic in Narcotics. New York: Funk and Wagnalls.

AUSUBEL, DAVID P. 1958. Drug Addiction. New York: Random House.

BECKER, HOWARD S. 1963. Outsiders. New York: Free Press.

BERGER, PETER L. 1967. The Sacred Canopy. Garden City, New York: Doubleday.

BERGER, PETER L. and THOMAS LUCKMANN. 1966. The Social Construction of Reality. Doubleday.

BIEBER, IRVING et al., 1962. Homosexuality. New York: Basic Books.

BLOOMQUIST, EDWARD R. 1968. Marijuana. Beverly Hills, California: Glencoe Press.

BRILL, HENRY. 1968. "Why not pot now? Some questions and answers about marijuana." Psychiatric Opinion 5, no. 5 (October):16–21.

CHEIN, ISIDORE et al., 1964. The Road to H. New York: Basic Books.

DAVIDSON, BILL. 1967. "The hidden evils of LSD." The Saturday Evening Post (August 12):19–23.

FARNSWORTH, DANA. 1967. "The drug problem among young people." West Virginia Medical Journal 63 (December):433–437.

FARNSWORTH, DANA and SCOTT T. WEISS. 1969. "Marijuana: the conditions and consequences of use and the treatment of users." in Rutgers Symposium on Drug Use. New Brunswick, New Jersey: The State University.

FINGL, EDWARD and DIXON WOODBURY. 1965. "General principles." in Louis S. Goodman and Alfred Gilman (eds.), The Phamarcological Basis of Therapeutics. New York: Macmillan.

FORT, JOEL. 1967. "The semantics and logic of the drug scene." in Charles Hollander (ed.), Background Papers on Student Drug Involvement. Washington: National Student Association.

GINSBERG, ALLEN. 1966. "The great marijuana hoax: manifesto to end the bringdown." Atlantic (November):106–112.

GOODE, ERICH (ed.). 1969. Marijuana. New York: Atherton Press.

GROSSBARD, HYMAN. 1962. "Ego deficiency in delinquents." Social Casework 43 (April):171–178.

HALLECK, SEYMOUR. 1967. "Psychiatric treatment of the alienated college student." Paper presented at the annual meeting of the American Psychiatric Association.

HUXLEY, ALDOUS. 1963. The Doors of Perception (bound with Heaven and Hell). New York: Harper Colophon.

ISBELL, HARRIS et al. 1967. "Effects of $(-)\Delta^9$ trans-tetrahydrocannabinol in man." Psychopharmacologia 11:184–188.

KEELER, MARTIN. 1967. "Adverse reactions to marihuana." American Journal of Psychiatry 128 (November):674–677. 1968. "Marihuana induced hallucinations." Diseases of the Nervous System 29 (May):314–315.

KENNEDY, ROBERT E. 1962. "The protestant ethic and the parsis." The American Journal of Sociology (July):11–20.

KISSIN, BENJAMIN. 1967. "On marihuana." Downstate Medical Center Reporter 2, no. 7 (April):2.

LOURIA, DONALD B. 1968. "The great marihuana debate." The Drug Scene. New York: McGraw-Hill.

LUDLOW, PETER. 1965. "In Defence of pot: confessions of a Canadian marijuana smoker." Saturday Night (October):28–32.

MAYOR LAGUARDIA'S COMMITTEE ON MARIHUANA. 1944. The Marihuana Problem in the City of New York. Lancaster, Pennsylvania: Jacques Cattell Press.

McLUHAN, MARSHALL. 1964. Understanding Media: The Extensions of Man. New York: McGraw-Hill.

MERTON, ROBERT K. 1968. "Puritanism, pietism and science." in Social Theory and Social Structure, 3rd ed. New York: Free Press.

MUNCH, JAMES. 1966. "Marihuana and Crime." United Nations Bulletin on Narcotics 18 (April–June):15–22.

NEEDHAM, JOSEPH. 1956. "Buddhism and chinese science." Science and Civilization in China, Volume 2, Cambridge: Cambridge University Press.

NEW YORK ACADEMY OF MEDICINE. 1964. "Homosexuality." Bulletin of the New York Academy of Medicine 40 (July):576–580.

ROSEVEAR, JOHN. 1967. Pot: A Handbook of Marihuana. New Hyde Park, New York: University Books.

SCHOOL MANAGEMENT. 1966a. "A schoolman's guide to illicit drugs." School Management (June):100–101. 1966b. "How one district combats the drug problem." School Management (June):102–106.

STONE, GREGORY and HARVEY A. FARBERMAN (eds.). 1969. Social Psychology Through Symbolic Interaction. Waltham, Massachusetts: Blaisdell.

TAURO, G. JOSEPH. 1967. Commonwealth v. Joseph D. Leis and Ivan Weiss, Findings, Rulings and Order on Defendants' Motion to Dismiss. Boston: Superior Court of the Commonwealth of Massachusetts.

UNGERLEIDER, J. THOMAS et al. 1968. "A statistical survey of adverse reactions to LSD in Los Angeles county." The American Journal of Psychiatry 125 (September):352–357.

YOUNG, LEONTYNE R. 1945. "Personality patterns in unmarried mothers." The Family 26 (December):296–303. 1954. Out of Wedlock. New York: McGraw-Hill.